THE
STREETS *of* PARIS

THE STREETS *of* PARIS

A Guide to the City of Light

FOLLOWING IN THE FOOTSTEPS OF FAMOUS PARISIANS THROUGHOUT HISTORY

WITHDRAWN

SUSAN CAHILL

PHOTOGRAPHS BY MARION RANOUX

ST. MARTIN'S GRIFFIN ⚑ NEW YORK

THE STREETS OF PARIS. Copyright © 2017 by Susan Cahill. Photographs copyright © 2017 by Marion Ranoux. All rights reserved. Printed in China. For information, address St. Martin's Press, 175 Fifth Avenue, New York, N.Y. 10010.

www.stmartins.com

The Library of Congress Cataloging-in-Publication Data is available upon request.

ISBN 978-1-250-07432-4 (paperback)
ISBN 978-1-250-13015-0 (e-book)

Our books may be purchased in bulk for promotional, educational, or business use. Please contact the Macmillan Corporate and Premium Sales Department at (800) 221–7945, extension 5442, or by e-mail at MacmillanSpecialMarkets@macmillan.com.

First Edition: June 2017

10 9 8 7 6 5 4 3 2 1

For Joey, beloved son, and for Marion,
chère belle fille

Remembering your gifts of photographs, computer wizardry,
the pleasures of your hospitality and our years of walking
the storied streets of the City of Light

CONTENTS

INTRODUCTION

"Beauty is in the streets," they say in Paris. We travelers know our favorites, Parisians know theirs. Jean Genet liked to stand with his friend Giacometti at the foot of *rue Oberkampf,* taking in its long uphill from the Marais to Belleville. Simone Weil loved walking *the quays* of *Île Saint-Louis* in her native river city. The scruffy streets of the ninth were François Truffaut's muse and mother.

As cities evolve and erupt, streets change; Parisians come and go. But the beauty remains. The gray light shifts, we see from new angles the stunning mosaic that is the City of Light. One by one, the streets of Paris, their multiple personalities—charming, broken, lyrical, dirty, elegant—wind along the past and present, through the storied worlds of Parisians ancient and modern. Walking in their footsteps, we sense the hauntings of history, connect with sites of memory.

The Streets of Paris focuses on twenty-two life stories of brilliant and passionate Parisian characters in their physical settings, along the streets that tell the stories of their inspiration, of how they became the icons that Paris—and history—still celebrate. In this book, the streets *are* stories. To paraphrase Rebecca Solnit's words about the *where* of all our lives: "*Places are stories.*"

Travelers who love to walk in cities, searching out the backstories in the narrow old streets, are walking in imitation of so many famous people of Parisian history who also walked their city and took its street life to heart. As the

Anglo-French historian and indefatigable walker Richard Cobb put it, "*Paris should be both walkable and walked, if the limitless variety, the unexpectedness, the provincialism, the rusticity, the touching eccentricity are to be appreciated.*"

With *The Streets of Paris* as your guide, you'll walk the *quartiers* of such original geniuses as Patrick Modiano, Édith Piaf, Colette, Jean Moulin, good king Henri IV—you'll find all these names in the book's Contents. Exploring the contexts of their life stories, we enter the complex mind and heart of Paris from the Middle Ages to the present. It comes through in these twenty-two portraits of writers, philosophers, lovers, patriots, royals, rebels, painters, composers, scientists, saints, and filmmakers. Each one reveals a major theme of the Parisian mosaic, the city's ambiguity, the courage and wit, the *élan*.

A few examples of their stories that do not show up on historical plaques or in the voice-overs of flag-waving tour guides:

- *Honoré Daumier* of *Quai d'Anjou* on the *Île Saint-Louis,* caricaturist, political satirist, for whom "the streets of Paris were his school and college, his occupation and pastime, his career," to quote one biographer. Daumier went to jail for his subversive cartoons of the powerful.
- Seventeen-year-old *Héloise,* the first troubadour, who, waiting for her lover Peter Abelard, hid in the shadows of the medieval *Notre-Dame Cathedral Close,* its winding unlit streets still winding today, a labyrinth of secrets and intrigue. "*Heloise is worth a thousand Abelards,*" said Henry James, preferring the passionate girl and her unrepentant love letters to the great medieval theologian (and father of her child) turned repentant monk.
- The antifascist hero *Jean Moulin* of *Montparnasse,*

leader of the French Resistence, sometime bohemian and artist, who lived a double life along the streets of southern Paris.

- *Albert Camus,* philosopher, writer, *Résistant.* He walked everywhere, Left Bank, Right Bank, recording the particulars in his *Notebooks.* *"Camus loved the world. He was uneasy with those indifferent to its beauty,"* wrote a recent biographer.

- *King Henri IV,* lover, urban designer, and pluralist, made Paris a miracle of tolerance and beauty after a century of the brutal Wars of Religion. He even thought to put sidewalks on his *Pont Neuf*—all the better for strolling and opening up what many feel is the most beautiful prospect in Paris.

- Walking south, into the *Latin Quarter,* you'll find the beloved statue of *Michel de Montaigne* along the *rue des Écoles,* a street dating from the Middle Ages when Paris became the academic star of Europe. The father of all enlightened moderns, Montaigne adored Paris as the inscription on his statue, a quote from his essay "of Vanitie" shows:

I love that citie for hir own sake . . . I love hir so tenderly that hir spottes, hir blemishes and hir warts are deare unto me. . . .

No sedentary philosopher, he loved to walk the streets of Paris: *"My business is to keep myself in motion. . . . I walk for the sake of walking. . . . "*

(Four centuries later, Julia Child echoed Montaigne. As she said in *My Life in France*, "You learn Paris on your own two feet.")

Following in the footsteps of such Parisians, you walk the city's main geographic *quartiers*: Île de la Cité; Île Saint-Louis; the Left Bank and its *quartiers* (Latin Quarter, Saint-Germain); Southern Paris (Montparnasse); Western Paris (Passy); the Right Bank and its *quartiers* (Pigalle, Montmartre, the Marais); Northeastern Paris (Picpus, Belleville, Ménilmontant). Hitler came close to bombing the northeast into the ground because it produced nothing but insurrection, those detestable noisy unions. And windmills.

The Contents names all these areas, organizing the stories in the clear way that travelers found helpful in my book *Hidden Gardens of Paris: A Guide to the Parks, Squares, and Woodlands of the City of Light.* This organization is an easy plan that helps travelers—with such street maps in hand as the little red book, *Paris par Arrondissements*, available at most news kiosks or bookstores; and/or the folding map *Streetwise Paris*—find their way without having to join an organized tour.

With *The Streets of Paris* as your guide, explorations of the city are original and leisurely rather than superficial and exhausting. (To quote Julian Green, *"Paris . . . is loath to surrender itself to people who are in a hurry; it belongs to the dreamers. . . . "*) And, as many travelers and travel writers have commented in *The New York Times*, although they pack and carry their electronic devices, in the interests of depth and originality of content, they still buy and bring along the travel *book*.

There's no need to join an organized tour if you're not in the mood; you can sit and rest your feet, eat lunch in any park or square—like the Parisians do—whenever you feel like it. The book tells you which métro to take (maps of the métro are available inside the métro stations) and which street(s) to follow on the way to your destination, say, the quiet streets of the southern Marais leading to the *Hôtel de Sens* at the end of pretty *rue du Figuier* where Queen Margot—*La Reine Margot*—earned her undeserved reputation as a bloodthirsty sex maniac.

A number of Parisian streets are havens of peace and solitude, perhaps unlike the tenor of the stories they tell: *Reine Margot's rue du Figuier. Daumier's Quai d'Anjou* on the north side of *Île Saint-Louis. Marie Curie's Quai de Béthune* on its south side, facing the back of Notre-Dame. On a Sunday morning, the deserted quad of *Simone Weil's L École Normale Supérieure* in *rue d'Ulm*. Colette's *rue de Beaujolais* bordering the exquisite Palais Royal.

A popular feature of *Hidden Gardens of Paris* that appears in *The Streets of Paris* is the listing of *"Nearbys"* that follows each selection: a few good cafés, bookstores, movie theaters, gardens, museums, churches, *pâtisseries*. The "Nearbys" help travelers find the rich—and often hidden—variety of a particular *quartier.*

What this guidebook does not offer is a listing of hotels or Best Shopping and practical tips about doing the laundry, finding a taxi, or a dentist.

For armchair travelers, the Sources—or bibliography—at the end of the book enlighten a journey whereby the places and people profiled in the book can come to life in the imagination if not on the actual Parisian streets. Nancy Mitford's novel, *Voltaire in Love*, for instance, serves as a wonderful companion while sitting, in your imagination, in the *hôtel* (now a shadowy café on *Quai Voltaire*) where this brilliant *bon vivant* died.

Like reading a great novel—or a fat biography that's never gone out of print—walking the streets of Paris helps us experience the sources of the love of life so vital in this city. We see transactions of friendship, love, work, beauty; we taste the good wine, the incomparable bread. So many wonderful books in the countless *librairies*, the good newspapers in the green kiosks. The laughter in so many dark eyes, the quickness in the air, of conversations overheard. The courtesy. We remember and cherish these pleasures long after we go home.

Victor Hugo named the most important source of his art: He said he got the ideas for his novels *by chance*, *in the streets*.

The striking photographs of streetscapes included in this book present the proof that the Paris of genius and beauty is as seductive and irresistible and possibly as life-changing as it ever was. The physical evidence of the photographs make the case: Paris lives, its radiance and *esprit* intact and largely the effect of the people who have lived and worked there.

And the effect of the river Seine must always be spoken: Its presence and power are at the heart of the city's joy and sensuality. Paris, as one old mapmaker once said, is a gift of the Seine.

—Susan Cahill
New York City

THE
STREETS *of* PARIS

ÎLE DE LA CITÉ

Héloise & Abelard: Rue des Chantres

THE SCANDALOUS LOVE
OF HÉLOÏSE AND ABELARD

LOCATION: *9–11, Quai aux Fleurs, Notre-Dame Cathedral Close*
MÉTRO: Cité

The passion of Héloïse (1095/1100–1163) and Peter Abelard (1079–1142) caught fire here, on *Quai aux Fleurs* next to the Seine, on the eastern tip of the *Île de la Cité,* and soon, raging beyond the controls of secrecy, was exposed, then cruelly punished, as if in the end the ice of winter had become the main character in their lives. But it is the passionate lovers—the Seine in summer—that the city's collective memory embraces to this day.

They wrote their story into the many letters* they exchanged during their affair and about fifteen years later, after they'd been separated: the ecstasies, despair, then Abelard's—but not Héloïse's—repentance for his sins of lust. *"Héloïse is worth a thousand Abelards,"* said Henry James.

In 1115 Canon Fulbert, a cathedral staffer, gave some rent-free rooms to teacher/theologian Peter Abelard in exchange for his services as a tutor to the canon's intellectually precocious niece, Héloïse. She read French, Latin, and Greek; she wanted to learn Hebrew; she was interested in Abelard's unorthodox philosophical project: to use dialectics to understand the ambiguities and contradictions of religious faith. Ortho-

---

*LETTERS, in Betty Radice, ed. & trans., *The Letters of Abelard and Héloïse* (London: Penguin, 1974).

dox scholars refused the very notion of ambiguity and contradiction. Absolutism—religious, moral, political—defined
the very ground of being.

Abelard at thirty-five was the master teacher of Paris,
at the school of Notre-Dame first, and later, to escape the
clerical censure at the Cathedral school, at the Abbey of
Sainte-Geneviève on the hill of the Left Bank's *Montagne
Sainte-Geneviève*. His students adored him, his shocking
humanism and open-mindedness freed them to think outside
the prescribed boxes. Abelard, for instance, was the defender
of sexual pleasure, rejecting the bachelor theologians' dogma
that marital intercourse is always sinful. Saint Augustine
had preached that pleasure itself is a sin; Pope Gregory the
Great echoed him: "*There can be no sexual pleasure without sin.*"

Abelard also dissented from the hatred of Jews. He criticized the First Crusade's slaughter of Jews en route to Jeru-
salem. He discussed Judaism with the rabbis from the *Île*'s
synagogue that dated back to the Roman occupation.

Héloise, like Abelard, had studied classical literature (they
both could quote long passages of Ovid's erotic poem, the
Metamorphoses). Having no living parents, she was raised by
nuns in the convent at Argenteuil, a few miles downstream
from Paris. She moved to Paris in 1115 (as a teenager or
twenty-year-old) to continue her studies under the protection
of Uncle Fulbert, her mother's brother, or maybe, according
to some, her father. Uncle or father, Fulbert was notoriously
jealous when it came to his beautiful black-haired, dark-eyed
niece. (What was he thinking, installing the handsome, sexy,
intellectual star of Paris under the same roof with his stunning niece?)

The lovers met in the dawn of the twelfth-century French
Renaissance, which blossomed more than a century before

Dante was even heard of. In the words of Alistair Horne's *Seven Ages of Paris,* it was a time that (except for the celibate clergy and hierarchy) "had little difficulty in squaring love of God with love of worldly beauty and of the sensuous world." Like Héloise and Abelard, this era of beatitude would come to a bitter end. From their secret sanctuary on the Seine, where to the sound of the flowing river they consummated and reveled in their love, they could look across the river at the marshy Right Bank, its ***Place de Grève*** almost directly opposite, not yet feared by Parisians as the place of public execution. Many writers believe that had the free-spirited Héloise lived in the thirteenth century or later, she, for refusing to repent of her love of Abelard as well as to deny their mutual sexual pleasure, would have been convicted of heresy and burned alive on the Right Bank.

Abelard's academic reputation suffered once he and Héloise became lovers. Their letters reveal they became more and more sexually insatiable, ignoring texts for the pleasure of their bodies (once Uncle Fulbert was out of the house). The master teacher became absent or unpunctual on the ***Petit Pont,*** his lectures stale and repetitious. As he remembered those nights and mornings in a confessional letter, written many years after their catastrophic breakup:

> *with our lessons as a pretext we abandoned ourselves entirely to love. Her studies allowed us to withdraw in private, as love desired, with our books open before us, more words of love than of our reading passed between us, and more kissing than teaching. My hands strayed more often over the curves of her body than to the pages; love drew our eyes to look on each other more than reading kept them on our texts.*

Nothing compared with Héloise. Novelist Helen Waddell, in her book *Peter Abelard*, describes these two as "drenched with love as the air is drenched with light."

Most of the letters Héloise wrote in the course of their two-year affair have the same erotic charge as Abelard's.

> *To one flowing with milk and honey, the whiteness of milk and the sweetness of honey, I send the flood of delight and the increase of joy. . . . I give you the most precious thing I have—myself, firm in faith and love, steady in desire . . .*

She called him "my only love," whom, she wrote in a later letter, she loved more than God. They wrote to each other every day.

When Héloise became pregnant, Abelard disguised her as a nun and took her north to his native Brittany where their son, Astrolabe, was born. Later, on a return trip to Paris, he convinced her to marry him, to placate the insanely angry Fulbert who felt betrayed. In the ***Chapel of Saint-Aignan,*** Héloise, very reluctantly, whispered her marriage vows: "*I looked for no marriage bond. I never sought anything in you but yourself.*" She believed, rightly, that a married cleric could not rise in the Church, that their marriage, kept secret or not, would ruin his brilliant career. Nor was she drawn to the constrictions of married domesticity: she preferred "love to wedlock and freedom to chains." Both lovers were aware of the Church's esteem for clergy and monks as an elite body on the ground of their celibacy.

What happened after their marriage is confusing. Refusing to ruin Abelard's career, Héloise either withdrew to or was urged to retreat to the convent she grew up in. Abelard followed her there, and later revealed that they made love in the only private space available, the convent refectory. Fulbert, however, presumed that Héloise's disappearance from Paris meant that Abelard had abandoned her and planned to divorce her (for the sake of his career in the Church). Late one night, the crazed uncle (or father) sent his hired thugs to Abelard's rooms to avenge Héloise's humiliation. They castrated her lover, husband, father of their child.

The confusion of the historical record continues, but a few facts are clear. Abelard, impotent, left Paris, where overnight he'd become an object of pity, to become a monk at the ***Abbaye de Saint-Denis*** (now the Basilica of Saint-Denis), in northern Paris.

Héloise, fully aware of her hypocrisy, professed her religious vows in the convent that had been her childhood home. She was no nun. Always her heart and soul would belong to Abelard. *"It was your command, not love of God, that made me take the veil."*

Fifteen years later, she came across a letter written by Abelard to a friend in which he recounts the joys and torments of his life. The letter of twenty thousand words—*Historia Calamitatum Mearum* (*The Story of My Misfortunes*)—is often referred to as Abelard's autobiography or *Confession*. He writes about his passion for Héloise, the details of their lovemaking, the birth, the marriage, his castration, and their separation, Abelard retreating to the Saint-Denis cloister where he repented his sins of lust, Héloise to a convent where she, too, according to Abelard, had found comfort in religion. The passionate girl of the ***Quai aux Fleurs*** was now the abbess of her convent, highly respected by bishops.

Héloise's response, in her first letter to Abelard since their separation, sets him straight. For her, nothing has changed

since their ecstatic nights and days in Paris. She is possessed
not by religion but by anguish and longing for him:

> *God is my witness that if Augustus, emperor of the
> whole world, thought fit to honor me with marriage and
> conferred all the earth on me forever it would be sweeter and
> more honorable to me to be not his empress but your whore.*

In her next letter, the Abbess Héloise repeats that her sexual self is still her most essential self:

> *Even at Mass, . . . lewd visions of the pleasures we shared
> take such a hold upon my unhappy soul that my thoughts
> are on their wantonness instead of on my prayers. Every-
> thing we did, and also the times and places, are stamped
> on my heart along with your image . . . I live through it all
> again with you.*

The lovers of the *Quai aux Fleurs* ended as victims of
the Church's law of celibacy already on the books of canon
law, its violation by a cleric a mortal sin, the penalty eternal
hellfire. At the time that uncle Fulbert had Peter Abelard
castrated, it was not clear whether Abelard had decided to
choose the priesthood instead of Héloise. After the tragedy,
the shamed husband's only refuge seemed to be a celibate
monastery.

For the rest of his life as teacher and writer, he was attacked and persecuted by jealous mediocrities, theologians,
ambitious clerics, fanatics (Saint Bernard of Clairvaux) who
convicted him of heresy and made him burn one of his own
books. Abelard was lucky. A century later, he himself would
have gone up in flames.

Héloise never wavered. To the end, she was a woman in love. No law or tradition or vow could crush her passion for Peter Abelard. Her intelligence, her refusal to be bullied into a fake repentance or conversion, and the intensity and warmth of her writing, place her front and center in a long line of bold, self-possessed French women, women who loved unconditionally. To this day she is a heroine of France.

For the Traveler

Go at night. After nine or ten o'clock as the tourist crowds thin to nothing. Exit the Cité métro and from the Parvis, the vast plaza in front of the cathedral, walk straight toward it and then bear left along *rue du Cloître-Notre-Dame*—the cloister walk. The souvenir shops on your left will be closed or closing. Bear left again into the narrow winding side streets. Within this labyrinth is the oldest part of the *Île de la Cité*: the Celts or Gauls (the tribe *Parisii*) lived here, long before the Roman conquest in 52 BC and the first Roman streets. In the Christian Middle Ages, these cathedral precincts were the heart of Héloise and Abelard's world.

Along *rue Massillon,* and then *rue Chanoinesse,* the main artery of the *Close,* you pass low-slung lintels and doorways leading into ancient sloping courtyards, shadowy buildings that huddle together. The very narrow *rue des Chantres* and *rue de la Colombe* (with its mark of the old Roman wall high on no. 6) and the sunken *rue des Ursins* (with its delicate small doorway of medieval tracery at the east end), each street winds at last into the clearing of *Quai aux Fleurs.* At night no cars and few people move along the cobblestone streets. From this northside edge of the *Île de la Cité,* you see, from the quay's embankment, the river Seine gleaming in the moonlight. *"Paris is a gift of the Seine,"* said the old map-makers. In prehistoric times the river was one hundred feet higher than it is today.

The contrast of seasons on the river—the calm flow of summer, the tempestuous current under the wind of winter—suit the love story of the *Quai aux Fleurs*.

The medallions set above the doors of the tall double house at nos. 9 and 11 on *Quai aux Fleurs* identify their residence, now much restored but still on the site of the home of Fulbert.

Bisecting the Île from the *Le Grand Pont* on the north side to the *Petit Pont* on the south side was the old Roman road spanning the two channels of the Seine, leading to *rue Saint-Martin* in the north and *rue Saint-Jacques* to the south. In Héloise and Abelard's time it was known as the *rue de la Juiverie* (the street of the Jews, now *La rue de la Cité*) where the synagogue, the Jewish market, and houses stood midway between the two bridges, a lively district crowded with knights on horses, merchants, a market, pilgrims, rabbis and their community. This Jewish quarter of Paris was mentioned in 1119, but the first Jews had come north to Paris with Caesar, settling on the Left Bank. Abelard wrote about Judaism with respect in his book *Dialogue Between A Philosopher, A Christian, and A Jew*. A celebrity, with a huge student following, he got away with all of it.

A true Renaissance man, Abelard also composed ballads and songs which he and his students sang in the taverns, around the *Petit Pont,* and along the narrow muddy streets of the *Close*. He had a thrilling powerful voice. No doubt his stirring choruses carried to the *Quai aux Fleurs* where Héloise awaited their rapturous tutorials.

His students listened to his lectures inside the *Close,* or on *rue du Fouarre* (see p. 13) or on the *Petit Pont* which was crowded with students, jugglers, canons, singers, dog and bear trainers, and pickpockets. (It has been rebuilt fourteen times.) Abelard's controversial ideas, shouted above the bridge traffic—"*The spirit of man is the candle of the Lord. . . . I said, Ye are gods . . .*"—attracted students from all over Europe. The debates that enlivened the Île de la Cité, the Left Bank—especially *rue du Fouarre* and the hilly vineyards rising on *Montagne Sainte-Geneviève*—marked the beginnings of the University of Paris. But it was Abelard's music and his lusty singing that first caught the attention of Fulbert's niece.

You can wander the streets of the early university, now the heart of the *Latin Quarter* (so named for the language spoken and written by the scholars): walk the quays below the *Petit Pont;* climb the slopes of Montagne Sainte-Geneviève (one of the lovers' hideaways), best accessible from *rue des Écoles,* up *rue de Montagne Sainte-Geneviève,* bearing left at the fountain, then past *Jardin de Navarre* (a sprawling vineyard in 1120 and later, when Henri IV was a boy in Paris, the campus of the Catholic College of Navarre he attended). At the top of the hill turn right into *rue Clovis.* Abelard lectured in this area, the site of the ancient *Abbaye-Sainte-Geneviève,* now the campus of Lycée Henri IV (see p. 93).

Descending in the direction of the *Île de la Cité,* you can visit the churches the lovers would have known—Saint-Julien le Pauvre, Saint-Séverin (a ruin in 1115, soon to be rebuilt), Saint-Germain-des-Prés, a short walk west along *boulevard Saint-Germain*—as the story goes, the handsome theologian and the beautiful student made love in these churches in the evenings, when they were empty and dark.

A remnant of the *Chapel of Saint-Aignan* is believed to

stand today within the *Close* as one stone wall in the rear courtyard of a medieval inn on 24, *rue Chanoinesse,* "**Au Vieux Paris d'Arcole.**" (Open every day except Saturday lunch.) The manager makes no claims for the wall's authenticity but graciously points your way, beneath the very low ceilings of the dimly lit old dining room, and out into a mysterious rear courtyard. At night this ruin of a wall and its ancient setting make a spell-binding impression. The wall of *Saint-Aignan* is also accessible from *19 rue des Ursins,* except that the gate leading to the courtyard is usually closed. A famous statue from this chapel, *Virgin of Paris,* stands now in the south transept of Notre-Dame, to the right of the main altar, with its "elegant lassitude," according to one art historian, a reminder of Héloïse's indifference to the sacrament of matrimony and motherhood.

Héloise and Abelard were buried together on the grounds of Héloise's convent, the Paraclete: a large cache of their letters was found in the Paraclete archive after Héloise's death. In the nineteenth century, their remains were transferred to *Père Lachaise* where they rest beneath an ornate stone canopy near the southern entrance.

MÉTRO: Père Lachaise; Gambetta; Philippe Auguste
ENTRANCES: Boulevard de Ménilmontant; avenue du
  Père Lachaise; rue de la Roquette
HOURS: Easter–Sept, 8–6; Oct–Easter, 8–dusk

Nearby

CRYPTE ARCHÉOLOGIQUE DU NOTRE-DAME *At the edge of the **Parvis** (entrance on **rue de la Cité**; 10–6, closed Mon) descend into the **Crypte** where architectural remains as well as* *wooden models, dioramas, and maps of various periods help us imagine the looks of early Paris and how it evolved. In the years of Héloise and Abelard's love affair (1114–1117) the **Cloître** and the maze of the cathedral precincts were studded with the church spires of the Île's fourteen parishes. Deep in the shadowy **Crypte** you can imagine the church bells ringing from bell towers, the sounds of the cathedral choir practicing chant and hymns in the cathedral school (still in existence, in a newer building), the music filling the narrow streets of tall wooden houses lit with torches. (Fires were frequent.) The old maps show the bishop's palace, to the right of the cathedral, then as now hugging the southern border of the Île, rebuilt after it was torn down in a riot.*

The Crypte *shows the identity of Paris as formed by the river, geography, the weather, invasions, the changing topography, and the life histories of people—Héloise and Abelard—who entered the city's soul.*

LE MARCHÉ AUX FLEURS   *The Flower Market along **Quai de la Corse**, behind the Hôtel-Dieu de Paris, built on the site of the razed twelfth-century Jewish community.*

LA MÉMORIAL DES MARTYRS DE LA DÉPORTATION   *Off Square de l'Île de-France, the eastern tip of Île de la Cité. Cross **Quai Archévêque** and enter the small rose garden surrounded by the Seine and facing Île Saint-Louis. Beneath the garden, down a narrow staircase, the writings on the walls of the memorial to the 76,000 French Jews, the martyrs of the Nazi/French Deportation, are by Saint-Exupéry, Aragon, Éluard, Sartre. Tues–Sun, 10–12; 2–7.*

LA FOURMI AILÉE   *Left Bank, **8, rue du Fouarre**, paris.resto .com. Open seven days from noon to midnight. A students' café, good food, atmosphere, service. **Rue du Fouarre** was originally named **rue des Écoliers** (street of the scholars); then it became **rue***

Feurre which means **paille**—*straw*—*after the bales of straw the students sat on to hear the lessons of their masters.* **La rue du Fouarre,** *the site of the first University of Paris, was celebrated by Dante, Petrarch, and Rabelais. The southern part of the street was renamed* **rue Dante** *after he visited here at the end of the thirteenth century.*

SHAKESPEARE AND COMPANY *Left Bank,* **37, rue de la Bûcherie** *10–11, seven days. An English-language bookshop packed with customers and from floor to ceiling with new and used books, the descendant of the original shop in* **rue de l'Odéon** *where owner and publisher Sylvia Beach published James Joyce's* Ulysses *in 1922. A fun place on Bloomsday, June 16, with readings and wine-tasting upstairs. There's a good selection of books about Paris, French writers, and history plus a new café.*

ABBEY BOOKSHOP *Left Bank,* **29, rue de la Parcheminerie,** *abbeybookshop@wanadoo.fr. Originally* **rue des Écrivains** *in 1273, named for the scribes who were the heart of the book trade. Just south of the front entrance of Saint-Séverin, the street is now named for the bookbinders and illustrators who worked here from the twelfth century. Its owner, Brian Spence, can put his hands on any title you request.*

Louis IX: Sainte Chapelle

LOUIS IX AND THE DARK SIDE
OF SAINTHOOD

LOCATION: *8, boulevard du Palais,* Sainte-Chapelle
HOURS: Daily, Mar–Oct, 9:30–6; Nov–Feb, 9–5
MÉTRO: Cité; Saint-Michel

I f you wonder why there are always crowds lined up on the *boulevard du Palais* near the corner of Pont Saint-Michel, the draw is *La Sainte-Chapelle* (the Holy Chapel), one of the most extraordinary masterpieces of Gothic architecture in Paris. People wait patiently in all seasons, looking up at the flying buttresses. Once inside, visitors enter what remains of the ancient *Palais de la Cité*—underneath and adjacent to the massive *Palais de Justice.*

Then a dark stone corridor leads to the entrance of *Sainte-Chapelle,* the creation of King/Saint Louis IX (1214–1270). The chapel feels so recessed in the bowels of the ancient buildings, you feel as if you've come upon a royal secret from a faraway past.

The first sight of it—the upper chapel on a sunny day—and there is no point in visiting this place if the sun is not shining—is so ravishingly beautiful it's startling. The walls of stained-glass windows blaze with gloriously rich sparkling colors. The colored light flooding the chapel, falling in gorgeous fragments on the chapel floor, leaves you without words. The blue has a mystical intensity. *Medieval blue* it's called, evoking a harmonious mystical universe. The rose window, as you turn to look up at it, you face what seems a soaring variation on or perhaps the final explosion of the miracles that inspired this architecture. The colors express a faith so joyful and *sure* it seems to pulse in another world.

The biblical stories contained in the windows—the childhood of Christ, the Passion of Christ, Saint John the Baptist, the Hebrew prophets Judith and Esther, the stories of Genesis and Exodus, in all 1,100 scenes from the Old and New Testaments—make visual the sources that aroused King Louis IX's religious passion. In the sunlight, you can read the plots and characters of the stories—including one about Louis himself, in the last window on the right, dressed as a penitent, carrying the sacred relics on foot to Paris—and come to understand or at least visualize the myths and miracles fueling the faith of medieval Catholic Europe. Statues of the twelve apostles, Christianity's founding fathers, surround the nave.

That King Louis IX conceived the beauty of **Sainte-Chapelle** does present an enigma. For it's hard to find an aesthetic dimension in his politics and policies. It is true that he looked out for the poor, and the lepers, the blind, and prostitutes. Possessed of a radical humility, he washed the feet of his nobles, sat beneath an oak tree in the *Bois de Vincennes* to hear the complaints of his subjects and administer royal verdicts. Such concern for social justice was unusual among kings.

But the stunning **Sainte-Chapelle** coexists with its creator-king's twisted psychological profile, usually omitted from the catalogs and booklets sold outside the chapel and inside the Conciergerie.

Louis had always been terrified of his mother, Blanche of Castile, who in turn taught him to be terrified of the devil who was everywhere. To protect his soul and safeguard his salvation, he wore a hair shirt, day and night, heard many masses, genuflected fifty times a night at bedtime, got out of bed at midnight to recite the *matins* part of the Divine Office, fasted and mortified his body to the effect of unhealthy thinness and a stooped posture. He disliked seeing people enjoy themselves. His marital sex life was furtive: He and his wife conceived their eleven children on a back stairway between their two bedrooms on different floors of the *palais* in order to avoid Blanche's unannounced nighttime visitations to their respective bedchambers. Though Blanche told Louis she'd rather see him dead than know he'd committed a mortal sin, the good son claimed to love his mother madly. As French historian Maurice Druon puts it in *The History of Paris from Caesar to St. Louis* "he was one of the great neurotics of history. Had he not inclined to saintliness he might have been a monster. Neros are made of the same fibre. . . . he would have made an admirable subject for psychoanalysis."

Louis's ascetic practices aroused the ridicule of many of his subjects who called him "Brother Louis" and the "king of priests." But what matters is whether his neurotic psyche made any difference to his governance of France. King or no, he was not above the law of the human condition: Those to whom cruelty is done do cruelty in return.

The sinister side of his character turns up in the Inquisition. In utter contradiction of the mood of the twelfth-century French Renaissance—Abelard's tolerance, his condemnation of torture—Louis IX established the Inquisition as a strategic policy of the throne in service to the papal throne in Rome. As you gaze up at the spire of his exquisite chapel from, say, the *Quai des Grands-Augustins* on the Left Bank, you don't want to but can't help remember that the saintly

king who built this sanctuary consented to the torture and ex-
tinction of the Albigensian heretics in the southwest just as
he would order the expulsion of the Jews from these Left
Bank streets and alleys (and other Jewish districts), where
they'd lived and worked since they came north with Caesar's
legions. Eventually, in 1254, Louis ordered their expulsion
from the entirety of France. (His grandfather, King Philippe-
Auguste, had expelled the Jews from Paris because he wanted
their money and property to pay his debts; once paid, he allowed them to return.)

Louis's anti-Semitism was not primarily about money and
property. For him the persecution of the Jews was a religious
mission. Obeying the order of the Vicar of Christ on earth,
Pope Gregory IX, Louis oversaw the public burning of
twelve thousand volumes of the Talmud, in twenty-four cart-
loads, in Paris. "For the Jews of Paris to watch copies of the
massive Talmud—each one copied laboriously by hand—go
up in flames must have been heart-rending. . . . Only the very
pious King Louis IX of France—celebrated all through his
life as the model of a Christian monarch . . . responded to the
papal call."*

What made the pope order the burning in 1242 was
Jewish disrespect of the Blessed Virgin Mary: the Jews did
not believe in the Virgin birth. Louis had counseled that
no Christian should argue with a Jew over any doctrine but
when one of them calumniates the Christian faith, the believer should run his sword through the Jew's body "as far
as it can go." His friend and biographer, Jean de Joinville,
kept track of Louis's doctrinal obsessions.

And though he may have delivered a merciful justice to

* Robert Chazan, *The Trial of the Talmud: Paris, 1240.*

his humble subjects on the grass of *Vincennes*, Louis did not shy from punishing criminals and heretics. For the sake of their souls' salvation, he wanted them to realize the consequences of heresy and evildoing. Accordingly, he ordered the erection of the gibbet of Montfaucon in northeastern Paris (near the Buttes-Chaumont park in the nineteenth *arrondissement*). There evildoers were executed, their corpses exhibited on sixteen high columns. Scores of evil bodies hung and swung at one time, for years, as dogs and rats and crows and sometimes wolves devoured the stinking rotting flesh. The stench reached the western districts, reminding the city that punishment was everywhere, in the air, like the devil. Lest any infidel thought he could escape the royal justice, Louis IX, also in obedience to the pope, ordered the Jews to mark their clothing with a piece of red or yellow cloth, in the shape of a circle or square or star.

A militant crusader, he was hellbent on destroying the Muslim infidels in the East. He led the Seventh Crusade, winding up in jail for a few years until the Knights Templar bailed him out; he could get no support from his own knights and nobles for the campaign of the Eighth Crusade. He went anyway, without allies, and died of typhus before he reached his destination. Pope Boniface VIII (despised by Dante who sent him to the eighth circle of hell with the simoniacs in *The Divine Comedy*) canonized Louis shortly after his death to signal his approval of the French monarch as preeminent crusader. The loss of life and the savage violence involved in these wars were considered necessary to the success of the Christian West as it tried to eliminate the heretical East.

Paris would have to wait three-and-a-half centuries for a monarch who broke the dogmatic mold of Louis IX. Had Louis and his mother been around in 1594 to witness the

coronation of the Protestant-turned-Catholic Henri IV—
the down-to-earth *bon vivant* committed, like Abelard and
Henri's friend, Michel de Montaigne, to religious tolerance—
they might have judged him a likely candidate for their notorious gibbet.

For the Traveler

Joining a tour led by a knowledgeable guide is a good idea
if you want to read the intricacies of the stained-glass windows accurately. Sign up in the Lower Chapel. *(Combined
ticket for Sainte-Chapelle and Conciergerie on site. Sainte-chapelle.
monuments–nationaux.)*

Louis built this private chapel—*chapelle haute*—for the
use of the royal family living here in the *Palais de la Cité* and
to serve as a repository worthy of the relics he had bought in
the aftermath of a Crusade launched to convert the Muslim
East to Western Christendom: Jesus' Crown of Thorns and
pieces of the True Cross. Supposedly he bought them from
the emperor of Constantinople, Baudouin II, at a higher price
than it cost to build the chapel; others say the seller was a
pawnbroker. Whoever it was, Louis had his double chapel,
upper and lower, designed and built within six years (1242–
1248) by an architect who also worked on the basilica of Saint-
Denis and Notre-Dame Cathedral.

Outside *Sainte-Chapelle,* from multiple angles you can
look up at the spire that many consider the most exquisite
example of Gothic art in France. Aimed at the sky, its high
delicate tracery, its refinement, the entire edifice supported
by outside buttresses, *Sainte-Chapelle* is visible from the boats
on the Seine and the quays of the Left Bank. It has survived

riots, the Revolution, foreign occupations, and the bombs and guns of two World Wars. Perhaps the king who built it believed the Christian relics inside his chapel would protect the monarchy itself.

Despite his inept military adventures in foreign lands, at home in Paris Louis was a successful administrator. He set up structures for the courts, the treasury, and a parliament albeit without powers. He founded the **National Archives,** which holds important documents from the seventh century to the present, located now in the Marais.

> MÉTRO: Rambuteau. Or a fifteen-minute walk from Sainte-Chapelle across the Seine to the Right Bank, then north on *rue des Archives* to the entrance at 60, *rue des Francs-Bourgeois.* Open daily, May–Oct, 8–7; Nov–Apr, 8–5. Four lovely gardens surround the archives' buildings.

King Louis IX's confessor, Robert de Sorbon, gave his name to the Sorbonne, which he and Louis founded in 1253.

> MÉTRO: Cluny-La Sorbonne. Walk south, crossing *rue des Écoles,* then left and up the hill of *rue Saint-Jacques,* and at the marked entrance on the left side of the street, the guards will permit you to enter the large courtyard of the Sorbonne. It helps to have a photo ID or better, a student or faculty ID. Originally a theological college devoted to teaching a strict scholasticism, the Sorbonne, true to its founders, maintained its original inflexible character over the centuries. Its hard-line faculty helped the English captors of Joan of Arc manipulate the so-called

theological evidence that convicted her of heresy and witchcraft. The Sorbonne faculty also justified the Saint Bartholomew's Day Massacre (see p. 40); twenty years later, administrators and faculty fought in the streets against the acceptance of the Protestant Henri of Navarre as king (see p. 38).

In the end, the bright side of Louis IX's reign shines and dazzles through the stained-glass windows of the ***Sainte-Chapelle***. And his Sorbonne made Paris the envy of intellectual Europe, the model for Oxford and Cambridge. The **National Archives** he founded have preserved the history of the city, sustaining centuries of professional historians and their readers. His building campaign to house prostitutes, beggars, and the blind should not be omitted from his royal accomplishments.

But there's no ignoring the dark side. The coexistence of Louis's beautiful light-drenched chapel with his monstrous acts of cruelty remains an enigma, one of many contradictions in the life histories of the City of Light.

There are concerts held in the chapel in the early evenings (tickets at the door), affording time and space to contemplate the imponderables as you sit surrounded by an architecture of jeweled radiance and a history colder than stone.

Nearby

PLAQUE: QUAI DU MARCHÉ NEUF AND BOULEVARD DU PALAIS *On the corner of the north side of Pont Saint-Michel, on the left as you face the Seine, a bronze plaque in memory of the Algerians killed by the French police of Maurice Papon at a peaceful protest march against the war in Algeria on October 17,*

1961. The crime was covered up. The bodies—as many as two thousand—were dumped in the Seine. The massacre was not acknowledged until 1997.

LES AUGUSTINS *Across Pont Saint-Michel, bearing right, a few minutes walk down Quai des Grands-Augustins. The Café des Augustins is laid-back and fun. No need to dress up. Sit outside at sunset for the magnificent view of **Sainte-Chapelle** and the Louvre.*

Olympe de Gouges: Conciergerie, the Seine, and Pont Neuf

OLYMPE DE GOUGES:
ROBESPIERRE'S VICTIM

LOCATION: *2, boulevard du Palais,* Conciergerie
HOURS: Mar–Oct, 9:30–6:15; Nov–Feb, 9–5
MÉTRO: Cité; Saint-Michel; Pont Neuf

Olympe de Gouges (1748–1793) was one of the 2,800 death row inmates in the *Conciergerie* murdered by order of Maximilien Robespierre or one of his appointed judges. For many years after the Revolution, hers has remained an obscure story and a name belittled by male historians. Now, late in the twentieth century and into the twenty-first, the memory of her heroic courage has been resurrected: her writings, dead to the world in the National Archives for almost two centuries, have now been reprinted and translated; a square in the northern Marais bears her name; a recent bust of her image now holds a place of honor in the National Assembly (the Palais Bourbon); a large assembly hall bearing her name stands in the square de la Roquette on the site of what was once a prison for "incorrigible" girls, women, and four thousand Résistantes. In 2015 she was one of the heroes of France nominated to have her remains transferred to the Panthéon.

In the beginning, Olympe de Gouges supported the Revolution. In 1770 she'd moved to Paris from her native Montauban in the southwest as a twenty-two-year-old widowed mother of a young son. She'd changed her name from Marie Gouze to Olympe de Gouges. An aspiring writer and early feminist who expressed her bold antiestablishment opinions with verve and humor, she was befriended by politicians, journalists, intellectuals, and theater people. A free spirit with a mind of her own, she was invited to attend their salons which lived and breathed the ideas of the Enlightenment. The mathematician and philosopher Marquis de Condorcet and his wife Sophie, friends of Voltaire (see p. 115), held a prestigious salon in Auteuil; they welcomed Olympe, an advocate like themselves for human rights. She was by then writing her own plays, some of which were produced. *The Slavery of the Blacks* had a successful run. Theater, she believed, could change the politics of audiences. Her essays and fiery pamphlets opposing the death penalty and advocating for the abolition of slavery, the equality of the sexes, women's right to divorce (and to retain custody of her children) established her reputation as a voice of the Enlightenment.

She supported the Revolution as conceived by the leaders of the Girondists (or Girondins or the Gironde), a political group composed mostly of lawyers, intellectuals, journalists, and businessmen. More moderate than the fanatical Jacobins ruled by Robespierre, the Girondists favored a constitutional monarchy; they opposed the execution of the king and queen. Robespierre, the Jacobin dictator who designed the blood-soaked Reign of Terror, had the Girondist leaders arrested in June 1793 and guillotined in October. For her association with this moderate group—which the Jacobins attacked as "royalist"—he had Olympe de Gouges arrested in July and imprisoned in the *Conciergerie*.

Her writings were used against her: for opposing the death penalty for the imprisoned king and queen, she was accused of supporting the monarchy and sedition. She had also condemned Robespierre's Reign of Terror. He despised Olympe's most famous tract, *Declaration of the Rights of Women and of the Female Citizen* (1791), a protest against the omission of women's rights in the French *Declaration of the Rights of Man and of the Citizen* (1789), a copy, "almost word for word," in the words of Eric Hazan, of America's Declaration of Independence (1776). (Her essay inspired Mary Wollstonecraft's *A Vindication of the Rights of Woman,* published in London in 1792. French women were denied the right to vote until 1945.)

For its silence regarding women's right to equality with male citizens as well as its omission of the issues of slavery and of women's suffrage, Olympe denounced the Revolution: It was clear there would be no justice for women (or slaves) under the patriarchal version of *Liberté, Egalité, Fraternité.* She called the Revolution a fraud.

Locked up in the **Conciergerie,** she was denied a lawyer; she was quite capable, the judge sneered, of arguing her own case. Her polemical pamphlets, attached to lampposts all over Paris, were well known. More were published while she was in prison. Her last one, *A Female Patriot Persecuted*, was said to be the one that so infuriated Robespierre he condemned her to death after three months in jail, denying her right to appeal. (Perhaps, more than her writing, he detested her reputation for attracting and accepting the sexual attentions of a number of lovers.)

She knew she had never stood a chance in a judicial system controlled by Robespierre, the director of the infamous Committee of Public Safety. As described by André Maurois in *A History of France*, Robespierre "hated women with the mad fury of some chaster men, angered by femininity itself. . . . There dwelt within him something of Mohammed and of Cromwell, and this Mohammed was ambitious to be Allah."

On November 3, 1793, perhaps in silence, Olympe de Gouges climbed into the tumbril that would carry her across the Pont au Change, up *Quai de la Mégisserie,* right at the *Pont Neuf* into *rue de la Monnaie,* left into *rue Saint-Honoré,* and up beyond the Louvre and the Tuileries into the *Place de la Revolution* (now the *Place de la Concorde*), its air thick with the stench of severed heads and the blood of innocents.

As she mounted the scaffold, Olympe de Gouges's face was described by an anonymous bystander as calm, serene, and beautiful. But the only hard evidence about this brave woman lives in the writings she left behind, now for sale in Paris bookstores and online. Her sculptured image rests in the National Assembly across the bridge from the place where she died.

The nineteenth-century historian Jules Michelet, a hard-line republican who never forgave her for urging clemency for the king and queen and opposed all participation in politics by women, for a time set the tone for other male historians of the Revolution :

> *She allowed herself to act and write about more than one affair that her weak head did not understand.*

For the Traveler

From the *Sainte-Chapelle*, walk one block north toward the Seine and Pont au Change; or from the Pont Neuf, walk up *Quai de l'Horloge,* passing the huge Palais de Justice on your right, which stretches from one side of the Île to the other. Turn right at the clock: the entrance to the *Conciergerie* is on the right, two minutes from the corner. Inside, you're on the site of the palace of Roman governors and French kings. Formerly part of the palace and to this day an impressive monument of medieval architecture, the **Conciergerie** became part of the ancient "seat of royal justice," the Palais de Justice, just south at **8, boulevard du Palais** (Charles V moved the royal residence to the Louvre at the end of the fourteenth century).

This hulking fortress, however, is most significant as a major seat of historical *injustice*. Its most notorious function was to serve as the prison for political dissidents during the French Revolution. These days, as you walk its creepy passages, you're seeing the site of a massive death row, the antechamber to the beheading of innocents on any number of Paris scaffolds with guillotines.

The **Conciergerie**, a closed dark abyss of stone and iron locks, stands as de Gouges's most appropriate commemorative space: She opposed everything this place represented in the life of Paris and the Revolution.

To see her final residence, either take the guided tour or explore on your own. Once through the vaulted Gothic *La Salle des Gens d'Armes* just inside the entrance (the oldest medieval hall in Europe), you move to the western end—to your right is the *Salle des Gardes* where Robespierre's Revolutionary Tribunal heard and sentenced plaintiffs, who, in 1794, included the Carmelites of Compiegne (see p. 253).

The small stairway at the end of the massive hall leads left into what was called in 1793 the **rue de Paris** (named for the executioner, Monsieur de Paris); prisoners (*pailleux*) too poor to pay for a cell slept here on straw. (This is now the gift shop where Olympe de Gouges's *Declaration of the Rights of Women* [in French] is on sale.)

To the left, as you leave the ***rue de Paris*** and ascend a short stairway, you'll find a room with marble walls incised with the names of the 2,800 prisoners held in this prison and guillotined during the Revolution, including those of Olympe de Gouges, André Chénier, Charlotte Corday, and Georges Danton. Farther on, you'll see Marie Antoinette's cell and chapel, near the death row chapel where the Girondists were held (and possibly Olympe de Gouges, who bore their taint). Also on display is the gigantic blade of a guillotine, "that shameful machine of human butchery," in the words of feminist and 1871 *communard* Louise Michel.

Outside, you can walk the *Cour des Femmes* where women prisoners, under the shadows of the fortress's high walls, did their laundry, washed themselves, and walked. That a special space was made available to the female victims of the Terror carries a bitter irony: It was women, numbering in the thousands, who marched all day on October 5, 1789, from Paris to Versailles, to bring the king back to Paris and bread home to their families. Paris was bankrupt, the harvests had failed, the poor *quartiers*—especially *Saint-Antoine* where the Bastille had been—were hungry.*

The king finally agreed to return to his capital on October 6, his procession protected by the National Guard who skewered loaves of bread on their bayonets; they were followed by carts with sacks of flour. The victorious women followed on foot. Many regard this action, organized and led by anonymous and poor women who risked their lives as they screamed for the king's attention and broke into the Versailles palace as a far more significant revolt than the razing of the Bastille.

---

* Eric Hazan, *A People's History of the French Revolution*.

Who knows what conversation passed among the women crowded around the stone washtubs in the *Cour des Femmes*, a sad place which—even now, more than two hundred years later—the rays of the sun do not touch. Did the women know the fate of their sister prisoners, a few of whom would enter the history books? The much demonized Marie Antoinette, judged guilty on all counts by the all-male historian jurors of the next three centuries, executed on October 16? Charlotte Corday who murdered the fanatic Jean-Paul Marat? Manon Roland who grew up on the *Quai de l'Horloge* just under the walls and high dark towers of the *Conciergerie,* a Girondist like Olympe de Gouges? Olympe's reputation as a witty conversationalist and playwright used to writing comic and irreverent dialogue—(her plays are available at www .olympedegouze.eu)—she would probably have had a lot to say inside the shadows darkening the fountain in the *Cour des Femmes*. Perhaps among those inmates, a few days before Olympe was murdered (and two weeks after Marie Antoinette) there were disobedient members of the Club of Revolutionary Republican Women Citizens, about two hundred radical democrats opposed to the Girondists, who had organized their club in May 1793, but in October had seen it outlawed for their excesses: *"women have little capacity for high conceptions and serious meditations . . . "* went the decree. *"They are disposed . . . to an exaltation that would be harmful in public affairs, . . . the interests of the state would soon be sacrificed to whatever the vivacity of passion might produce in the way of distraction and disorder."* One can only imagine how Olympe de Gouges might have answered the decree that silenced her sister revolutionaries.

Weekends, when the embankment beside the *Quai de la Mégisserie* is closed to traffic, you can follow Olympe de

Gouges's route to the guillotine. The light of the sun on a warm Sunday in February can seem to have the power to bleach the horrors of history to nothingness. Paris, the world's shining pride, luminous ground of the world's beauty, surely its bloody savage history is just a phantom.

Except that in our time there is nothing ghostly or even dated about the mad mind of Robespierre. In his book *Virtue and Terror* he declared the moral foundation of his Reign of Terror. His abstractions have all too contemporary a ring:

> *Terror is nothing but prompt, severe, inflexible justice; it is therefore an emanation of virtue . . . a consequence of the general principle of democracy applied to the homeland's most pressing needs.*

Nearby

CAFÉ BORDS DE SEINE   *Metro: Cité. 1, Place du Châtelet. 7–12:30. At the north end of **boulevard du Palais,** cross Pont au Change (or Pont au Changeurs where the moneylenders did business in Louis IX's time), originally called the Grand Pont. The brasserie is at the end of the bridge, on the corner. The terrace is heated in winter and you can sit as long as you like. Excellent service. The upstairs dining room has a view of the Seine, the three round towers of the **Conciergerie,** and the Gothic towers of Notre-Dame.*

QUAI DE LA MÉGISSERIE   *The buildings are nineteenth century, but the quay is of fourteenth-century origin. Animal lovers are happy here, crowding the quay's pet shops on weekends, visiting live animals, stuffed animals, plants, and flowers. The mégissiers (leather dressers) worked here before the pet merchants moved in.*

THÉÂTRE DU CHÂTELET *www.theatre-chatelet.com. On Place du Châtelet, a large busy square with the Châtelet fountain in the center, named after the Grand Châtelet, a twelfth-century fortress and fortified gate to the Cité, razed in the nineteenth century. The large theater highlights musical programs, some suitable for children. The New York City Ballet performed a twenty ballet tour at a summer festival here in 2016. Tickets online or at the box office.*

Henri IV: Place du Pont Neuf

HENRI IV'S BEAUTIFUL CITY

LOCATION: **Pont Neuf:** *Place Dauphine; Louvre; Square du Vert Galant; Place des Vosges*
MÉTRO: Pont Neuf

The story of Henri IV in Paris is best told from high on the *Pont Neuf,* the New Bridge, the best-loved creation of France's most beloved king. *Henri IV* (1553–1610) sits here on the bronze horse in the middle of this street over water, the longest and widest of the Parisian bridges that connect the Left and Right banks. The statue faces the elegant triangle of *Place Dauphine,* another jewel designed by the king who professed himself a simple cowboy: *"I rule with my arse in the saddle and my gun in my fist."* Centuries after his death by assassination, the streets of Paris were still singing his praises.

Vive Henri Quatre
Vive ce roi vaillant
Vive le bon roi
Vive le vert galant!

The religious fanatics of the war-torn city hated Henri. The mad Catholic who stabbed him to death sixteen years after his coronation was the one assassin—out of at least twenty-three others—who tried to kill him and actually succeeded. Jesuits, Protestants (called Huguenots, Calvinists, or Reformists), and the militant Catholic League, they never stopped plotting their murderous revenge against the soldier-king *bon viveur* who from 1589 (when Henri III died, making Henri IV next in line to the throne) to 1593 had led his Protestant troops against the rebel Catholics of Paris. Bombarding the city from the heights of Montmartre and the bell tower of Saint-Germain-des-Prés, he had hoped to force and finally starve it into submission to a Protestant king.

But then Henri IV renounced his heretic past in the abbey of Saint-Denis in 1593 and six months later was crowned king in Chartres Cathedral. After thirty years of civil war between Catholics and Huguenots, followed by Henri's four-year Siege of Paris, ordinary Parisians didn't care, at this point, whether Henri's conversion was pure or cynical. What mattered was that his submission to Rome meant *no more war.* According to Desmond Seward's *The First Bourbon: Henri IV of France and Navarre,* there is no evidence that he ever said, *"Paris vaut bien une emesse."* (Paris is worth a Mass.)

He had once written to a friend, *"Those who genuinely follow their conscience are of my religion—as for me, I belong to the faith of everyone who is brave and true."* The Catholic League, in thrall to a dogmatic hierarchical authority, sneered at this shameful twist, the new heretical standard of individual conscience. So Protestant! So *moderne!* But ordinary city dwellers—merchants, craftsmen, bankers, artists, masons, burghers, the poor—they were all sick of hunger, sick of the ruins which papists and Huguenots and Henri himself had made of their city. The streets ran with feces—animal and human—the mud thick with blood and rotting body parts. The economy of France was another ruin.

Henri made sure not to burden the workers with the costs of his extensive building and reconstruction projects. To pay for the **Pont Neuf**, for instance, he taxed every cask of wine that came into the city. Enthroned in the Louvre palace, issuing pardons to all combatants, making his visionary plans for the restoration of the broken city, he won the people's allegiance. *"We must be brought to agreement by reason and kindness,"* he wrote, *"and not by strictness and cruelty which serve only to arouse men."* In this magnanimous spirit, he drafted and signed the Edict of Nantes, granting tolerance and freedom of worship to the reformist religion in 1598 (the same year he undertook the *Pont Neuf,* originally planned by the Valois king Henri III). Such was his popularity that even the most rigid Catholics chose not to make war against Henri's mandated tolerance.

Born into the House of Bourbon and raised in the southwest, in the kingdom of Navarre, at the time a small independent realm in the Basque country between France and Spain, he had the Gascon temperament described by Balzac as "bold, brave, adventurous, prone to exaggerate the good and belittle the bad, . . . laughing at vice when it serves as a stepping stone." At every stage, he was a charmer, "his eyes full of sweetness, . . . his whole mien animated with an uncommon vivacity," to quote one magistrate. The northern, more cerebral French regarded the men of the South, who spoke Provençal, as foreigners.

He was baptized in the Catholic Church but was given a Protestant tutor after his parents converted to Protestantism. When his father—but not his mother—returned to the Church, he gave his son a Catholic tutor. The boy, however, kept his mother's reformed faith, even while studying in Catholic Paris at the College of Navarre on the hill of Sainte-Geneviève.

The Wars of Religion raged during his adolescence when

he left the College of Navarre and returned to his family's kingdom. He saw for himself the torture and barbarism each of the warring sects inflicted on the other. In 1572, he once again left home to travel north to Paris where his arranged marriage with the Catholic Marguerite de Valois (*Margot*), sister of the Valois king Charles IX and daughter of the royal poisoner Queen Mother Catherine de Medici, was seen at first as an occasion of joy, a sign that the papists and the Huguenots would now stop killing each other. (For Marguerite's bridal emotions, see "La Reine Margot: Legends and Lies," p. 229.)

Thousands of Protestant nobles came to Paris to enjoy the party. They were invited to occupy rooms in the Louvre. (Some stayed home in their châteaux, possessed of a strange sense of foreboding.) The marriage festivities, despite the bride and groom's distaste for each other, obvious during the ceremony outside the Cathedral of Notre-Dame, lasted almost a week. Then, to the signal of triumphant Christian church bells, horror exploded. What became known as the Saint Bartholomew's Day Massacre, of Protestants by Catholics—raged throughout the next three nights and days.

The Protestant bridegroom, expecting death, hid in the Louvre and later, under "house arrest" in the corridors of the *Château de Vincennes*, at that time a state prison.

Plotting but failing to escape from Paris over the next four years, Henri played the game of pretending to enjoy the pleasures of the city, hunting in the royal forests landscaped under François I (*Bois de Boulogne* and *Fontainebleau*) as well as gambling, tennis, women, strolling through the gardens of the Louvre. The new bride tried to help her husband escape. Alexandre Dumas's novel *La Reine Margot* portrays her as Henri's loyal protector.

Finally he got away, home to Navarre, hoping never to set eyes on Paris again. Following the Saint Bartholomew's Day Massacre, there were eight more civil wars involving Catholics and Protestants. Henri saddled up to join the nonstop bloodletting over whose religion was the *True* one, the surest ticket to paradise. No wonder he came to detest the absurdities of partisan religion, wanting no part of it once he was king. The slaughter ended only on the day he genuflected to Rome in Saint-Denis. War had not worked; conversion, he realized, was the only way to win over Catholic Paris and be crowned *Rex Christianissimus*, Most Christian King. (Montaigne believed that though a firm Calvinist under his mother's influence, Henri's warm earthy personality was more suited to the Catholic faith than to the icy purity of Protestantism.)

What was not understood about Henri in 1594 when as king he settled into the *Louvre* palace and took jubilant carriage rides onto the *Île de la Cité* to hear High Mass at Notre-Dame was his love of beauty. He was determined to transform the filthy ruins of Paris into a place fit for civilized human beings: *"To make this city beautiful, tranquil, to make [it] a whole world and a wonder of the world."* A visionary and a pragmatist, by the time he was murdered, he had made the medieval city of Paris into a modern capital: "the Capital of the World" as it came to be called, for centuries.

For the Traveler

From the day it opened, in 1606, the **Pont Neuf,** like its creator, delighted Paris. People came in droves to enjoy its wide openness—unclogged by houses or shops—where musicians and acrobats engaged the strolling crowds making merry along the never-before-seen sidewalks, a wonder of Europe. According to seventeenth-century travel writers, the *Pont Neuf* offered the most magnificent view in the entire world. Parisians and tourists could gaze at the river, the monuments and *hôtels* along the riverbanks, and the trees and hills in the distant silvery light.

And still we come, day and night, our delight quickened with the colors of the sky, the Seine a kind of music.

Leaving behind Henri in his bronze saddle and twenty-first-century tourists, we walk north from the *Pont Neuf* onto the Right Bank en route to the *Louvre* palace where Henri's friend Montaigne had first set eyes on the beautiful *Reine Margot* (see p. 229).

Bearing left into *Quai du Louvre* and, in two blocks, right into *rue de l'Amiral de Coligny,* you will soon pass the lovely parish church of the ancient royal families, *Saint-Germain l'Auxerrois,* where the devout Margot, the new Queen of Navarre, attended Mass. Built on the site of a Viking camp, the church faces the great door of the Louvre, which admits you to the *Cour Carrée* (Square Courtyard), the oldest part of the Louvre. It was from the belfry of Saint-Germain, that the church bell—"*la Marie*"—rang out in the dawn of August 24, summoning Catholics to launch the Saint Bartholomew's Day Massacre. Encouraged by Henri's new Valois mother-in-law, Catherine de Medici, and her crazy son King Charles IX, Catholic mobs trapped the Protestant wedding guests inside the Louvre and hacked them to death. "*Kill them all, kill them all!*" the insane king screamed from the palace windows as corpses and body parts were hurled from the roof, landing in the courtyards. Lingering in the hush of the *Cour Carrée* on blue summer nights when the

Louvre stays open late (Wed and Fri until 9:45), the story of the royal bloodbath feels like a blood-and-guts movie plot—not real, this could never happen!

The slaughter lasted for more than three days. Thousands of Huguenots were killed in Paris, most dumped in the Seine. Ten, possibly thirty thousand died throughout provincial France. In Rome, the pope and his College of Cardinals attended a triumphant *Te Deum*, the cannon of the *Castel Sant'Angelo* fired salutes in celebration of mass murder. King Philip of Catholic Spain was said to smile for the first time in his life.

Returning now to the ***Pont Neuf,*** (leaving Henri behind, hidden in his new bride's closet as Alexandre Dumas has it), descend its staircase behind the *cheval de bronze* to ***Pointe de la Cité*** which is occupied by the lovely ***Square du Vert-Galant,*** a garden at the original level of the *Île de la Cité*. It's named for the lusty *galant* up on the bridge, the "gay blade" astride his horse. Here, away from the crowds, you can contemplate, through a screen of willow trees bordering the square, the lifeline of Paris, the city's main street, ***the river Seine***. From the tip of the *Île,* you can see the majestic "power" architecture of the Louvre: in the distance its celebrated long gallery—***Grande Galerie*** or ***Galerie du Bord de l'Eau***—which Henri had built. From the beginning of his reign, he worked on the enlargement of the Louvre though the gallery project itself—to connect the royal Louvre with Catherine de Medici's Tuileries palace. As a prisoner after the Saint Bartholomew's Day Massacre and then as king, Henri loved to stroll the length of the Louvre, his riverfront ***Grande Galerie*** adding a quarter of a mile to his walk. He also designed the original *Orangerie* at the far end of what is now the Tuileries gardens which were first planted by his homicidal mother-in-law. (Today's *Musée de l'Orangerie* was built in 1852 on the site of the original gallery, next to the Place de la Concorde.) The best view of the *Grande Galerie* is from one bridge west of the **Pont Neuf,** on the **Pont des Arts** (recently liberated from its Love Locks), which extends between the Institut de France on the Left Bank and the Louvre, on the Right.

King Henri's transformations of war-zone Paris survive today in some of his most glorious projects: the most celebrated is the **Place Royale,** now known as the **Place des Vosges;** the lovely **Place Dauphine,** dedicated to his son who became Louis XIII; **rue Dauphine,** the extension of the **Pont Neuf** into the Left Bank; and the **Hôpital Saint-Louis** in northeast Paris, just off the Canal Saint-Martin. Proud of his urban renewal projects and the cleaned-up city streets, he wrote to Cardinal de Joyeuse, the French ambassador to papal Rome:

> *This is to give you news of my buildings and of my gardens and to assure you that I haven't lost any time . . . In Paris you will find my long gallery which goes to the Tuileries completed. . . . a pond and many beautiful fountains . . . my plantings and my garden very beautiful; the Place Royale which is near the Porte St Antoine . . .*
>
> *At the end of the Pont Neuf, a beautiful street which goes to the Porte de Buci, plus two to three thousand workshops which work here and there for the embellishment of the city, so much that it is unbelievable how much you find changed.*

Place Royale (Place des Vosges)

MÉTRO: Saint-Paul; Chemin Vert
DIRECTIONS: Or a twenty-minute walk east from Pont
    Neuf along the quays to rue Saint-Paul; turn left and
    walk a few blocks north to rue Saint-Antoine; a short
    walk east to rue de Birague, which leads through the
    Pavillon du Roi into the Place.

Architecture, Henri told his friends, along with war and women, was his greatest delight. A legendary lover (though he seldom bathed and was said to reek of garlic), he had many mistresses. The children of-the-blood lived in a royal nursery in Saint-Germain where they were raised on an equal footing and visited frequently by their father. As a husband he was a failure. He and Marguerite Valois, *La Reine Margot* (see p. 229), finally divorced so that Henri could marry Marie de Medici for her fortune and pay off France's war debts. But the Italian Marie of Tuscany was less accepting of his infidelities than the unfaithful Margot had been. The bedrooms of the Louvre palace rang with her operatic screaming and weeping sometimes lasting all night.

Abroad in the city, Henri enjoyed himself. He liked the nearby *quartier* of the *Marais* (marshland) on the northern bank of the Seine, where charming *hôtels* had been built in the sixteenth century. He had friends here and sometimes partied all night with one mistress or another, returning to the Louvre and the furious Marie at eight o'clock in the morning. Maybe it was at the end of a long high-spirited night in the *Marais* that the urban visionary king, noticing in the light of dawn all that vacant land of the *quartier* Tournelles—including a dump and a horse market—conceived the idea to build there a large open beautiful public space . . . surrounded by buildings of brick and stone, a gorgeous red brick and golden stone . . . with vendors in arcades and workshops for artisans and for silk workers in the factories he would open, making silk a French industry, thus eliminating the Italian competition, this lively colorful site, bordered by rows of lime trees, would offer commerce and entertainment, music, literature, art, and sex in the salons of the handsome brick and stone pavilions to be built around a large square, a rich cultural mix . . . a *Place Royale . . . a Royal Square*! As his carriage rumbled west on **rue Saint-Antoine,** a street since the Roman occupation in 52 BC, Henri imagined the particulars of the *Place* that would be his masterpiece. All the way back to the Louvre, as the sun rose over the city, he dreamed it. To this day, *Place des Vosges,* in all seasons, is a ravishing dreamworld in the early morning light, private and silent, waking up at noon with the arrival of schoolchildren and visitors. Sundays are festivals of families and tourists looking for brunch.

Henri ordered his *Place* built in eighteen months, visiting the construction site every day. But problems arose, slowing things down, changing his plans.

And then the king who loved tolerance and beauty and the city of Paris was dead, his aorta punctured by a dropout monk with a kitchen knife on **rue de la Ferronniere** (still clogged today with the traffic that in 1610 stalled Henri's carriage to the mad François Ravaillac's advantage). *All Paris changed . . . everyone began to wail and cry, with women and girls tearing their hair out* . . . Henri, who had once declared kindness and mercy the primary virtues of a prince, would hardly have approved his assassin's punishments—torn limb from limb in the Place de Grève, drawn and quartered, boiled alive.

His reign had been a golden age. He gave the city peace, a measure of prosperity, and a culture of beauty and energy. These days he probably would not turn up his nose at the tourists strolling south off the **Pont Neuf** onto his very commercial **rue Dauphine** on the Left Bank, the glut of hotels, bars, the giddy foreign teenagers, pierced and coiffed in the colors of a rainbow, their elders pointing out the pretty cross streets. **Rue Christine**—the couples making out, accordions playing "I Love Paris," the poodles in arms, the crowded **rue de Buci** just ahead. Neither bigot nor snob, the king of pluralism loved the carnivalesque of Paris streets, the exuberant and improvisatory freedom of a great city.

Nearby

VEDETTES DU PONT NEUF   *www.pontneuf.net. Sightseeing boats depart from the north side of the* **Square du Vert-Galant.** *An enchanting ride, especially at night.*

LA TAVERNE HENRI IV   *13,* **Place du Pont Neuf,** *75001. Tel: 01.43.54.27.90. Every day except Sunday, noon–3; 7–12:30. A small old wine bar, also serving delicious charcuterie, tartines, hot plats du jour. "The archetype of the great bistro à vin" in the words of* The New York Times, *for Parisians one of the best wine bars in Paris. On the western tip of Place Dauphine just across from Henri IV's statue on the Pont Neuf.*

ACTION CHRISTINE   *Métro: Saint-Michel; Odéon. 4, rue Christine, off rue Dauphine. Henri called rue Dauphine his "beautiful street." Tel: 01.43.25.85. A small movie theater with deep red velvet seats, showing restored classic American films.*

ÎLE SAINT-LOUIS

Honoré Daumier: The Seine at Quai d'Anjou

HONORÉ DAUMIER'S HUMAN COMEDY

LOCATION: *9, Quai d'Anjou: Along the North Bank of Île Saint-Louis*

MÉTRO: Pont Marie

P icasso compared him to Michelangelo. The solidity of his bodies, his sense of their burdens, their grace. Others, especially Vincent van Gogh, mention Rembrandt, the dramatic play of light and dark evoking the humanity of Daumier's washerwomen, bargemen, grandmothers, clowns. His neighbor, the poet Charles Baudelaire (1821–1867), called him "one of the most important men . . . in the whole of modern art. . . . He draws as the great masters draw." Some say Daumier prefigures film, citing him as a major influence on avant-garde Russian filmmakers, especially Sergei Eisenstein.

In Daumier's lifetime (1808–1879), he was best known as a caricaturist, lithographer, and sculptor. *"What a sculptor!"* Rodin exclaimed on his first encounter with one of Daumier's clay figures. His fellow painters—Corot, Manet, Delacroix, Courbet, to name a few—praised his paintings. But they did not sell. *The Laundress,* for instance, this empathic image of the working mother and her child whom he observed from his studio on the *Quai d'Anjou* was hung so high on the wall of the *Salon* that visitors couldn't see it. When Daumier's masterpiece, *The Third-Class Carriage* (now in the Metropolitan Museum of Art in New York) was shown at an exhibition of his work at the Durand-Ruel gallery the year before

he died, artists (Degas) and critics wrote about it in superlatives. But the public didn't show up. This modest man, a
lifelong radical democrat who detested the pretensions and
greed of the nouveau-riche bourgeoisie would have found the
idea of self-promotion, self-"marketing" repugnant.

Born in Marseilles, he came to Paris when he was eight
years old and never left. More than any other influence—
the South, art classes, his would-be artist father, his artist
friends—it was Paris that shaped his genius. The streets of
nineteenth-century Paris—before Haussmann—became his
school and college, his inspiration. Baudelaire said he had a
"divine memory" for the faces and bodies he saw and studied all over the city; Daumier used no models. His parents
were poor. Daumier worked in a bookstore and as a "gutter
jumper," an errand boy for notaries and lawyers. At fourteen,
announcing he would become a painter, he studied in a few
studios and art schools. And then he learned lithography—
the art of printing from stone—which had just arrived in
Paris. "You have the touch," a teacher told him. And in the
lithographs, caricatures, and engravings he sold to newspapers, he found a steady if extremely modest source of income. He worked constantly and prolifically.

Like all of antimonarchist Paris, he was optimistic in
July 1830 when troops and citizen rebels, reacting to the extreme urban poverty of the Restoration years as well as the
threat of press censorship, drove the last Bourbon king,
Charles X, into exile. There was relief at first when Louis-
Philippe, the elected ruler of "the people," abandoned royal
pomp and circumstance, walking around Paris with a green
umbrella tucked under his arm, greeting workers as "my
friends." The bourgeoisie liked the prospect of peace and
their increasing prosperity.

But nothing changed in the lives of the poor. Hordes of immigrants arrived from the provinces to find no jobs, no food, no housing. The streets of Paris remained filthy and muddy and crowded with thieves and prostitutes. By 1831, riots turned the streets violent and deadly; a cholera epidemic in 1832 killed thousands. On and off *rue Saint-Antoine,* life felt as hopeless as before the Revolution of 1789. The suffering of the working poor was one of Daumier's lifelong themes. You can see his sympathy in the way he paints faces, eyes, the curve of backs stooped beneath their burdens.

Daumier and the other republicans of Paris saw early on Louis-Philippe's July Monarchy as an empty show. His ministers were encouraged to *"enrichissez-vous."* Get rich yourselves, leave the politics to us. The maxim of the day, in the words of George Sand, was "Everybody by himself, for himself." As the corruption swelled, the ministers got fatter, Louis-Philippe more bloated and oppressive, the money gap between the rich and poor larger. Louis-Philippe's appointees in the National Assembly approved a tax increase that allowed the Citizen King an allowance 37 times greater than what Napoleon Bonaparte had received and 148 times greater than what the president of the United States was paid at the time.

Daumier took on the powerful in lithographs and political caricatures that were published in a left-wing newspaper. Inspired by the bawdy Rabelais, his caricature of a gross and gluttonous Louis-Philippe as Gargantua—entitled *La Poire* (*The Pear*) in imitation of the shape of the king's head (now in the *Bibliothèque Nationale*)—became wildly popular. But the artist, who was the sole support of his elderly mother and father, was sentenced to prison for six months. By specific order of the Pear, four of those months transpired in a mental hospital.

For the Traveler

He never stopped satirizing the rapacious government. He visited the ***National Assembly*** regularly, scrutinizing the faces of the members, then sculpted their heads with clay.

> (The public entrance to the beautiful Assemblée
>   Nationale/Palais Bourbon—Delacroix, its major
>   artist—is at 33, Quai d'Orsay. Métro: Solférino or
>   Assemblée Nationale. Guided tours have been
>   temporarily canceled. En.parisinfo.com/Assemblee-
>   Nationale.)

Thirty-eight of the forty unbaked painted clay busts that survive can be seen today in the ***Musée d'Orsay*** on the ground floor, to the left of the entrance as you enter, in rooms 4–6.

> (Métro: Solférino; 9:30–6; Thurs until 9:45; closed Mon.
>   Long lines except for ticket holders; tickets sold on
>   line. www.musee-orsay.fr.)

On the politicians' faces you see the distortions left by hypocrisy, greed, and the genius of Daumier's hands. He saw his busts as so many masks demonstrating the collective soullessness of Louis-Philippe's reign. The series was called *Les Célébrités du Juste Milieu*. Seen in the ***Orsay,*** the busts, like the *La Comèdie Humaine* novels of Daumier's friend Honoré de Balzac, show the cruel dark side of nineteenth-century

Paris, a powerful counterpoint to the sentimentality of conventional artists. ("He's a scoffer and a skeptic," opined one loud visitor in 2015. "Let's get out of here." Gone with a sneer, the man missed other Daumiers in the same gallery: the magisterial *La Blanchisseuse* [*The Laundress*], *Les Fugitifs,* and *Ratapoil.*)

Hand in glove with the king's ministers were the lawyers who made their living in the *Palais de Justice* on boulevard du Palais, next to the entrance to the Sainte-Chapelle (see p. 17), a huge building, much altered since it served as the Capetian kings' residence. Daumier watched the lawyers coming and going, up and down the long front staircase, knowing from his own experience the heartless injustices orchestrated inside the *Palais* under Louis-Philippe: the evictions, the homelessness, the forced emigrations, the neglect of poor children. Thousands of his lithographs on these subjects—the politicians, lawyers, and their victims—can today be found in museums and private residences all over the world. His lawyers' faces show up in Serge Eisenstein's *Battleship Potemkin*.

You may visit the courtrooms in the *Palais,* observing the interactions of robed lawyers, the bewigged judge, plaintiffs, and defendants. If you can find your way to the sixteenth *chambre correctionnelle,* you can look in where Baudelaire's *Les Fleurs du Mal* was tried for obscenity in 1857, the same year Flaubert's *Madame Bovary* was tried on the same charge.

DIRECTIONS: (*Palais de Justice,* formerly the Palais de la Cité—its parts ranging from the thirteenth to the twentieth centuries. 10, boulevard du Palais, 75001.

8:30—6:30. Métro: Pont Neuf/Saint-Michel. Robespierre's tribunal pronounced the death sentence on
Marie Antoinette in the chambre Dorée.The grossly
huge western façade of the Palais, a nineteenth-
century addition, towers over Henri IV's gracefully
proportioned sixteenth-century Place Dauphine. See
p. 44.)

Daumier had had many addresses in the city by the time
he moved to the top floor of *9, Quai d'Anjou* on the *Île Saint-
Louis* in 1841, staying until 1863. He converted the attic space
into a studio, installing a window in the roof, plastering the
walls white, making a large bare room with enough light for
a painter as well as a living space for him and his beloved
Didine (Marie-Alexandrine Dassy). His caricatures and lithographs paid the (affordable) rent, but more than anything,
Daumier wanted to paint. (Many painters have set up their
ateliers behind the long "French" windows on the banks of
the Seine—Matisse, for example, on *Quai Saint-Michel.)*

Four bridges connect the mainland to the island. From the
southern *Marais* the **Pont Marie** has direct access to the north
bank: turn left onto *Quai d'Anjou*. On a gray February afternoon, the view from the empty street is haunting, the muted
colors, the silence, the choppy gray-brown river. These days
real estate on the Île Saint-Louis attracts billionaires, discour-
aging local buyers; the restaurants are pricey, the streets and
shops well-heeled and buttoned-up. But in early evening or
morning, as you walk along *Quai d'Anjou,* you enter the
mystery of old Paris. The past becomes a presence.

It was once just a small islet in the Seine, the backyard of
the *Île de la Cité*. Henri IV had the idea to join the two is-
lands; his son Louis XIII executed the plan and the great

French architect Louis Le Vau built the imposing mansions, including one for himself. Two centuries later, many of the tall noble *hôtels* had been broken up into small apartments, occupied by artists, merchants, and the working poor. It was a diverse neighborhood, quiet and shaded by trees. As Zola described it in *The Quarry*,

> *the island communed sleepily with itself in a quarter sel-dom troubled by the noise of carriages. . . . You would think yourself a thousand miles away from that modern Paris alive and swarming . . . loud with the roars of mil-lions.*

Daumier had friends nearby, painters, writers, most nota-bly Baudelaire who lived in the Hôtel de Lauzon (no. 29), known back then as Hôtel Pimodan. Baudelaire's art criticism, collected in *The Painter of Modern Life* (1863) includes his brilliant commentary on Daumier. Known as "the father of modern art-criticism," Baudelaire, who despised sentimental-ity, was a passionate defender of the devastating honesty of Daumier's work. He visited him in his *atelier* and spread the word about his genius to other artists, including his friend Manet. Another friend wrote that

> I admired his face glowing with strength and good nature, his small piercing eyes, his nose uptilted as though by a breeze, his gracious mouth, his fine art-ist's head.

Daumier's muse on *Quai d'Anjou* was the Seine in all its moody river life. The Paris sky above, the buildings on the Right Bank's *Quai des Célestins*, the workers on the river—

bargemen, longshoremen, water carriers, and the washer-women who washed the dirty laundry of Paris while keeping an eye on their children. Daumier's *Laveuse au Quai d'Anjou* (Albright-Knox Art Gallery in Buffalo, New York), *La Sortie du Bateau à Lassive.* (Metropolitan Museum of Art), and *La Blanchisseuse* (**Musée d'Orsay**) comprise several versions on the theme of the working women and the river, each one a life force, eternal. He painted what he saw every day from his high windows: the mother coming up the steps from the river, her heavy bulky laundry under one arm, helping the child with the other. The steps leading down to the embankment are still there on the quay as are the stone washhouses across the river on *Quai des Célestins*, but the water has been cleaned up. No longer a public laundry, it's fit for fish.

Couples, children, people of all ages walk along the quays these days. At night the lights of boats and buildings are reflected on the water. It's a scene foreign visitors never forget.

The sympathy with which Daumier saw these working mothers who carried the burdens of the world comes across with profound conviction. (This same blend of realism and idealism, the movement of dark into light, animate his most famous painting, *The Third-Class Carriage*. The figure of the grandmother has often been compared to Rembrandt's and Michelangelo's old women.)

Some critics consider Daumier's figures among the most moving in French painting. "They are alive with the charity, the strength, and the understanding poured into them by the great soul of the artist," to quote Thomas Craven. "Of all the French painters, he is the most democratic." For all his sympathy, in his *Bluestockings* series he caricatured the feminists of the 1840s as ugly harridans, a misogynistic lapse usually explained away as evidence of his contempt for ideologues and polemics, not for women. He was a lifelong socialist who did not join in partisan politics, rallies, or letters to the editor.

He stayed quietly loyal to what he loved. Without public comment he refused the medal of honor from the Légion d'Honneur. It was offered by Emperor Napoleon III whose name Daumier could not bear to hear mentioned. After he and his wife moved off the increasingly expensive Île Saint-Louis to working-class Montmartre, he was walking one day with a friend on the *boulevard de Clichy*. (The Daumiers lived at no. 36.) Always hard up for money but never complaining, he stopped to look at the people in a poor Montmartre street: "We have our art to console us," he said. "But they, unhappy creatures, what have they?"

Nearby

*One of the most beautiful prospects in Paris is **Place Louis Aragon** on Quai de Bourbon on the western tip of Île Saint-Louis. Turn left at the end of Pont Saint-Louis, leading from the Île de la Cité, walk a short distance to the bench and its sign bearing words by Aragon (1897–1982): "Connaissez-vous l'Île? Au cœur de la ville. Où tout est tranquille. Éternellement." You could sit here forever on the edge of the Seine, under the trees, looking over at Héloise and Abelard's **Quai aux Fleurs**. Aragon's novel, Aurélien, numbered among the one hundred best French books of the twentieth century, is set here, on Île Saint-Louis.*

36, QUAI DE BÉTHUNE *From Place Louis Aragon, walk east up the quays (past the elegant Hôtel Lambert, which Voltaire owned at one point (see p. 120), around the little square at the eastern tip, and, then, up Quai de Béthune to no. 36, the final residence of Marie Curie (see p. 87). The view from here, of the back of the Cathedral of Notre-Dame, the curve of the Île on its southern edge, and the swans and ducks on the Seine is sublime, in all seasons. Crossing the* **Pont de la Tournelle,** *past the statue of Sainte Geneviève, bear right and stop to look over the Seine at the apse of Notre-Dame.*

BERTHILLON ICE CREAM   *29–31,* **rue des Deux Ponts,** *on the right as you head south on the Île Saint-Louis toward the Left Bank.*

THE LEFT BANK

Montaigne: Statue of Montaigne on rue des Écoles

The Latin Quarter

GOING SANE WITH
MICHEL DE MONTAIGNE

LOCATION: ***Rue des Écoles,*** *Statue: Square Paul-Painlevé;*
Collège de France; Louvre; Latin Quarter
MÉTRO: Cluny-La Sorbonne; Maubert–Mutualité

One way to appreciate the pleasure Parisians still take
in the memory of Montaigne (1533–1592)—called vari-
ously the first modern philosopher; a Christian humanist; a
humanist; a realist—is to watch them on ***rue des Écoles*** as they
pass his statue. It faces the street and the uphill ***rue de la Sorbonne*** and ***rue Saint-Jacques***; its back is to the *Square Paul-
Painlevé* and the Cluny museum.

> DIRECTIONS: (From the Cluny-La Sorbonne métro, walk
> up—south—on "Boul'Mich"; turn left into rue des
> Écoles.)

As they pass the statue, more than a few pedestrians of all
ages, tweedy professors, kids, students, pause to touch—
caress, really—the bronze foot of Montaigne's crossed right
leg. Some smile. Foot touchers have confessed to asking his
help on exams. The smile on Montaigne's face would inspire
trust. Stefan Zweig called him "the patron saint of every free
man on earth. He cheers me up."

Paris, as the words incised on the statue show, was the darling of Montaigne's heart. By comparison, his native Bordeaux didn't score. To this day his famous words have the

power to stir the hearts of even the city's most disenchanted natives:

> *However much I rebel against France, I look warmly on Paris. It has had my heart since I was a child. . . . the more I have seen other fine cities, the more Paris's beauty gains in my affections. I love it for itself, and for itself alone. I love it tenderly warts and all. I am only French through this great city . . . the glory of France and one of the noblest ornaments of the world. May God drive out of it all divisions!**

And though the statue shows a sitting Montaigne, he was not a sedentary man: He loved to walk the streets of Paris. "*My business is to keep myself in motion. . . . I walk for the sake of walking.*"

Born and raised in the small Château de Montaigne thirty miles east of Bordeaux and educated in the law, he served his native city as a public servant, in its parliament, its law courts, and as its mayor. In these official roles (and as a child), he visited Paris many times. Following the deaths of his much beloved father and his best friend, Étienne de La Boétie in 1571, he retired from public life in a state of deep depression to read and write alone in his library. The fruits of his cloistered meditations he called the *Essays*. He used the word *essay* in its original sense, meaning "test, trial, or experiment."

Throughout the years of their composition (1571–1592), the furies of the Wars of Religion raged on. Catholic and Protestant corpses, thousands of them, rotted in the streets of French villages and cities. Catholic himself, Montaigne,

---

*Michel de Montaigne, *The Essays: A Selection*, trans. M. A. Screech.

like his Protestant friend Henri of Navarre (see p. 37), another man of the South, the future *Henri IV*, despised the intolerance of both versions of Christianity. Each sect saw itself fighting a "holy" war, with God on its side, justifying every atrocity, which in the words of historian Lauro Martines, included "the murder of children, the disemboweling of pregnant women, and the bizarre configuring of massacred body parts."

The heinous politics of sixteenth-century France aroused in Montaigne not only disgust but a profound skepticism. Received truths from blowhard zealots, submission to what clergy and theologians called the "Will of God," none of the era's manipulative dishonesty and its consequent cruelties escaped or fooled him.

He found a purpose in this brutal history: he would figure out and write about how to live as a human being; he would describe how a person with a mind of her own could be happy. It was a wild idea in the context of a society so blood-soaked with competing religions. His method was also strange for the times. He shaped the content of the essays by exploring his own consciousness. He told his readers not what he knew from authority but what he'd come to learn as an individual man: reason has its limits. A man full of contradictions, doubts, skepticism, he himself became the subject of his 107 essays, which he published in three separate books over the next twenty years. In his words, "I offered my self to myself as theme and subject matter."* As the subject under scrutiny he confessed that he could never pin down a stable "I." He was ever-changing. He offered no apologies. That's how he was; that's how human beings are.

---

*Michel de Montaigne, *The Essays: A Selection*, trans. M. A. Screech.

He portrayed becoming rather than being, life and existence as process. Life came down to moments. In the words
of biographer Donald Frame, his point of view anticipates
Proust and Joyce:

> *Long before Freud . . . Montaigne had a strong sense of*
> *the conflicts within the psyche, of the myriad parts that may*
> *rebel, openly or covertly, against our will . . . . The absurd*
> *is almost a creed today . . . [but] few men before our time*
> *have been more aware of what Montaigne . . . prefers to call*
> *our absurdity. We are not, he reminds us, "so full of evil as*
> *of inanity, . . . Man is . . . all in all, the fool of the farce."**

In his processive world, absolutes are dead ends. Wise men
are tentative, moderate. They laugh and smile more than they
frown with worry and anxiety.

No wonder academics like to touch his bronze foot on the
rue des Écoles. The first man to present the destabilized self
as a fact of human psychology—perhaps explaining the ab-
surdity of existence—deserves respect!

Shakespeare caught his spirit, reading the *Essays* while
writing *The Tempest*. Flaubert and Camus read the *Essays*
throughout their lives. Joyce had Montaigne in mind at the
end of *The Portrait of the Artrist as a Young Man*, declaring
his intent to explore the consciousness of his own soul, the
way to free himself from the imprisoning dogmatism of his
native country and religion.

As Montaigne left his library behind for long periods,
traveling in Europe, spending time in Paris, he made up his
own mind about all that he saw. Of course it helped that he

---

*Qtd. in Montaigne: *A Biography*, 1965, by Donald M. Frame.

had studied history, philosophy, law, and languages. He said he could write about anything, even a fly, and clearly his essays reflect an original mind curious about weird particulars. By the time he returned home from various travels and trips to Paris to write about flies or sex or cannibals or marriage (he had a wife and child) he was richer in understanding than when he'd last sat contemplating in his solitary library. He came to insist that the body has equal dignity with the soul. Ignoring the body, he said, is a form of madness; only saints and madmen (and Plato) can pretend or aspire to be angels. In his final essay "On Experience," he voices his unequivocal acceptance of the human condition: *"Upon the highest throne in the world, we are seated, still, upon our arses."*

For the Traveler

Montaigne's Paris was the creation of King François I (1494–1547), the importer to France of the body and soul of the Italian Renaissance. As royal curator and godfather of this new world, he launched a number of projects that shaped the reputation of Paris as the artistic and intellectual heart of France.

As a member of the Bordeaux parliament Montaigne had traveled regularly to participate in the Paris parliament. By the time François had died and his Catholic sons were on the throne, Montaigne, on the strength of his essays and his having served as intermediary and negotiator between Protestant Henri of Navarre and François's son, the Catholic king Henri III, was widely respected and trusted by both factions.

He was not popular with everyone. He was suspected of being a secret Protestant or atheist because of his lack of deference to the clergy's opinions as well as his attachment to the "pagan" classics—Ovid, Seneca, Socrates—and to his friend Henri of Navarre. André Maurois believes that Montaigne is no more Christian than Voltaire; others judge him a Catholic skeptic, claiming that his faith in the Church enabled him to enjoy his universal doubt and to remain himself. Montaigne wrote:

> *I remain where God put me. Otherwise I would not know how to save myself from endlessly roiling.*

The *Essays* belonged to the cultural revolution that marked the beginning of François I's French Renaissance, revolutionary because it marked a definitive break with the medieval belief in revealed truth. It valued the beauty and wisdom of Greek and Roman art and philosophy more than the texts of the Bible. The *Essays* established Montaigne as a true Renaissance man: He believed that every human being can shape for himself a philosophy, and decide how to live and act on his own. He prized freedom, a far happier condition than the constraints of dogma.

In addition to the Renaissance ethos the king's vision of this larger new world translated into highly visible reconstruction projects. He rebuilt the Louvre, ordering the demolition of the old gloomy medieval fortress's west and south sides built by Philippe-Auguste and their rebuilding as an anti-austere lavish palace. The elegant new sculptural decorations on the oldest part, the *Cour Carrée*, were a proud expression of worldly rather than heavenly glory.

During the reigns of François I's descendants, Montaigne visited the Paris court off and on until the end of his life. The exact dates of his visits are not known. But his life as a courtier in Renaissance Paris gave him great pleasure as Stefan Zweig shows in his biography. Pleasure was his guiding star leading him always to Paris. *Paris la ville que Montaigne aime depuis toujours and qui toujours l'enchanté.* (Paris, the city Montaigne loved forever and which enchanted him always.)

To follow in the footsteps of Montaigne the courtier, visit the palace he knew best, the *Louvre* on the Right Bank, which later became one of the world's largest museums. To get a fuller sense of the court life of the sixteenth century, its intimacies and intrigues, travelers might enjoy Madame de Lafayette's novel, *The Princesse de Clèves,* a masterpiece of historical French fiction, which begins in 1558, in the royal palace of Tournelles (which Montaigne knew well), before Catherine de Medici razed it and moved the royal family to the Louvre after the death of her husband Henri II. Beneath the façades of court protocols and constricted morality, you can feel the heat of a woman in love, her divided conscience, her sexual desire, the terror of disobedience, of carnal pleasure.

The Louvre's much restored three wings or pavilions, the *Sully, Denon,* and *Richelieu,* were once the galleries where courtiers enjoyed royal hospitality and entertainments (and *The Princesse de Clèves* her secret surges of immoral passion). On a quiet uncrowded evening visit to the Louvre, it's easy to imagine the masked and dancing couples in these pavilions, the rustle of silk, the whisperings of lovers, the royal entourage.

The Louvre's art collection was the result of François I's enterprising enthusiasm for Italian art. He imported masterpieces by Uccello, Titian, Giorgione, and, most notably, Leonardo da Vinci himself, whose Mona Lisa—*La Joconde* in French—was and remains the most valued painting in the royal collection. Montaigne does not mention the paintings or the Italian sculptor Benvenuto Cellini whom François also imported to help transform gloomy Paris into a city of bright and saucy opulence.

> DIRECTIONS: (The ***Louvre*** is open daily, except Tues,
> 9–5:45; evenings Wed and Fri until 9:45. Closed May 1,
> Jan 1, Aug 15, Dec 25. The main entrance is at the glass
> pyramid in the center of the Cour Napoleon. To avoid
> long lines, buy tickets in advance online (www.louvre
> .fr) or from stores (FNAC, Virgin, Galeries Lafayette,
> Printemps). The Paris Pass includes entry to the
> Louvre. *www.parispass.com/free-download-centre.php.*

Returning to the Left Bank and Montaigne's statue, a short walk to the east along ***rue des Écoles*** leads to the ***Collège de France*** on the south side of the street.

François I opened the ***Collège de France*** in 1530 as another testament to Renaissance independence and humanism, a non-theological institution in opposition to the conservative Sorbonne which since its founding (see p. 23) had taught a narrow scholasticism. He appointed six royal lecturers, two in Greek, two in Hebrew, one in math, and one "Independent." The classes were free, open to the public, no entrance exams required; it escaped, by royal design, the Sorbonne's censorship. It is thought that sometime after he turned thirteen, Montaigne was allowed a few years of school holiday, free to live in Paris at court and study with scholars at the ***Collège de France.***

To further his investment in education, François I, the humanist king, committed himself and his wealth to the promotion of letters. After 1537 the royal bibliophile worked to create new "national" libraries, traveling to his royal abbeys to collect manuscripts and books in many languages and send them on to Paris. He also visited in person the printing/

bookshops of the Latin Quarter along *rue Saint-Jacques* (publishing and bookselling were combined in the early years), including the shop of Robert Estienne, printer to the king in Greek, Hebrew, and Latin, a Catholic who became a Protestant and fled to Geneva because the "divines" of the Sorbonne censured and attacked him relentlessly. The bibliophile Montaigne no doubt knew these early publishing houses himself. François I and Montaigne would also have known *rue de la Parcheminerie,* at that time the *rue des Écrivains,* home to writers and papermakers, next to Saint-Séverin, the current address of the Abbey Bookshop (see p. 14).

> DIRECTIONS: (The entrance to François I's *Collège de France* is in the Place Marcelin-Berthelot in *rue des Écoles.* There is a sloping garden in front of it, blazing with flowering shrubbery in June, shaded in all seasons by chestnut, lime, and plane trees. Students sit on the steps next to the statue of Dante. Farther east is Square Pierre de Ronsard, its profusion of pink and white roses in late spring a symbol of Ronsard's sweet and delicate poetry.)

The *rue des Écoles* takes its name from this sprawling quarter of prestigious schools, many originating in the Middle Ages when Latin was the language among scholars. Along the side streets off *rue des Écoles* and at the top of *rue Saint-Jacques, rue de la Sorbonne,* and *rue de la Montagne Sainte-Geneviève,* you will pass *Le Collège des Bons-Enfants* (1254); *Lycée Henri IV* on rue Clovis; *École de Medécine,* the original *École Polytechnique;* the Jesuit *Collège de Clermont,* now *Lycée Louis-le-Grand* on *rue Saint-Jacques* where Molière, Voltaire, Robespierre, Delacroix, and Hugo studied; the

École Normale Supérieure in **rue d'Ulm,** where Simone Weil (see p. 91), Sartre, and Simone de Beauvoir were students; and Pierre and Marie Curie's *École de Physique et de Chimie Industrielles* (see p. 79) in *rue d'Ulm.*

Montaigne's statue on the street of the schools commemorates him as progenitor of the tradition of French intellectual brilliance, wit, and moral seriousness. As André Maurois put it, Montaigne is "an essential part of every French mind" and this area is a kind of homage to his influence.

And yet there's an irony to his likeness presiding over the streets where the schools began. For though his father, like François I, worshipped men of learning, *"receiving them at his house like holy persons having some particular inspiration of divine wisdom . . . myself, I like them well enough, but I do not worship them."* As a boy in Bordeaux, he had detested schoolrooms and the discipline of schoolmasters.

> *Schools are a real jail of captive youth. . . . Go in at lesson time: you hear nothing but cries, both from tortured boys and from masters drunk with rage. What a way to arouse zest for their lesson in these tender and timid souls, to guide them to it with a horrible scowl and hands armed with rods!*

Thanks to a tutor who let him alone, he learned to love books on his own, gorging himself on Virgil's *Aeneid*, Terence, Plautus, and Italian comedies.

One can only speculate about what Montaigne would have to say these days about the schools of Paris, the punishing stress of the *Bac*, the fears of failure among careerist students and faculty, the intimidating culture of meritocracy.

In addition to his reconstruction of the **Louvre** and the founding of the **Collège de France** and the libraries of Paris,

François I undertook an extensive reconstruction of the *Hôtel de Ville*—the city's town hall—which faces the Seine from the Right Bank, across from the Île de la Cité (*Métro: Hôtel de Ville*). There's no record of Montaigne visiting the construction site or commenting on this center of administration with the large square on its western side, the *Place de Grève*.

For centuries this square was the open space where during the centuries of the Inquisition (and later), Protestants, Jews, and other heretics and witches were tortured and executed in public. (Today it's an ice-skating rink in winter, an outdoor movie theater in summer.)

Montaigne, an indefatigable walker, may have heard of the *Place de Grève*. Perhaps he crossed the Grand Pont (now Pont au Change) at Châtelet and walked east along the quays to observe the atrocities himself. He was unusual in his time for his unequivocal condemnation of torture:

> *All that goes beyond plain death seems to me pure cruelty.*
> [He thought Brazilian cannibals were morally superior to the "civilized" cruelty of his own time.] *There is more barbarity in eating a man alive than in eating him dead; and in tearing by tortures and the rack a body still full of feeling, in roasting a man bit by bit . . . and what is worse on the pretext of piety and religion . . .*

Montaigne's ancestors in Spain, on his mother's side, had been Jewish before "converting" to Christianity and moving to Provence after having lost many family members to the crimes of the Inquisition.

During a visit to Rome in 1580–1581, he was rebuked by the papal censors for his essays' subversive opinions on torture (and a few other things). He was told to change them. But he preferred not to. The Vatican would then list on its Index of Forbidden Books the radically humane *Essays* of Michel de Montaigne, along with four thousand other renowned works. They would remain off limits to Catholic Christians, under "pain of sin," until 1854.

Nearby

LIBRAIRIE COMPAGNIE   *58, rue des Écoles, across the street from **Square Paul-Painlevé**, with a complete inventory of French literature, reviews, journals.*

BRASSERIE BALZAR   *Diagonally across from Montaigne's statue at 49, **rue des Écoles**. Good food, service, mirrors, plants.*

GALERIE DE LA SORBONNE   *52, **rue des Écoles**. A good bookstore, a block east of the statue, opposite rue Saint-Jacques. Art books on sale, Montaigne's Table, contemporary philosophy.*

BOULANGERIE RÉGLAIT   *38, **rue des Écoles**, north side, opposite rue Jean-de-Beauvais. In season, you can sit on the outdoor terrace, facing the statue of the Romanian romantic poet, Mihai Eminescu (1850–1889), surrounded by trees.*

ACTION ÉCOLE CINEMA (*Le Desperado*)   *23, **rue des Écoles**. Old black-and-white American movies.*

Marie Curie: Panthéon and Bibliotheque Sainte-Geneviève
at rue Valette

THE LONELY PASSION
OF MARIE CURIE

LOCATIONS: *10, Place du Panthéon, Bibliothèque Sainte-Geneviève; 11, Rue Pierre et Marie Curie, Musée Curie; 36, Quai de la Béthune, Île Saint-Louis,* Marie Curie's last residence in Paris
MÉTRO: Cluny-Sorbonne; rue Monge; Cardinal Lemoine

The only money Marie Curie (1867–1934) had with her when her train pulled into the Gare du Nord in 1891 went to pay the fees for attending science classes at the Sorbonne. With little money left for expenses, she ate almost nothing except buttered bread, tea, and chocolate over the two and a half years she lived in a series of garrets around the Latin Quarter—*3, rue Flatters, 11, rue des Feuillantines,* and a private house on *boulevard de Port-Royal.* All were sixth-floor walk-ups without heat, light, or water. In winter the water froze in the washbasin. She slept in her clothes; her blanket the black woolen coat she'd brought from Poland. She was twenty-four years old. Alone. Hungry. Passionately determined.

A brilliant teenaged student in Warsaw who won all the first prizes, she was locked out of the university not only because she was a woman. Poland was occupied by Russia; the tsar controlled every aspect of Polish life, outlawing the use of the Polish language in schools and homes, sentencing dissidents to Siberia. There was no future in Poland for the likes of Manya Sklodowska as she was called then. To keep her spirit alive she held close the dream of the faraway

Sorbonne. Her secret paradise. She worked for four years as a governess in a remote province, saving her money, teaching herself math, physics, chemistry, and French in the middle of the night and at dawn before her job of caring for four children began, finally saving enough to pay for the train ticket out.

As a student living in the Latin Quarter, Marie Sklodowska—she changed the Polish "Manya" to the French "Marie"—lived on three francs a day. She did nothing but study, work in the labs of the Faculty of Science, and sleep four hours a night. A few times she fainted from fatigue and hunger, once in the *Bibliothèque Sainte-Geneviève.* Occasionally she treated herself to an egg and a walk into the country on the outskirts of Paris. She loved open green space, the world of nature.

In 1893 she passed first in the Master of Science exam in physics. The following year she came in second in the Master's in math.

Degrees in hand, she still felt guilty about not returning to Warsaw to look after her aging father. But she was now a successful resident of paradise, a star among the students in the Sorbonne's Faculty of Science. The leading men of French science talked to her about her work, made her welcome in their labs. The high intellectual energy of the Latin Quarter, the Sorbonne in particular, had proved true to its reputation: it had captured her soul, her dream became real. This new world she lived in intensified her determination to succeed as a scientist, to do something extraordinary. More and more, her work in the library and the labs intoxicated her.

When a professor assigned her a study that required a workroom larger than the small lab where she was working, a friend introduced her to a physicist/director of the School of Industrial Physics and Chemistry of the City of Paris (EPCI) in *rue Lhomond* who had some extra work space.

Pierre Curie, born in 1859 in Paris, was another genius, his discoveries known all over Europe. In France, though, because he had not attended any of the prestigious *écoles*, he received little attention. At first he and the strange Polish woman talked only science. She told him that when her studies ended and she had her teaching certificate in hand, she planned to return to Poland to care for her father.

But on their first meeting both of them realized the immediate sympathy they felt for each other. That they shared an absolute devotion to science intensified that bond. In summer 1895, they married. Their "wedding tramp" was a bicycle trip in Brittany and the Auvergne. By the time they came home to Paris in October, they were deeply devoted to one another. She loved his peaceful eyes, serene, deep. He never raised his voice. Their first child, Irène, born in 1897, would one day win a Nobel Prize herself.

Pierre found a small workspace for Marie at the EPCI where their professional collaboration became the pattern of their life together for the next almost nine years. (EPCI has been relocated to rue Pierre-Brossolette, named for a great leader of the French Resistance—see p. 219.) Marie notes in her autobiography that the couple's work that began at the end of 1897—in "a miserable old shed" of a lab— culminated in their achievement of the "great work of our lives." Her choice of topic for her doctoral studies produced that achievement: She would study the radiation of uranium, in the process discovering other substances hidden in it, polonium—named for her native Poland—and thorium. They were also radioactive substances.

They emitted rays which she and Pierre saw as signs of

the hidden wonders and miracles alive in the invisible universe of science. In time she realized that the rays signified an atomic property. For years she sifted and analyzed and purified pitchblende, an ore of uranium, four times more radioactive than pure uranium, trying to discover other elements. Husband and wife invented their methods of research, so ingenious and difficult and wild from both a nonscientist and a scientist's point of view. *"I sometimes passed the whole day stirring a mass (of pitchblende) in ebullition, with an iron rod nearly as big as myself. At night I was broken with fatigue."* And yet, she wrote, in this old shed they spent the best and happiest years of their life.

She took breaks from the backbreaking work, bicycling home to **rue de la Glacière** to nurse the baby, check on the nanny who took Irène to Parc Montsouris, put on the dinner, cook up fruits, make jam, and note in her journal when Irène spoke, smiled, shook hands, laughed, walked for the first time. Biking back to the shed, sometimes in the middle of the night, she loved to walk in and see the luminous rays emitted in the dark from the tubes in their lab. And yet in Poland, where there is national pride in her scientific achievements, she is often described as a "bad mother." She worked so many long hours outside the home. She didn't smile, or cuddle her daughters for photographers. She had a freakish, unfeminine love of math and science. Her second child, Eve Curie, a professional musician, wrote a biography of her mother, *Madame Curie* (1937), still in print, that is heartstopping in its affection as well as its understanding of the woman and her science.

The discovery of radium made the Curies famous. But it took four years to produce the kind of evidence which chemical science demands: that radium is truly a new element. In

1902 they were able to establish the existence and character of radium. Their study became the basis of the new science of radioactivity. They wanted no patent, no material profit. Radium should be of use in treating disease. At last the Sorbonne came through with a chair in Physics for Pierre.

In June 1903 Marie defended her doctoral dissertation at the Sorbonne, becoming the first woman in France to receive the doctorate. Still the Sorbonne provided no lab for the Curies' work, no job for Marie. The Curies, after all, were nobodies, one of them an immigrant, the other "home-schooled" because his father knew his son's originality would be destroyed in the rigid French schoolrooms. To the men who delivered the truckloads of pitchblende (donated by Austria) to the miserable shed in *rue Lhomond,* they were that pair of "French lunatics."

When the Nobel committee wrote to Pierre Curie in November 1903 that for his discovery of radium he would receive the Nobel Prize for Physics, Pierre declined the award: He insisted that the committee add the name of his wife Marie Curie to the citation. In December they were jointly awarded the prize for the discovery of radioactivity and new radioactive elements. Marie never seemed irritated by the gender bias of various institutions, the universities, the Swedish academicians, the family. Although she was responsible for childcare, meals, sewing baby clothes, what sustained her was the opposite of resentment: her gratitude for the freedom to do science, to work as an equal with the man she loved. Did she even realize that she belonged to "the weaker sex," in France as in Poland? Or, as biographer Barbara Goldsmith tells it, that at the turn of the century, wealthy Parisians saw commitment to an insane asylum the solution to the problem of a wife with a mind of her own?

The Curies despised the publicity machine that went into overdrive after they'd won the Nobel Prize. Pierre had always hated competition, hierarchies, classifications. And yet, looking back after April 19, 1906, none of the noise and fuss mattered. On that dark rainy day in Paris, absentminded Pierre was knocked over by a horse and cart coming off the Pont Neuf, dragged by the horse into *rue Dauphine*. His skull was broken in pieces, his brains left on the cobblestones. Marie's grief and depression almost finished her as a scientist. "A cope of solitude and secrecy fell upon her shoulders forever," writes her daughter. She became icy, lifeless, an automaton, "cold as a herring," in the words of Albert Einstein, a friend, colleague, and hiking companion.

For the Traveler

At night, after a long day of classes, the pale thin ash-blonde student from Poland found refuge and delight in the *Bibliothèque Sainte-Geneviève* on *Place du Panthéon* where the gas was lit, it was warm, and she could study at one of the long tables until the closing bell rang at midnight. Besides the warmth, she loved the silence and the atmosphere of concentration. Heading back to her garret, she could ignore the drunken students roaming the streets of the Latin Quarter, the loud nightlife of the many student cafés (now gone). Since the time of François Villon the Quarter had belonged to the young.

After the solitary hours in the library, she walked home as if detached from the material world, possessed by the mysteries of physics and chemistry. Her love of science and her desire to study were the forces that had moved her to abandon Poland and her family and risk a new life in the City of

Light. As Luther had said centuries before, "It is in Paris that we find the most celebrated and most excellent of schools: it is called the Sorbonne."

The walk from the ***Bibliothèque Sainte-Geneviève*** to the streets where she lived takes about twenty minutes if you follow ***rue Saint-Jacques*** past ***rue Pierre et Marie Curie*** to your left, then crossing ***rue Gay-Lussac*** and bearing left into the nondescript ***rue des Feuillantines***. The half-starving Polish girl might have thought her mind had collapsed had anyone prophesized in 1892 that a street in the ancient quarter of the great schools would one day be named after her.

To visit the second-floor reading room of the ***Bibliothèque*** present your passport to someone sitting behind a table to the left in the first-floor entrance hall. He/she will accompany you up a long stairway and through a wide doorway into the vast Labrouste Reading Room. Here you see students and visitors sitting at long rectangular tables with small green lamps under a magnificent curved iron and glass roof, a sort of shapely, beautifully designed skylight. The reading room's calm brings to mind a monastic setting filled with light. In fact, the library occupies the site of the library of the Abbaye Sainte-Geneviève where Peter Abelard starred in the twelfth century (see p. 11).

The building (built 1844–1850, see www-bsg.univ-paris1 .fr/), one of the masterpieces of architect Henri Labrouste, is an early example of a metal-framed building made out of wrought and cast iron. It holds some 150,000 volumes from the sixteenth to nineteenth centuries, including original manuscripts of Baudelaire, Rimbaud, Verlaine, Gide, and Valéry. In the stillness of the reading room, you might feel the presence of scholars' past, the wisdom of great literature, the joy of Manya Sklodowska: *"All that I saw and learned was a new*

*delight to me . . . the world of science which I was at last permit-
ted to study and know in all liberty."*

The library's exterior façade, resembling a Renaissance
palace, is covered with the incised names of great men who
have shaped the mind of Europe and Asia: Abelard's appears
directly above the front door, next to Suger, and then Ma-
homet, Petrarch, Dante, Marco Polo, Chaucer, Bruno, Spi-
noza, Cervantes, Rabelais, Luther, Calvin, Vico to name only
a very few. No women made the cut. *Place du Panthéon,*
which the library faces is a wide open generous space, sometimes crowded with students lining up to enter the library
as well as tourists headed for the Panthéon. Again, Manya
Sklodowska might have feared she suffered from the hallu-
cinatory effects of malnutrition had she heard or felt any in-
timation that she would one day be buried inside the great
temple of French heroes.

Five minutes away from the *Bibliothèque,* bearing right
around the corner of rue Soufflot and downhill onto rue
Saint-Jacques, you can enter the courtyard of the Sorbonne. (Sometimes you'll be asked to show a photo ID.)
Marie Curie heard the results of her exams of 1893 and 1894
in the Grand Amphitheatre of the Sorbonne. *(To book a tour
of "this most excellent of schools," visit www.sorbonne.fr/en/the
-sorbonne/visiting. Tel: 01.40.46.23.48 or go to visites.sor
bonne@ac-paris-fr. The tour is well worth the two hours and 9
euros you'll spend.)*

After Pierre's death, the Sorbonne hired his widow to take
over Pierre's physic classes. A statue of Professor Marie
Curie sits high in the Sorbonne's *Salle des Autorités* in the
Faculty of Science. She looks like a young girl.

The *Musée Curie* (www.musee.curie.fr), a ten-minute
walk from the Sorbonne, is the best place in Paris to get a

clear sense of the scientific genius and moral seriousness of the Curies. You'll find it at *11, rue Pierre et Marie Curie* off *rue Saint-Jacques*. *(Hours: Weds–Sat, 1–5. Métro: rue Monge; Cardinal Lemoine.)*

Exhibits include extensive neon timelines showing important events in the developing study of radioactivity, the contributions made by Pierre, Marie, and their daughter Irène and her husband Frédéric Joliot, both of whom won the Nobel Prize in Chemistry in 1935. The original Institute of Radium, funded by the Sorbonne, and the Pasteur Institute, comprised two parts: a lab of radioactivity in the front building, directed by Marie Curie, and behind it, across the garden, a lab for biological research into the treatment of cancer, directed by an eminent physician: the two institutes worked in cooperation for the development of the science of radium.

The lovely garden between the two buildings, which Marie designed and planted herself, still provides a spot of calm and a place to sit. You'll find the entrance through the excellent small museum bookshop and out the rear exit from her research pavilion. At an angle, near the *rue Saint-Jacques* side of the building, an expressive sculpture of Marie and Pierre shows their almost mystical seriousness. Before the foundations of the buildings had been laid, Marie planted lime trees and plane trees as well as the rambler roses that are so fragrant in June and still thriving in early November. Above the garden, you see the large second-story windows of her lab which flooded her research halls with sunlight.

But before she and her staff could move into the new labs and research rooms, World War I began.

Marie stayed in Paris but all work stopped in the lab. "Even though she had been excoriated," as Barbara Goldsmith writes, referring to Curie's imputed love affair with the married-with-children physicist Paul Langevin and the hate attacks of the right-wing press in 1911, who, while Marie was away from Paris collecting her second Nobel Prize, stoned and graffitied her house in Sceaux—*Jew, foreigner, whore, go back to Poland*—Marie Curie "resolved to put all my strength at the service of my adopted country."

Commandeering X-ray equipment from labs and doctors' offices, she designed "mobile X-ray units" to use in war-zone hospitals to diagnose the maimed and wounded on the battlefield so they could be treated immediately. Wealthy Parisian women donated their cars. Marie and her women volunteers, though bureaucrats had at first forbidden them to drive to the front, drove to the field hospitals, where Marie and her technicians X-rayed the wounded, found the location of their bullets and the shrapnel in their bodies, directing the surgeons where to operate, little time wasted. Her chief assistant was Irène, her seventeen-year-old daughter, who often ran things on her own. Sometimes working through the night, both mother and daughter were exposed to heavy doses of X-rays and radon gas.

The last time Marie Curie visited her lab, in May 1934, she walked out the rear door and noticed that some of the roses looked unhealthy. Because she had a fever and was close to the end of her life, she couldn't attend to the flowers herself. Her last request to a staff member was to ask the gardener to take care of the roses.

It took two more months before her undiagnosed pernicious anemia finally killed her. For a lifetime she had worked unprotected from radium, her bones and organs gradually destroyed by the effects of radiation.

There has always been the question: How did she and

Pierre not know how dangerous their discovery could be to the human body? She did admit that sometimes in the lab she felt a "discomfort." And in a letter to her sister, complaining of her failing eyesight, she wrote, "Perhaps radium has something to do with these troubles, but it cannot be affirmed with certainty." Doctors called it a miracle that she lived to the age of sixty-seven. After the war, she made exhausting fund-raising trips to the United States, worked long hours in her lab to the end, and spared little time to enjoy the view from her apartment at *36, Quai de Béthune* on the south side of the Île Saint-Louis.

There's a way in which a part of her was always a child, curious, simple in her likes, ignoring what she didn't understand, ignoring danger, and hunger, and the freezing temperatures in her Latin Quarter garrets. She was obsessive about her radium, which she referred to as "my child." Albert Einstein wrote of her, *"Marie Curie is, of all celebrated beings, the only one whom fame has not corrupted."*

In 1995 Marie and Pierre's remains were transferred from the simple country cemetery where they'd been buried to the august Panthéon, France's temple of heroes. She was the first woman to be admitted to the Panthéon on her own merits, not because she was a great man's wife. In her lifetime her achievements had often been ignored or belittled in academe.

In her own words, she expressed her credo, the source of her tendency to ignore malice:

I am among those who think that science has great beauty. A scientist in his lab is not only a technician, he is also a child placed before natural phenomena, which impress him like a fairy tale . . .

Nearby

PLACE DE L'ESTRAPADE   *A quiet small square to the right off rue d'Ulm as you walk south, with a café and pâtisserie. It has the feel of a secret place: It began in 1515 as a site of torture and execution of Calvinists.*

RUE LHOMOND   *Bear left off rue d'Ulm. The original building (shed) where Marie Curie worked sometimes through the night stirring pitchblende is gone, replaced by a newer science lab.*

IRISH CULTURAL CENTER   *Open Tues–Sat, 2–6; Weds until 8; Sun 12:30–2:30. Turn left off rue Lhomond; on the right at 5, **rue des Irlandais** (Métro: Place Monge). www .centreculturelirlandais.com. A long garden, with tables, chairs, a few students from the surrounding college buildings where foreign students study French in summer. A good eighteenth-century library above Saint Patrick's chapel, another library open to the public to the right of the entrance. Spring and summer, evening theater, and poetry readings in the garden.*

Simone Weil: Quai de Bourbon, Île Saint-Louis

SIMONE WEIL:
SOUL ON FIRE

LOCATIONS: *23, rue Clovis, Lycée Henri IV;*
    45, rue d'Ulm, École Normale Supérieure;
    17, rue de la Sorbonne, The Courtyard
MÉTRO: Cluny-La Sorbonne; Maubert–Mutualité

Camus called Simone Weil "the only great spirit of our time." For André Gide she was "the best spiritual writer of this century." T. S. Eliot, not given to superlatives, considered her "a woman of genius, of a kind of genius akin to that of the saints." Polish poet Czeslaw Miłosz believed that "France offered a rare gift to the contemporary world in the person of Simone Weil." American poet Adrienne Rich valued this "visionary" woman's "stunning insights into domination and oppression."

Though Simone Weil (1909–1943) is not exactly a starred name on the cultural map of Paris, since her death at the age of thirty-four, there have been more than twenty volumes of her writings published in Europe and the United States. Between 1995 and 2012 over 2,500 scholarly works about her philosophy have appeared. It was Camus, who, as an editor at Gallimard, began the posthumous publication of her books and essays after the war (see p. 136), including *The Need for Roots*, *Waiting for God*, and *Gravity and Grace*, a compilation from her many notebooks.

Born into a well-to-do, agnostic Jewish family, Weil's religious identification is neither Jewish nor Christian. She did not "convert," as some erroneously claim. Her life story has been called "tragicomic," "mad," masochistic. Always an outsider, she was misunderstood and ridiculed by some of her contemporaries (who nicknamed her the "Red Virgin"). Yet to this day she remains for many readers—who include believers and nonbelievers—a beacon of light and courage in a soulless world.

Growing up in Paris, she was a brilliant child, later the *enfant terrible* of the top Latin Quarter schools. As much as she enjoyed visiting cities in Spain and Italy, for her, Paris was always the most beautiful city in the world. As fervently as she, a devout disciple of Plato, loved any earthly thing, she loved Paris. The beauty of the world, she wrote toward the end of her life, was one of the signs of the presence of the hidden God.

Simone Weil thought about the idea of God throughout her childhood, the possibility and impossibility of his existence; coming up with no solution, no certainty, she decided to forget about it. Her parents never brought her to synagogue or any religious establishment. She did not like the observant orthodox Jews in the family, finding them rigid and legalistic. Her upbringing, entirely secular, like the enlightenment city that nurtured her on its own sacramentals—books, music, philosophy, mathematics, physics, activist politics, travel—consumed her "creative attention." (In later years "creative attention" was her definition of prayer.)

As a student, hanging out through all-night discussions and debates in the Latin Quarter's student cafés (most are gone), she expressed respect for Christianity, but she considered the institutional Catholic Church contaminated by its centuries-old alliance with the Roman Empire, inheriting its will to domination rather than honoring the original Christian command to serve the oppressed and the common good.

Further, after the fall of the Empire, the Church established its own sort of totalitarianism in Europe in the thirteenth century, after its extermination of the Albigensians on the order of the pope and Saint Louis IX (see p. 20). Although she admired the liturgy of the Church, especially Gregorian chant, and later told of a mystical experience in Assisi and again, while she read George Herbert's poem "Love bade me welcome"—she said that afterward she felt the presence of Christ for the rest of her life—she rejected the Church's embrace of power deriving from its militaristic Jewish and Roman sources; she also disliked its hierarchy and its historical record that included the Inquisition and the Crusades. Perhaps the thing she abhorred most was the Church's practice of excommunicating heretics, those who dissented from a particular dogma. The formula *anathema sit* ("let him be anathema") repelled her, as it had Peter Abelard. "The proper function of the intelligence demands total freedom," she wrote.

For the Traveler

In 1913, the family moved to an apartment at *37, boulevard Saint-Michel* (now a Benetton, which is funny because the absentminded student-professor dressed like a bag lady). In 1925, as a teenager, she entered the *Lycée Henri IV* at *23, rue Clovis*. A short walk from home, up the hill of "Boul'Mich" and heading east over the *Montagne Sainte-Geneviève* around the Panthéon, *Henri IV* is perhaps the most prestigious of all the elite Parisian high schools.

MÉTRO: Saint-Michel; Cardinal Lemoine; Place Monge.
Closed to the public except on conference and

performance days, *Lycée Henri IV* occupies the sixth-century site of the church founded by the barbaric King Clovis—the Abbaye Sainte-Geneviève—named for the brave warrior woman who converted him to Christianity. In 1200 Peter Abelard taught classes here in the well-preserved Cloister, visible from the front entrance foyer. The monks' refectory of 1220 is now the school's chapel on rue Clotilde, named for Clovis's devout wife. More than Clovis or Saint Genevieve or Peter Abelard, however, in modern Paris the most revered name connected with *Lycée Henri IV* is "Alain," the philosophy teacher who was born Émile Chartier in 1868. Alain was considered by André Maurois and many generations of students and Parisian intellectuals "the greatest man of our time." Alain's lectures were the reason sixteen-year-old Simone Weil desperately wanted to win admission to *Lycée Henri IV.*

Henri IV prepared students for the rigorous entrance exams for *École Normale Supérieure,* a highly competitive division of the Sorbonne, where the teachers of France are educated. One of Alain's best students, Simone became a *normalienne* in 1928, earning her *agrégée de philosophie* in 1931, outranking all her fellow students including Simone de Beauvoir and Sartre. If you want to understand "the mystery of French intellectuality," wrote Tony Judt, "you must begin here at ENS." Since 1850, "virtually every Frenchman of intellectual distinction . . . graduated from it."*

MÉTRO: Place Monge; Censier-Daubenton. *L'École Normale Supérieure at 45, rue d'Ulm,* a ten-minute

* Tony Judt, "Historian's Progress," *New York Review of Books*, March 11, 2010.

walk from *Lycée Henri IV,* along rue Clotilde behind the Panthéon and left into rue d'Ulm, has a lovely students' garden that's open to the public on weekends and some weekdays.

Sitting here on a calm Sunday morning, a plashing fountain at the center encircled by magnificent tall trees, you can observe the rituals of French intellectual seriousness. Here and there students on benches discuss and argue back and forth, attentive like lovers to the words spoken. Clouds of cigarette smoke drift above their slim bodies, the intense dark eyes. Normaliens study here in the sculptured presences of French genius: the stone heads of Foucault, Louis Aragon, Lavoisier, Descartes, Pascal, Pierre Corneille, Molière, Racine, La Fontaine, Jacques-Bénigne Bossuet, Voltaire, Rousseau, Chateaubriand—a pantheon of secular gods. Simone Weil, who ate little, was never without a cigarette. A top student, aggressively idealistic, antiauthoritarian, leftist, committed to activism on behalf of workers, unions, and the poor, the ENS administration was glad to be rid of her in 1931 when she went off to her first teaching job. Had she studied here ten years later, during the Occupation, she, whose resistance to fascism throughout the thirties was constant, public, and dangerous—a volunteer in the Spanish Civil War, she almost lost a foot when she stumbled into a pot of boiling oil—she probably would not have survived the surveillance and censorship of the Nazis. The ENS student body, which identified with and participated in the Resistance, provoked four raids by the Gestapo in 1944 alone as well as the arrest of its director, Georges Bruhat, who died at Buchenwald.*

* Alice Kaplan, *The Collaborator.*

What she worshipped throughout her years at *Lycée Henri IV* and *École Normale Supérieure* was the moral seriousness of these schools which kindled her desire to make the world a more just place for the "unfortunate." (Camus was committed to giving a voice to the "lost causes.") She sought to solve the scandal of social injustice in action, not in the abstract theories of the lecture halls. At the age of eleven, and then as a teenaged student at *Henri IV*, she became determined to share the fate of the downtrodden, live as they did. (Though she never ran away from her parents' comfortable apartment to a squat in eastern Paris.) Throughout these years she joined demonstrations for disempowered workers, attended union meetings, wrote petitions, tried to bully her professors into signing them, and, despising materialism and bourgeois complacency, practiced the self-denying habits of an ascetic. (Except for the cigarettes.)

She loved walking the streets of Paris and along the quays on the Seine, especially on the *Île Saint-Louis,* where a favorite tutor lived. "There were not many places she liked as much as the quays," according to her school friend, Simone Pétrement, who often walked with her and later became her biographer.

A graduate herself of *Henri IV* and *ENS*, Pétrement realized in the course of their long walks through the Latin Quarter and the Luxembourg that though Alain's ideas did influence Simone, she had conceived some of them on her own, before she became his student. In particular, the obligation to act in solidarity with the poor was her own deepest moral conviction and in her view the core morality of all religions; though a professed agnostic, she was especially inspired by the Christian Gospels' predilection for the poor.

For Alain, philosophy was a commentary on religion.

Each religion, he said, has its own kind of truth, its own validity. Simone never abandoned Alain's open-minded respect for all strata of religious experience. Years later, when she and her parents were running from the Nazis in Marseille, waiting for an escape ship to the United States, she told a priest confidant that she loved Christ but did not feel that God wanted her to enter the Catholic Church. One reason was the admiration she had for other religious traditions. She loved Krishna, Hinduism, the *Baghadavita*, the Book of Job, the Psalms, the Song of Songs, the Egyptian mysteries. She didn't want to attach herself "exclusively to Christianity."*

After fighting in World War I, Alain had become a radical pacifist, convincing his Paris students in the twenties and thirties of the futility of war (some blamed his influence for the unpreparedness of the French army before the Nazi invasion); Alain also insisted it was necessary to have fought in order to have the right to judge. Alain's pacifism influenced but did not create Simone's hatred of force and violence. The basis of her hatred stemmed from her critique of the Roman Empire, Homer's *Iliad*, and the Hebrew Bible's Jehovah who crushed Canaan. Her animus against militarism culminated in her 1939 essay "The *Iliad*, or the Poem of Force"—"one of the most moving and original literary essays ever written," to quote Elizabeth Hardwick—in which Simone argued that the effect of the cruelty of combat depicted in Homer's epic was the destruction of the human spirit: the force that kills turns anybody who is subjected to it into a *thing*.

And yet Simone supported the war against the totalitarian dictatorship of Hitler. She had no use for the totalitarian mysticism of Marxism, the U.S.S.R., and the Communist

*Simone Pétrement, *Simone Weil: A Life*.

Party (though at *ENS* some called her a communist for her leftist sympathies). For her, the party was, as Pétrement quotes her, "a bureaucratic, military, and police dictatorship that has nothing socialist or communist about it but the name."

Simone Weil never did anything to please others or to sugarcoat her intransigent opinions. Simone de Beauvoir remembered seeing her one day walking through *the courtyard of the Sorbonne,* followed by a group of Alain's disciples, holding forth about the scandal of a famine in China. She and Simone Weil differed on what the solution should be (Weil said the starving needed food, Beauvoir said they needed meaning). The brief hostile exchange that followed cut off any friendship they might have formed as serious intellectual women.

MÉTRO: Saint-Michel; Cluny-La Sorbonne. You may enter the *courtyard of the Sorbonne at 17, rue de la Sorbonne,* asking permission of the guards at the entrance, maybe having to show a photo ID depending on their moods. It's an inspiring space, alive with eight centuries of students' energy and fractious history: the Church's conservative control in the beginning (see p. 23), followed by royal control, eventually undone by the Revolution, evolving since then into many different schools in many Parisian locations. The dome (and façade) of Richelieu's chapel at the southern end, the wonderful compass/sundial to the north, the elegant façades to the west, and to the east, the sculpture of Louis Pasteur. Schoolchildren from the suburbs who visit the courtyard between semesters find the compass/sundial, in particular, thrilling. Individual tours are available on Saturdays; you must book at least three months in advance of your visit. www.sorbonne

.fr/en/the-sorbonne/visiting. Tel: 01.40.46.23.48 or go to visites.sorbonne@ac-paris-fr.

Simone Weil is remembered today at *Lycée Henri IV* and at *ENS* as one of the most brilliant prodigies of the Sorbonne's educational institutions. Her strange conflicted life reflects the glory of the *Latin Quarter,* the *quartier* of youth in all its contradictions and extremes of idealism and courage. She qualifies as a true descendant of Peter Abelard, the spiritual founding father of the hill's first great school. Both Christian father and Jewish daughter are souls in exile, anti-establishment originals who died young, at once vilified and cherished by the city they loved.

When she took breaks from her teaching jobs or stints on the assembly lines to come home to Paris, she walked the streets she'd known since childhood with old school friends and the union members she knew and worked with in the provinces; they went to the Odéon Théâtre and concerts; she visited many churches and bookshops. She continued to publicly protest France's abuse and exploitation of its colonies in Africa and Indochina. She wrote and wrote and wrote, the articles and notebooks and essays that now, thanks to Camus, belong to world literature. In *Gravity and Grace* and in the essay "Forms of the Implicit Love of God" she expresses her personal credo: God is really, though secretly, present in religious ceremonies; in one's friends; neighbors; and in the beauty of the world. Like the Greeks (and Blake and Teilhard de Chardin), she saw no line separating the spiritual and the secular. The work of seeking justice for the "unfortunate" she sees as a kind of obedience, an imitation of the "divine" model presented in the Gospels.

Compared to Simone de Beauvoir, who spent the

Occupation years in Paris (1940–1944) attending concerts and theater and writing to Sartre (see *Letters to Sartre*), Simone Weil's antifascist convictions turned her into what some more cautious *Résistants* considered a wild-eyed fanatic. She worked for the Resistance in Marseille, also helping imprisoned Vietnamese refugees to escape. Finally, she left France for New York and then made her way to London, where she worked again for the Resistance, intent on activating her plan to parachute nurses—including herself—onto the front lines of France to save wounded French soldiers from bleeding to death. De Gaulle thought her plan "mad." It was in fact a plan similar to the one Marie Curie activated successfully on the front lines during World War I.

Because Weil hardly ate, accepting only the same number of rations as the people of France were surviving on, her always frail health deteriorated, she contracted tuberculosis, refused surgery. There was mutual dislike between her and the attending doctor at the British hospital where she died; he reported her death as a suicide, that she starved herself to death. Years later, medical records and archival research have found that the hospital food was inedible, she actually asked for food (to be cooked in the French way: she could not stomach English potatoes). She was never intentionally suicidal: the doctor was hostile to this strange woman with a mind of her own and hellbent on parachuting into France. Cardiac arrest was a factor in her death in Ashford, England, in August 1943.

When Albert Camus received word in 1957 that he had won the Nobel Prize for Literature, the story goes that he went immediately to the home of Weil's parents at *3, rue Auguste Comte* (Métro: RER B, Luxembourg) to declare that it was Simone who deserved the prize much more than he did. Until his own early death in 1960, as an acquiring editor for

Gallimard, he continued to visit the Weils, reading Simone's manuscripts, sitting at the large table—it looked down over the hedges and the southwestern corner of the **Luxembourg Gardens**—where Simone had done much of her writing. *Rue Auguste Comte's* prospect from the high floor of the Weil's apartment—where, at their daughter's request, they had hidden refugees from Nazi Berlin after 1933—is the site of the original Carthusian monastery, the Chartreuse (Charterhouse) de Vauvert built on the abandoned Château de Vauvert in 1258. After the Revolution, the French Directory confiscated the land though they preserved the famous "pépinière"—nursery garden and vineyards—at the south end of the park. In the 1860s Haussmann extended the Luxembourg by cutting off and transforming the old nursery garden into an English garden with winding paths, planting a fruit garden in the southwest corner, which is still there. Simone often walked here—a ten-minute walk from **Lycée Henri IV** and **ENS** down the hill of the Panthéon through the Luxembourg's east entrance on **boulevard Saint-Michel.** She loved the ancient branching trees reaching down to the lawns, she did not like the statues. Just over the hedges along the southern border, there is a plaque on the façade of her parents' building: *Simone Weil, philosophe, a habité cette maison de 1929 à 1940.*

Nearby

CHURCH OF SAINT-SÉVERIN   *Between* **rue Saint-Jacques** *and* **rue de la Harpe.** *There's a certain resonance between this church and Simone Weil's story. Originally the site of the hermit Séverin's sixth-century retreat, it developed into a church in the twelfth century and then was enlarged to meet the spiritual needs* *of the growing Sorbonne congregation. Outside, on the south side, the galleries of the only surviving charnel house in Paris arc around a garden and a sculpture of a hermit. "Preserve your solitude," Weil wrote, perhaps in approval of Séverin. Inside, the oval-shaped Mansart chapel displays the lithographs of Georges Rouault entitled "Miserere," to accompany Psalm 50.*

GIBERT JOSEPH   *26, 30, 32, 34,* **boulevard Saint-Michel.** *Four stores on the west side of the boulevard stocked with books, DVDs, CDs, vinyl, full floors of classical music, jazz, current and classic movies. Jean Genet was arrested as a child for theft in the bookstore.*

LE CHAMPO   *The legendary movie theater, on the corner of* **rue Champollion** *at 51,* **rue des Écoles,** *showing classic and current films. Simone Weil's favorite actor and film was Charlie Chaplin's* Modern Times.

The Grand Mosque of Paris: Place du Puits-de-l'Ermite

BENGHABRIT, JEWS, AND THE GESTAPO

LOCATION: *2, Place du Puits-de-L'Ermite,* Grand
  Mosque of Paris
HOURS: Sat–Thurs, 9–12; 2–6
MÉTRO: Censier-Daubenton

The Grand Mosque of Paris was built between 1922 and 1926 to symbolize the eternal friendship between France and Islam. It was also meant to express gratitude to the half-million Muslims of the French Empire's North African colonies who had fought against the Germans in World War I. A hundred thousand Muslims died for France; without their sacrifice, it is said, the victory of Verdun would not have happened. The Mosque was particularly meant to honor the fallen Muslim *tirailleurs* (sharpshooters) from Algeria.

After the war many Algerians relocated to France, working in factories and on construction jobs mostly, sending money home to their families. Known as Kabyles—Berbers from Kabylia, the treacherous Atlas Mountains and impoverished villages of Algeria that Albert Camus wrote about (see p. 129)—the Kabyles became the dominant Muslim population in Paris. Many lived in slum housing in Belleville in northeastern Paris, forming bonds with their other immigrant neighbors and coworkers: Chinese and Vietnamese, Tunisians, Moroccans, Jews from North Africa, Russia, eastern Europe.

When the Nazis invaded in 1940 and began rounding up

Jews for deportation, many Kabyles joined the French Resistance. (It is also true that like Christians, many Arabs in North Africa and Paris collaborated with the anti-Semitic Vichy and German authorities.)

The successes of the Kabyle Resistance were intimately connected with the clandestine antifascist operations in daily progress in the cellars of the Grand Mosque where the Kabyles worshipped. Thanks to the heroism of the Mosque's rector, Si Kaddour Benghabrit (1868–1954), the Kabyles were free to bring their Jewish friends and coworkers to the Mosque for safe haven.

The first prayer offered at the Paris Mosque in 1926, in the presence of the president of France, was given by this rector who was also the Mosque's founder. Benghabrit, born in Algeria, a cultured diplomat in Paris and North Africa who wrote books, enjoyed Parisian salon culture, and loved music became the most important Muslim in Paris and the most influential Arab in Europe. He has now become a figure of historical interest and some acclaim because of his actions during the Holocaust.

When the Nazis and the Vichy government began arresting and deporting the Jews of Paris, Benghabrit committed himself and his congregation to making the Grand Mosque a sanctuary for endangered Jews. He devised a threefold rescue operation: first, he offered European and Algerian Jews shelter in the same apartments inhabited by Muslim families; second, he gave them fake identity certificates, to prove they were Muslims, not Jews; finally, he initiated the use of the cellars and tunnels beneath the Mosque as escape routes. The Jews-in-hiding crawled and dug their way through the sewers and tunnels (*souterrains*) under the Mosque to the banks of the Seine where empty wine barges and boats operated by Kabyles were waiting to smuggle them out of Occupied Paris. Benghabrit was arrested and interrogated by the Gestapo a number of times as rumors of the Mosque's resistance inevitably got out. A higher German command, however, ordered him released each time: The Germans could not risk Algerian riots in North Africa or Paris if the Reich was to hold North Africa against the allies. It was important that the Muslims on both fronts stayed submissive.

Salim Halali, a Berber Jew from Algeria, popular singer of North African songs and friend of Benghabrit, sought and found safety in the Mosque. The rector not only made him a Certificate of Conversion to show—falsely—that Salim's grandfather had converted to Islam; he also had an unmarked tombstone in the Muslim cemetery in Bobigny inscribed with the family name of Halali's grandfather. After the Nazis checked it out, they left Halali alone. He lived out the war in the Mosque, passing as a Muslim when the Nazis, responding to rumors of a Mosque underground, barged in regularly on a search-and-deport mission. (Benghabrit had a warning bell hidden in the floor under his desk that alerted everyone of another Nazi raid in progress.) After the Liberation, Halali went on to become the most popular "oriental" singer in Europe. He and Benghabrit remained good friends.

Albert Assouline, a North African Jew who with a Muslim friend escaped from a POW camp in Germany, surfaced in Paris without identity papers. The Mosque welcomed him and his friend. While hiding out in the basement, Assouline saw many other Jews in hiding: the children lived in the upstairs apartments with Muslim families, the adults in the basement. Because North African Jews and Muslims looked alike, had similar surnames, were circumcised, and spoke Arabic, the Jews, with their fake Muslim identity certificates, were able to pass as Muslim when the Gestapo came searching for evidence of a Jewish sanctuary movement. After the war, Assouline gave testimony that he witnessed 1,600 Jews passing through the basements and sub-basements of the Mosque and descending into the dark labyrinthine tunnels, eventually making it out onto the boats waiting at the *Halles aux Vins* on the Seine to carry them to safety in the Maghreb and Spain. In addition to Jewish refugees, the Kabyle boatmen also carried messages between the French Resistance in Paris and the Free French Army in Algeria.

Some sources dispute Assouline's estimate, claiming that at most five hundred Jews were given a home and then safe passage by Benghabrit and the Mosque. One Israeli scholar dismisses the story as exaggerated from start to finish. There is not much data available to provide the actual numbers of Jews rescued by the Mosque. But what there is—old newspapers, scholarly research,* and personal testimonies from Jews who after the war told of hiding for its duration in the Mosque's basements—supports the details of this hidden history.

Benghabrit was given the Grand Croix de la Légion d'Honneur after the war. But Eva Wiesel has noted in *The New York Times* that getting Yad Vashem in Israel to grant the honorific of "Righteous Among Nations" to a Muslim, even the Oskar Schindler–like Benghabrit, is and will remain very difficult. This heroic unsung leader of the Paris Mosque Resistance died in 1954 in the early stages of the war of Algerian independence. He is buried in the Mosque, facing in the direction of Mecca, as are all Muslims.

---

* Robert Satloff, *Among the Righteous: Lost Stories of the Holocaust from Arab Lands.*

For the Traveler

The domes of the Grand Mosque of Paris and the golden mosaics of the minaret dominate the skyline of this eastern edge of the Latin Quarter. The voice of the muezzin from the top of the minaret calling Muslims to prayer five times a day adds a backup of ancient chant to the sacred site.

Once inside the Mosque, you enter the courtyard, a calm bright space of grassy green plantings, turquoise pools of water, lovely tiled walls of white and black and shades of blue. "The desert culture of Islam," in the words of Garry Wills, "sees heaven as a garden perpetually rinsed with purifying waters." Palm trees and cypress rise along the aisles of intricately carved arches and columns bordering the cascading fountains, flowering bushes. The white ceiling is high.

Walking here, even on gray winter days, you notice the light from above brightening the tiled walls, the sounds of soft voices and flowing water infusing a sense of reverence. Approaching this place from the plain nondescript street outside, you'd never dream such a hushed and beautiful sanctuary existed so close by.

Beyond the courtyard is a large dimly lit prayer room for men and women, the floor and walls covered with magnificent carpets. Other rooms for prayer and study open onto more dim corridors. The downstairs of the mosque where women perform their ablutions are interesting to explore. If you take a guided tour, you can ask about the religious significance of the ritual baths. (Each of the Abrahamic religions—Judaism, Islam, and Christianity—have in different periods of their history required special cleansing rites for women.)

The Mosque has multiple functions. Besides being a place

of prayer it has in the past provided apartments to the people who work there, a health and social services clinic, archives, small gardens, a library of ancient manuscripts, steam baths, pools, a restaurant, café, and gift shop.

What many foreign visitors and Parisians have never heard of is the hidden history of the Paris Mosque: It played an important role in the French Resistance in World War II, until recently, a well-kept secret. The story of the Paris Mosque's role during the Holocaust has gone strangely neglected. Just as Arab countries, especially Qatar, Egypt, and Saudi Arabia, deny the very fact of the Holocaust, so Western historians have failed to pay attention to the contribution of the Mosque to the rescue of Jews during the Nazi Occupation. Arab Holocaust deniers, however, deny their own history when they ignore this story of courage.

Walking along the corridors, in and out of prayer rooms and a large library, it's easy to imagine this place as a sanctuary of secrets—intricate, rich, a labyrinth of life, death, and rescue.

It is inarguable that the Occupation years were a time of interreligious brotherhood between many North African Muslims and many of the hunted Jews of Paris. Without the Mosque, the number of Jewish deaths would undoubtedly have been higher. In July 1942 when the Nazis and the French police arrested thirteen thousand Jews in the *Vel d'Hiv* roundup, eight thousand of the arrested Jews came from the immigrant neighborhood of ***Belleville*** in northeastern Paris. Without the help of the Kabyle spy networks and the availability of the Mosque as a hiding place, there would have been many more Belleville Jews lost in that roundup.

Wise people saw then and acknowledge now the spiritual

bond that has always united the two cultures. "Whoever saves one life," says the Talmud, "it is as if they have saved the whole world." "Whoever saves one life saves the entire world," says the Koran. And, as Eric Hazan observes, in today's *Belleville* and *Ménilmontant* there is still a multicultural peace: Orthodox Jewish men, mothers in African robes, Chinese and Muslim families shop together in the markets along *boulevard de Belleville*. Old retired workers bask in the sun on the plaza of the Ménilmontant métro or inside the Kabyle café du Soleil; they speak in Arabic or Kabyle inside the Islamic bookshops on *rue Jean-Pierre Timbaud*. After the war, Albert Camus used to take his visiting Algerian friends to his favorite couscous places in the North African neighborhoods of Belleville, enclaves "full of tolerance and humanity."*

Several recent French movies (*Les Hommes Libres*, *A Forgotten Resistance*: *The Mosque of Paris*, *Together*), books, and journalism† have weighed in on the secret history of the Paris Mosque, realizing that the erasure of this story creates a tragic loss of opportunity for spiritual healing in an era of Islamaphobia and anti-Semitism. After the *Charlie Hebdo* massacre in January 2015, the media focused on the Algerian origin of the terrorists though they were born, raised, and educated in France. "Here in France," said an Algerian man living in Paris, "anti-Algerian racism is everywhere. Because of a group of feebleminded extremists, we have all been stigmatized."†

The media also warned travelers not to wander beyond the tourist hubs into the "dangerous" Muslim "ghetto" neigh-

* Eric Hazan, *The Invention of Paris: A History in Footsteps*.

† Amir Jalal Zerdoumi, "French-Algerian or Algerian-French?," *New York Times*. See also George Packer's "The Other France," August 31, 2015, *The New Yorker*.

borhoods of northern and northeastern Paris. But regular visitors to Paris walk easily in the multicultural streets—*Romainville,* ending at Square Belleville where the kids of Orthodox Jews and Muslims play on a Sunday afternoon; *Couronnes,* running uphill to the crowded rose gardens of Parc Belleville; young boys in *rue Raponeau* playing soccer in early spring evenings. On market days along the boulevard, shoppers bargain with the merchants, whom they know by name, artists descend from squats to pick up bargains, greet their neighbors. Ordinary street scenes. Nothing scary here.

Nearby

MOSQUE GARDEN AND TEAROOM   *Open daily, 9–midnight. Around the block from the Mosque entrance, on the corner of **rue Daubenton** and 39, **rue Geoffroy Saint-Hilaire,** opposite the Jardin des Plantes. A pretty terrace café planted with jasmine, olive bushes, and fig trees where singing birds nest and play. Surrounded by mosaics of dark blue and turquoise tiles on tables and fountain, the ambience here—on a weekday—is a lovely calm. (Very crowded on Saturdays.)*

JARDIN DES PLANTES   *Gardens, summer, 8–8; winter, 8–5:30. www.mnhn.fr. Spectacular garden walks starting at the main entrance on Quai Saint-Bernard (or from the direction of the Gare d'Austerlitz métro). Flowering cherry trees in April, beds of roses, peonies, iris, a laurel orchard, a hidden Alpine garden of two thousand species of flowers and plants, and a menagerie (open summer, Mon–Sat, 9–6; Sun, 9–6:30; winter, 9–5:30) where Delacroix and Cézanne studied and sketched botanical and animal anatomies. For readers of the novel* All The Light We

Cannot See *by Anthony Doerr, the Mineralogy Gallery is an evocative experience; palaeontologist Pierre Teilhard de Chardin worked on his studies—once thought heretical—in the Palaeontology Gallery. Inside the rue Cuvier entrance, the first Cedar of Lebanon planted in France in 1734 stands magisterially at the foot of the butte.*

INSTITUT DU MONDE ARABE   *1, rue des Fossés-Saint-Bernard. Daily except Mon, 10–6, entrance through the south-side façade. A building by Jean Nouvel, overlooking the Seine from the Left Bank. From the ninth-floor terrace the views are among the best in Paris; the Middle Eastern food served here is excellent. The gift shop on the main floor carries exquisite pottery and fabrics.*

Voltaire: The Seine and the Louvre from Quai Voltaire

Saint-Germain-des-Prés

VOLTAIRE: DYING INTACT

LOCATIONS: ***13, rue de l'Ancienne-Comédie,*** *Le Procope;*
2, rue Saint-Louis en l'Île: Île Saint-Louis, Hôtel
Lambert; 23, Quai de Conti, Institut de France;
27, Quai Voltaire: *Le Voltaire Café*
MÉTRO: Saint-Michel

*Born François-Marie Arouet. Nickname "Zozo." Brilliant
child, Paris bad boy, adored playwright. Bastille prisoner,
exile, scourge of l'Ancien Régime and the Catholic Church.
His* Treatise on Tolerance *condemned. Acid wit, ardent
lover: "Pleasure is the greatest reality of our existence."
Motto: "Get to the point."*

Voltaire (1694–1778) was lionized in the streets of his native city but not so welcome in the throne rooms of power. Royals and aristocrats feared his iconoclastic wit almost as if they intuited the threat that the precocious young man's critical spirit posed to their world. It would be, after all, "ideas that destroyed the ancient regime."* Orders of exile or warrants for his arrest were routine responses to his publications, his scrapes, his cheek when up against this duke or that king. But Paris audiences loved the iconoclasm of his plays. Without the bite and moral vision of his writings some say that 1789 would never have happened.

He was born in ***Rue Guénégaud,*** between Quai de Conti

* Roger Pearson, *Voltaire Almighty: A Life in Pursuit of Freedom.*

and rue Mazarine, a narrow old Left Bank street named for a disgraced finance minister. There is no plaque.

Voltaire's "father" moved his family across the Petit Pont to the Île de la Cité when Zozo (who was probably a bastard) was seven and newly motherless. Tutors and Zozo's godfather, Abbé de Châteauneuf, taught him to memorize and write long poems; from the time he was three he became known as a prodigy in the salons of Place Royale (now Place des Vosges), including the salon of Ninon de l'Enclos on rue des Tournelles (see p. 243).

His godfather also introduced him to religious skepticism years before Zozo moved up the hill to *123, rue Saint-Jacques* to board and study at the Jesuits' college, now *Lycée Louis-le-Grand*. (Virtual tours only on www.louislegrand.org.) The Jesuits were fond of Louis XIV for revoking, in 1685, Henri IV's wishy-washy Edict of Nantes which had made religious tolerance of Protestants the law of the land. Thanks to the Sun King, Protestants after 1685 were once again declared heretics, risking exile, prison, torture, and death for following their consciences. Such intolerance made Voltaire a lifelong opponent of organized religion. *"Papist fanatics, Calvinist fanatics, all are molded from the same shit, and soaking in corrupted blood,"* he wrote to another philosophe. But he was not an atheist as is often claimed. Like other philosophes, he was a deist: *"When I see a clock, I believe in a clockmaker."*

At *lycée* he was the Jesuits' star pupil, making friends with some of them, grateful for an education that despite all the "Latin and a lot of nonsense" taught him how to read literature, write prose, and think for himself. Law school, on the other hand, where his father forced him to enroll after *lycée*, served up "useless rubbish." He escaped by spending wild nights in the Place Royale and writing verse, staging plays, making love to actresses, hiding out at Le Temple, the twelfth-century property of the Knights Templar and in the early eighteenth century a free zone (the police could not enter) for freethinkers and aristocratic hedonists who could break wineglasses with their teeth. Le Temple is now the much reduced Square du Temple, a pretty garden on the Right Bank, in the northern Marais.

His father, disgusted by Zozo's debts and all-night carousing sent him to Holland as secretary to an ambassador. More disaster: a love affair and an attempt to elope with a Protestant, the luscious "Pimpette." Back in Paris, the law-school dropout with the sparkling eyes finally went too far. In pretend-funny verses he attacked the Duke of Orléans (the prince regent for the child king Louis XV) for his incestuous affair with his daughter; in 1717 the prince regent sent him off to an eleven-month incarceration in a dark windowless cell in the Bastille because he could. François/Zozo spent his jail time writing.

For the Traveler

His first play, *Oedipus*, ran as a sold-out success at the old Comédie-Française at *14, rue de l'Ancienne Comédie* (between **boulevard Saint-Germain** and **rue de Buci** and a five-minute walk west of the Saint-Michel métro, along the crowded boutique-y **rue Saint-André-des-Arts**). The Comédie-Française is now located on the Right Bank at the Palais Royal on Place Colette and rue de Richelieu, with a statue of a seated Voltaire by Houdon in the foyer.

The original theater took its name from the street where it was located, a street jammed with carriages and theatergoers as it is now with shoppers. It stood opposite *Le Procope* at *13, rue de l'Ancienne Comédie*. The city's first coffeehouse, started by a Sicilian, François Procope, served up two absolute necessities of eighteenth-century Paris, coffee and conversation. Voltaire, said to have drunk forty cups a day (afflicted with nervous indigestion, he said all ill health was caused by overeating) was a regular here along with fellow philosophes determined to overturn the dominant superstitions of the Middle Ages and enshrine the light of reason over affairs of state, religion, culture. The philosophes valued material evidence over blind faith, a defiant reversal of priorities. Over coffee, Voltaire, Diderot, d'Alembert, Beaumarchais, and others came up with the idea of the *Encyclopédie*, a book of definitions and commentaries on the main ideas relating to the Enlightenment, the most significant intellectual development of the modern era. But it was not radically new: it drew on an older tradition of Renaissance humanism.

Le Procope, café and restaurant, now done up in high neoclassical exuberance, is still open for business (daily, 11:45–midnight; reservations at: 1.40.46.79.00) and well worth a visit, mostly for the ambience—bookcases and walls crowded with the luminaries' books and images. Explore the upstairs dining rooms, imagining the very amiable Benjamin Franklin making an entrance in one of them, looking for his friend Voltaire whose desk and table are on display.

Voltaire's literary success intensified in 1724 with the publication of *La Henriade,* his epic poem in praise of his favorite royal, the tolerant *Henri IV* (see p. 37) whose monument is not a classical domed building but the very practical and useful-to-the-people *Pont Neuf* (see p. 41). All Paris (except for Henri's son King Louis XIII) adored the poem, embracing

Henri as "its Best and Favourite King"* and Voltaire as France's greatest living writer.

Then, because Voltaire had the nerve to fight back, arranging a duel with a swinish aristocrat who had had him beaten up, he found himself again locked up in the Bastille. He asked to be set free on condition that he exile himself in England.

That exile changed everything. A child of the bourgeoisie, unprotected by power and lineage, throughout his youth he'd suffered the double-edged despotism of the French state and the Catholic Church. Coming from a country in which the people had no say, he now observed a society marked by a high degree of religious tolerance, political freedom, a limited democracy, and enlightened ideas on science and philosophy, a country where writers and artists were respected. In *Letters Concerning the English Nation*—or simply *Letters on England*—published a few years after he came home to Paris, he praised the foreign land where he had even considered settling for life. (He'd learned English in three months.) The book was condemned and banned by the Paris Parliament, burned in front of the Palais du Justice; a warrant was issued for Voltaire's arrest. His praise of England was rightly interpreted as criticism of France, how unjustly things were done at home.

Fearing for his freedom—another sentence to the Bastille where one never knew if his case would be heard in court, where he could rot for the rest of his life depending on the whim of a royal judge—Voltaire again fled Paris, finding refuge in eastern France in the château of his lover Émilie, marquise du Châtelet (1706–1749), wife of an old marquis

* Nancy Mitford, *Voltaire in Love.*

who liked Voltaire and didn't care what he and his wife were up to after hours.

"A remarkable feminist exemplar of the Enlightenment,"* and a brilliant mathematician and scientist who translated Isaac Newton, Émilie—Voltaire called her the "she-philosopher"—lived in happy exile with Voltaire for ten years. They passed their days studying, reading and writing, making love, and savoring the pleasures of the table in the middle of the night: the daytime eroticism of the intellectual life fueled their passion. To him, she was "a prodigy."

Now and then they returned to Paris. Émilie missed entertaining and court gossip. In 1739, she bought, and Voltaire paid for, the magnificent *Hôtel Lambert* on the eastern tip of *Île Saint-Louis* at 2, rue Saint-Louis en l'Île. *(From the Sully–Morland métro, cross Pont de Sully onto the island; or walk ten minutes east from the Saint-Michel métro along the Left Bank quays to Pont de la Tournelle and onto Île Saint-Louis.)*

Palais Lambert, as Émilie called it, remains today the same luxurious mansion where Chopin, George Sand, and Lizst were hosted; the Rothschilds and other lords of finance lived; and the present owner, the brother of the former emir of Qatar plans to install an underground parking lot and interior elevators to the horror of preservation-conscious Parisians worrying about the stability of the original seventeenth-century architecture, gardens, frescoes, windows. The renovations continue, with 2019 the supposed year of completion.

Voltaire did not enjoy himself on these return junkets to Paris. He complained that "everybody is in too much of a hurry . . . not a moment to oneself, no time to write, to think or to sleep," as Nancy Mitford tells it. And he often had to

---

*Ian Davidson, *Voltaire in Exile*.

look over his shoulder for the censors or the police, sent by the king or one of the many aristocrats who loathed his subversive writings which the literate bourgeoisie devoured and read aloud in *Le Procope*. His enemies united to make sure that that "atheist," the most important writer in eighteenth-century France, was rejected several times over for membership in the prestigious *Académie Française*.

Walking west from *Île Saint-Louis*, across *Île de la Cité* and Henri IV's *Place Dauphine* where Voltaire and Émilie heard open-air concerts, bear left over the *Pont Neuf* and then right (west) along the Left Bank quays until you see on your left the domed beauty of the *Institut de France* (*23, Quai de Conti*): It overlooks the Seine and the Pont des Arts, facing the Louvre. Originally a college, it became the home of five academies, the most renowned of which is the exclusive *Académie Française*, which was, in Voltaire's day, housed in the Louvre.

Founded by Cardinal Richelieu in 1635, its primary function is to guard the purity of the French language, creating and updating the dictionary and defending French-speaking communities. Membership is restricted to forty illustrious members—*les Immortels*—each one nominated (after rigorous screening) and appointed on the death of one of the forty. Gaining acceptance was an extremely political business. Voltaire cared enough about admission that he whored himself continuously, manipulating and flattering the sitting members (and the pope who had a say in everything) until he was finally admitted in 1746.

> HOURS: The Académie Française and the other
> academies are open to the public once a year, in the
> third week of September, the French Heritage days.

Only the Institute's ***Bibliothèque Mazarine*** is open
to the public year-round (Mon–Fri, 10–6). To enter,
cross the Institute's octagonal courtyard to the front
entrance, show a picture ID, and continue into the
next courtyard and then left up the winding staircase
leading to the Bibliothèque named for and donated by
Louis XIV's hated chief financial minister, Cardinal
Mazarin, a Roman by birth.

Bibliophiles will want to settle in forever in this
seventeenth-century sanctuary. The first free public library
in France, it holds 650,000 volumes of French literature in all
genres. The exhibits of rare books, manuscripts, and maps
are tastefully displayed, there is not a sound in the long, dark,
wood-paneled reading room, lined on all sides with ceiling-
high bookshelves, the French windows (with window seats)
letting in the light from the river. Golden chandeliers and
reading lamps on the long tables create a well-lit serenity.
Busts of the ancients decorate the aisles; the beloved American, Benjamin Franklin, is honored on his pedestal.

Voltaire took his green academician's uniform with bicorn
and sword back to eastern France, now a permanent exile
after Louis XV told his mistress, Madame de Pompadour, a
friend of Voltaire, to let him know he was not *ever* welcome
at court. He'd had enough of his plays' and poems' jokes that
made the courtiers roar laughing and stop paying attention
to Louis.

In the last decades of his life, following the death of Émilie in 1749, Voltaire wrote his masterpiece, *Candide* (1759), renowned ever since for its prescription of moral health: *We
must cultivate our garden*. The garden is what there is: accord-

ing to his philosophy of activity, instead of a posturing pessimism and depression, we must work on the material and the local, on the cultivation of the earth or the city or wherever we find ourselves. He himself, as an urban reformer, urged greater hygiene in the streets of Paris as well as cleaner air, all of which would enhance the city's beauty. He cared deeply about the aesthetics of "the capital of the world" and in particular the design of its streets.

At a distance from Paris, he continued to crusade against what he called *l'Infame*, the persecution and intolerance practiced by the Church in alliance with the state. As he aged, he became an indefatigable advocate of human rights, working to overturn a number of unjust death penalty edicts of the French judicial system, and, posthumously, the unjust guilty verdicts of Protestant victims of the Catholic state and Church. He also took up the cause of the impoverished peasants who worked on his estates. He was caught up, too, in these years away from Paris, with business deals with Jews that went sour, leading to charges against Voltaire as an anti-Semite.

When his *Treatise on Tolerance* (1763) was published in Paris, he again feared for his freedom, so outrageous did the aristocracy find his ideas:

> *What is tolerance? It is the prerogative of our humanity. We are all fashioned of weaknesses and mistakes. Let us pardon each other for our blunders. This is the first law of nature.*

After the *Charlie Hebdo* massacre in January 2015, Voltaire's essay on "Tolerance" became a best seller in Paris, reprinted many times. Nearly half as many copies were sold in the three weeks after the killings as have been sold in the last twelve years. Intellectuals have been quick to draw comparisons between Voltaire and *Charlie Hebdo*. The *Société Voltaire*, a group that safeguards his legacy, called him the rallying symbol for those who do not accept violence in the name of religion. At a time when "our way of life, of being and living together has come under attack," wrote a spokesperson for Gallimard, Voltaire's publisher, "this book is an antidote, a way of resisting."

In 1778, in terrible health, making sure before he ordered the carriages that he was not a wanted *philosophe*, he traveled to Paris to see the production of his play *Irène*. He stayed in the **Hôtel de Villette** owned by his friends the Villettes and now called **Le Voltaire Café,** at the corner of the **rue de Beaune** and the **Quai des Théatins,** named **Quai Voltaire** in 1791 (between the Pont Royal and the Pont du Carrousel). He'd known the building intimately in his profligate youth; he'd rented an apartment there in his twenties and had an affair with the then owner, Madame de Bernières. The entrance to the apartments, restored but not open to the public, is around the corner on **rue de Beaune.**

Irène was another triumph. At one performance, the audience cheered as a bust of Voltaire was crowned onstage, in his presence, the actors placing wreath upon wreath on the marble head. Crowds mobbed his carriage, hailing him as "the defender of the poor and oppressed." Day and night many old friends came to visit, including Benjamin Franklin with his grandson by the hand; Voltaire dropped in at the Académie Française (in the Louvre) and was greeted at the door and celebrated by all the members except the bishops and clergy.

As he got sicker, priests from nearby **Saint-Sulpice** came to the *Hôtel de Villette,* at first to visit, then to harass. They wanted a deathbed confession, a recanting they could publicize for propaganda's purposes. There are varying accounts of what actually happened as Voltaire, in great pain, began to die. One witness claimed he was demented, gone mad; a priest said there was a smell of sulfur and smoke in the bedchamber as Voltaire's soul descended into hell; others disputed all of this except that he was in pain and told the badgering priests to get out.

For his deathbed integrity, he was refused a Christian burial by the Church. His hearse left Paris with his body, which was buried on the grounds of an abbey in Champagne where his nephew was abbot, following a funeral Mass. Until 1791 he rested in peace. Then the Revolution, claiming him as one of its founding rebels—*"he prepared us to be free"* was incised on his coffin—reburied him in the Panthéon. Voltaire himself would have denounced a Paris gone mad with everything he loathed: intolerance, injustice, cruelty.

Inside *Le Voltaire,* the café on the corner of *Quai Voltaire* (*open Tues–Sat for lunch and dinner, tel: 01.42.61.17.41*) in the building where he died, a glass panel at a right angle to the bar is incised with some of his final words:

Je meurs en adorant dieu, en aimant mes amis, en ne haïssant pas mes enemis en detéstante la superstition. (I am dying adoring God, loving my friends, not hating my enemies, hating superstition.)

The dimly lit wood-paneled café bar with the velvet banquettes is a good place to ponder Voltaire and his eighteenth-century Paris late into a fall evening, away from the traffic on *Quai Voltaire,* the Seine and the Louvre in full view. His genius, his flawed humanity (the philandering and anti-Semitic resentments), his humor, and courage as a champion of civil liberties—he knew the limits and the dangers of enlightenment thinking even then in 1778 when the world looked new.

Without him, in the opinion of Benjamin Franklin and Thomas Jefferson, the Declaration of Independence and the American Revolution would never have happened.

Nearby

SQUARE HONORÉ-CHAMPION   *Through an arch to the right of the **Institut de France,** a statue of Voltaire stands on a green mound landscaped with flowers and trees. There's an appealing modesty in this hidden site of memory.*

LE BISTROT MAZARIN   ***42, rue Mazarine.** Excellent for long lunches and good food. At the end of the street where Voltaire was born, in **rue Guénégaud.***

CAFÉ DE L'ODÉON   *www.theatre-odeon.eu. Inside the famous theater, up a grand staircase leading to the Grand Foyer. At the top of rue de l'Odéon, south of boulevard de Saint-Germain, surrounded by arcades. Quiet at midday, electric on theater nights.*

Albert Camus: Café de la Mairie, Place Saint Sulpice

ALBERT CAMUS: CONSCIENCE
OF HIS GENERATION

LOCATIONS: *Place Saint-Sulpice, Café de la Mairie;*
5, rue Gaston-Gallimard and environs, Éditions
Gallimard, Publishers
MÉTRO: Saint-Germain-des-Prés

I n the end, Camus (1913–1960) came to hate Paris, longed to be "rid of it." The gray weather, the cultural elites, the cynical politics, he detested it all, that "city without light, rising in the fog." On his visits back home to his native Algeria he said again and again that Parisians were cold or worse. "Our intellectual society, whether leftist or rightest, is almost always frightfully mean and nasty."*

At the same time, throughout the twenty years he lived there, his notebooks record his ambivalence about the city. Paris, he writes, reflects the beauty of the world. It is the city of his success and much personal happiness. His books were published there, his plays produced, his fame as "the conscience of his generation," the dominant voice of humanism and a compassionate morality, caught fire here, spreading across Europe and America. His children, whom he loved, were born here as were his passionate love affairs and many friendships. Francine Faure, who, like him, was born and raised in Algeria, was his loyal Paris wife. He considered her his best friend whom "I have never stopped loving in my bad

---

* Olivier Todd, *Albert Camus: A Life*. Todd's biography is the source of most of the details and quotations cited here.

way." Francine put up with his infidelities until she finally fell apart.

The landscape of Algeria, his homeland, was the place he loved most profoundly; his mother whom he called "his only love" lived in Algeria. Poor, half deaf, mostly mute, a widow in 1914 after the Battle of the Marne when Albert was one, a housecleaner for life, he left her and Algeria behind for the first time in March 1940 as the Germans were heading toward France.

Arriving in Paris, he moved into a seedy hotel in Montmartre in the eighteenth *arrondissement*. On staff at the newspaper *Paris-Soir* from early morning until midday, he spent the nights working on his novel *The Stranger*. His first three months in Paris were "cloistered," as he put it, without women or dancing or drinking in cafés. In May 1940, he wrote to Francine on the night that he had "just finished his novel. . . . I think I'd forgive Paris for everything, for having allowed me to live like this, completely concentrated upon what I was doing." The loneliness of the Montmartre streets intensified his lifelong self-consciousness as an exile, an outsider like Meursault, the protagonist of *The Stranger*.

When the Germans invaded Paris in June, *Paris-Soir* and Camus joined the exodus south. The manuscript of *The Stranger,* in a small case, was always close by. When the newspaper folded, Camus returned to Algeria. About a year later, after severe flare-ups of the tuberculosis that ravaged his lungs, he returned to German-occupied France to live in the mountains of southern France, going to a nearby town for treatments: It was wrongly believed that living at high altitudes—three thousand feet—would enable the tubercular patient to inhale high doses of pure oxygen whereas the opposite was true. The higher the altitude the less oxygen there is in the air; thinner air gives the patient less, not more energy. His disease, in remission at times, caused him pain, exhaustion, and depression for the rest of his life. But Camus, journalist and editor, novelist, playwright, director, essayist, philosopher, and activist never stopped working like a man possessed. He expected his lungs to fail, that he would die young.

His mountain retreat was near the village of Le Chambon where Huguenot pastor Trocmé and his congregation hid and saved five thousand Jews throughout the war. Camus, an atheist, shared the pastor's ethical commitment to the practice of resistance. Resistance was, for both men, "a way of seeing the world, one that makes manifest the moral imperative to acknowledge and respect the dignity of each and every fellow human being."* For Camus the world was absurd, but his absurdism became a kind of humanism: the irrational world, without meaning, assumed the meaning one gave it, as Olivier Todd puts it. The act of resistance gave the world meaning, fighting for lost causes. For the rest of his life, Camus resisted political and moral oppression. The cruel history of the war and postwar years marked him: either you resisted historical cruelty or your life was worthless.

For the Traveler

It's still possible to walk the streets of Camus's Paris though he might not recognize the gentrified bars and cafés where he was a regular.

He settled into Occupied Paris in late 1943, a twenty-nine-year-old writer whose novel *The Stranger* and essay

---

* Robert Zaretsky, *A Life Worth Living: Albert Camus and the Quest for Meaning.*

collection *The Myth of Sisyphus* had been published and well-reviewed in 1942. His play *Caligula* would be produced soon. He had a job as a reader for his publisher, Gallimard, on the Left Bank; he became a columnist and then editor of the Resistance newspaper *Combat*, "one of the best-written papers in the entire history of French journalism," to quote historian Raymond Aron. The punishment for writing anti-Nazi and anti-Vichy columns for the Resistance press was deportation to a concentration camp.

He worked on *Combat* in his apartment, and late into the night in the clandestine offices of *Combat* on the Right Bank in a building designed for the French press (1924) at *100, rue Réaumur* in the Bonne Nouvelle district. Though restored, the building still stands, with its bas-reliefs of reporters, typesetters, and printers. The story is told that one night Camus and his lover, the actress Maria Casares (the Occupation had trapped Camus's wife in Algeria) who worked as a courier for the Resistance, were stopped near the Réaumur-Sébastopol métro in a Nazi sweep. Camus was carrying a layout page (measuring 7 × 10 inches) with the heading "*Combat*." He passed the page to Maria: women were not body-searched by the Nazis, at least in public. Maria, so the story goes, swallowed the incriminating page,* a Resistance survival tactic shown in Jean-Pierre Melville's Resistance film, *Army of Shadows* (1969).

Handsome as a movie star, often compared to Humphrey Bogart, Camus was as irresistible to women as beautiful women were to him; fellow writers were drawn to his celebrity, charm, and wit. Early on his novel had been reviewed with condescending praise by the not-handsome philosopher

* Patrick McCarthy, *Camus*.

Jean-Paul Sartre, the pope of the Left Bank. After meeting Sartre and his partner Simone de Beauvoir ("the Beaver" and "Castor" were her nicknames) in June 1943, the trio became friends, socializing at night in the Left Bank cafés of the district of *Saint-Germain* where Sorbonne intellectuals, journalists, politicians, academics, theater people, and artists met in cafés to talk, argue politics and philosophy, drink, party, tell jokes, dance, and hook up with pretty girls. During the war, collaborators and spies were also part of the mix. He was working on a second novel, *The Plague,* more plays, and *The Rebel,* a long essay about political morality that would draw the contempt of Sartre and many Left Bank intellectuals when it was published in 1951. Feeling their long-suppressed hatred, Camus realized then, in retrospect, that his café and jazz-club nightlife of the forties had been a lie: "*these people were never my friends.*" The drunken carousing had distracted him from the fact that in Paris he was an outsider; that his companions— many were *normaliens*—deluded by their own privilege and abstractions, knew nothing about the experience of poverty and the ordinary people he loved in his Mediterranean youth.

He wrote about the influence of the light of Algeria with a very un-Left Bank lyricism:

> *Poverty prevented me from judging that all was well under the sun and in history; the sun taught me that history was not all.**

Sartre got quite enough of Camus as Mediterranean man (and the darling of Parisian women). Behind his back he called Camus an Algerian street urchin.

---

* Albert Camus, *Notebooks: 1951–1959*, trans. Ryan Bloom.

But while it lasted, the two friends had a lot of fun together despite each man knowing they thought very different thoughts and perhaps realizing their friendship would
not survive the enmities of intellectual Paris.

The cafés they liked have either closed down or like *Saint-
Germain* itself have changed so much the writers of postwar
Paris wouldn't recognize them. The district is now the most
expensive in Paris: luxury shops—Dior, Vuitton, Armani,
Cartier—dominate every block. The great *librairies*—the
legendary bookstores—unable to compete with billionaire
retail have closed. *La Hune* is the most recent victim.

The *Café de Flore (172, boulevard Saint-Germain*) and
*Les Deux Magots (170, boulevard Saint-Germain at Place
Jean-Paul-Sartre-Simone-de-Beauvoir)*—métro: Saint-Germain
-des-Prés—where Sartre and Camus and many other writers worked days and nights despite the Nazis strutting past,
keeping warm in the *Flore* around the sawdust-burning
stove, are decorated today with photographs of their long-
dead famous customers. Inside the brass railings the tables
(and outdoor terraces) and the red banquettes are crowded
in all seasons with tourists and Parisian shoppers fresh from
tanning parlors. Despite the glut of bling and poodles, the
Deux Magots' prospect from its east side is lovely: the tables
and *terrasse* face the *Place Sartre-Beauvoir* and the church of
Saint-Germain-des-Prés, which gives the ancient district its
name. (There was a church here in 542–559.) The Roman-
esque bell tower of the twelfth-century church rises toward
the night sky like a deliverance, a reminder in stone of what
Camus believed: "that history was not all."

A few hundred yards north of the cafés of *Saint-Germain*,
the small 150-year-old bistro *Le Petit Saint Benoit* at *4, rue
Saint-Benoit* near the corner of *rue Jacob* was a regular din-

ing spot for Sartre and Camus. (Ten years earlier it had been Antoine de Saint-Exupéry's favorite.) Its simple good food and down-to-earth feeling still suggests quintessential Paris. The writer Marguerite Duras lived across the street, at no. 5, where she and her husband held Resistance meetings. One story has it that Camus acted as a lookout during the Occupation after Duras's husband, Robert Antelme, was arrested, deported to Dachau, and it became a matter of the life and death of many *Résistants* in his network that his papers be removed from the apartment and destroyed.

Across *boulevard Saint-Germain* at no. 151, *Brasserie Lipp* also remains pretty much as Camus and Sartre knew it. They ate here once a week, sometimes for lunch and dinner, surrounded by the same mirrors, mosaics, and Belle Époque ceramic designs by Léon-Paul Fargue that make the place so attractive. The creation of two Alsatian refugees from the Franco-Prussian War in 1870, Leonard and Flo Lipp—"*Chez Lipp*"—was awarded the Légion of Honor in 1958 for having the best literary and theater salon in Paris. (Reservations are required. Tel: 01.45.48.53.91.)

The basement jazz clubs of *Saint-Germain* where Camus and Sartre often dropped in after dinner are gone. The bar of the *Pont Royal,* one of their favorite hangouts, though still small and convivial now caters to well-heeled tourists. Walk west along *boulevard Saint-Germain,* turn right into *rue du Bac,* soon bearing right into *rue Montalembert* where at no. 7 the *Hôtel Pont Royal* still calls itself the *Hôtel Littéraire.* More upscale now than in Camus's time (18 euros for a margarita, guests layered in luxury going and coming through the revolving doors), it's fun to sit in the bar in early evening surrounded by photographs of the literary stars of postwar Paris—Camus, Duras, Robbe-Grillet, Sartre, de Beauvoir, Gide—that look down from the dark paneled walls of the gracious lobby.

The *Pont Royal* is remembered as the writers' bar because it served the publishing house of Gallimard which was—and is—right around the corner at no. 5, *rue Gaston-Gallimard* (in Camus's time this street was *rue Sébastien-Bottin*).

Afternoons Camus worked in his office as a reader for Éditions Gallimard, named for the founder and patriarch of the Gallimard family a number of whose members worked as editors and executives in the building. Resistance members held secret nighttime meetings in Gaston Gallimard's office. After the war, Gallimard was criticized for keeping his doors open during the Occupation. Critics had perhaps forgotten the attacks of the collaborationist press on Gallimard, charging it had published books of propaganda for Israel as well as unhealthy Jewish writings by Sigmund Freud, filthy writers such as André Gide, André Malraux, Louis Aragon. Gallimard's deals and financial support on behalf of Resistance writers as well as writers whom the Nazis ordered him to drop from the list had remained a secret, in the years of Occupation.

Camus occupied an office on a high floor with a terrace that looked out over the Left Bank. If you enter the lobby today, the receptionists are friendly but strangely clueless. Asking to see the office of Albert Camus—whose books as well as a copy of *The New York Times* front page reporting Camus's Nobel Prize are displayed in a case to the left of the front entrance—I heard the amiable young women claim not to recognize the name. "Albert Camus?" *"Qui est-ce?"*

In 1946 Camus's series *Espoir* was launched by Gallimard. Camus published some of Sartre's friends, some of his own. In 1949 he discovered the unpublished writings of the philosopher and mystic Simone Weil. He read through Weil's handwritten manuscripts in her parents' apartment in *rue Auguste-Comte* (see p. 101). Some of her themes converged with ideas he cared and wrote about passionately: a detestation of the violence and force that characterize totalitarianism; love for the Greeks, their sense of limits and measure, and for the landscapes of Italy and Spain; the scandal of the French Empire's exploitation of its colonial populations; the hatred of the death penalty, and the immoral living conditions of workers. Both Weil and Camus were religious outsiders, not connected to any one tradition though Weil was drawn to Christianity's commitment to the poor. Weil's history of activist engagement on behalf of the working class Camus interpreted as a sign of deliverance from nihilism. Eventually, he published eight of her books, which gave her an international audience. Camus also published the poetry of the Resistance hero, René Char, which "dazzled" him. Camus and Char became close friends.

As the Cold War intensified in the fifties, most of the Paris Left was as partial to Soviet Communism as ordinary Parisians had been to the United States at the time of the Liberation. Camus's *The Rebel* condemns communism as totalitarian, murderous, a cruel system of slavery comparable to German Nazism and the Fascisms of Italy and Spain. *"An anti-communist is a dog,"* wrote Sartre. For his part, Camus, who had always refused the label of "existentialism," referred to it now as the province of "dusty old men," who lacked all compassion.

During these years of literary success—the novel *The Plague*, essays, plays—Camus avoided invitations, fans, official social events, and the old cafés. The unpopularity of his idealistic politics among the cynical *gauchistes* reduced him to a lone voice, ignored and ridiculed. He and Francine bought an apartment at no. 29, *rue Madame* (having moved from no. 18, *rue Séguier*). From the Saint-Sulpice métro, walk south along rue Madame until you come to no. 29 on the east side of the street. The name "Camus" still appears on the buzzer of the apartment.

Weekday mornings Camus walked north on *rue Madame* toward his office at Gallimard, crossing Place Saint-Sulpice with the *Fontaine des Quatre Points Cardinaux* in the center, then stopping at the *Café de La Mairie,* which faces the Place. The terrace today is packed with people most afternoons, but the indoor back room (and the upstairs dining area), plain and quiet, is where Parisian regulars, like Camus himself, sit turning the pages of that day's *Le Monde, Le Figaro,* and *Libération* while having their first coffee. No doubt the ordinariness of the café and its clientèle pleased him. From there he walked straight west to *boulevard Raspail,* then heading right to the Gallimard office. If you're following in Camus's late morning footsteps, it's rewarding to leave his route at *Place Saint-Sulpice* and detour through the streets that lead into it: *rue Férou* (with Rimbaud's poetry wall), *rue Servandoni* (where William Faulkner, Olympe de Gouges, Roland Barthes, Eugène Atget, Juliette Gréco, and others lived), and *rue Garancière*. This *quartier* holds the secret of why Paris can take such hold of you, live in your memory forever.

A few years after the fury over *The Rebel* came the vicious attacks on Camus for his position on the Algerian war for independence. He advocated negotiation (a civilian truce) between the government of France and the pro-independence Arab and French Algerians. Aside from René Char and Germaine Tillion (his *Résistante* friend whose body was recently transferred to the Panthéon) who both agreed with his antiviolence position, most of his Paris and Algerian friends deserted him. Camus, in their eyes, was a traitor to his native Algeria. (Fifty years later Camus's prescient position now receives a new respect.) Despite the shunning by the militant Left, Camus's next novel, *The Fall*, was a best seller. Then, for his writings against the death penalty which, quoting Montaigne, he called "a criminal act," he was awarded the Nobel Prize in 1957. Sartre and his disciples mocked him for accepting such a bourgeois honor.

Despite the loss of friends and the ugly war in Algeria—the French army tortured the Algerian rebels just as the Nazis and the French police had tortured the *Résistants* on rue Lauriston (see p.)—Camus never turned a blind eye to the beauty of the world. "I put the beauty of a landscape before all else. It's not paid for by any injustice and my heart is free there." In his Nobel address, he named the source of that beauty: "*I have never renounced the light.*" Asked which French writers had most influenced him, he named "Simone Weil and René Char," both poets of the light.

In the end, he still found joy in his nighttime walks through the streets of Paris. Observing the **Square du Vert-Galant,** he noted:

> *Night of the 15th. Stroll along the Seine. Beneath the Pont Neuf young foreigners (Scandinavians) are joined together around two of their own, a trumpeter and a banjo player, and lie on the street, couples embracing, listening to the improvisation. Farther, on one of the benches of the Pont des Arts, an Arab has stretched out, a portable radio by his head, playing Arab music.**

*Albert Camus, *Notebooks: 1951–1959*, trans. Ryan Bloom.

The vitriol of Paris intellectuals could not blind him to our common humanity.

He bought a house in Provence, in the village of Lourmarin, near René Char's village. The closeness to the sea and to "the secret of the light" reminded him of Algeria. He worked there alone on his next novel, *The First Man*. The silence and isolation, the same "cloistered" life he'd known while completing *The Stranger* in Montmartre, helped him concentrate. His family came down for Christmas. On his way back to Paris, on January 4, 1960, carrying 144 pages of his novel, he was killed in a car crash.

Nearby

PLACE RENÉ-CHAR   *Métro: rue du Bac. The marker at the Place identifies Char as "Poète et Résistant," 1907–1988. At the intersection of **boulevard Saint-Germain, rue du Bac,** and **boulevard Raspail,** the Place is along Camus's daily route to Gallimard, now mad with traffic. Char dedicated his* Leaves of Hypnos *to Camus. "Nous n'appartenons à personne sinon au point d'or de cette lampe inconnue de nous . . ." "We belong to no one except the golden point of light from that lamp unknown to us . . ."*

Jean Moulin: 26, rue des Plantes

JEAN MOULIN:
HERO OF THE RESISTANCE

LOCATION: *26, rue des Plantes, Hideaway*
MÉTRO: Mouton-Duvernet

June 14, 1940. Nazi troops goose-step down the Champs-Élysées. The forces of darkness are taking possession of the City of Light.

Jean Moulin (1899–1943), who would become the leader and hero of the French Resistance, was an hour southwest that day, in Chartres, the town with the glorious cathedral, part of the *departement* of Eure-et-Loir. As its prefect, one of the highest administrative posts in the government—the equivalent of being a major general in the army—Moulin had already earned the people's respect for not joining the panicked Paris exodus south in the days before the Nazi invasion. He *did* hit the road, but he drove in the wrong direction. He and his lover, Antoinette Sachs, went to Paris, to his *Montparnasse* apartment to retrieve government files he kept hidden in closets. A few days later, however, on June 18, when Brigadier General Charles de Gaulle made his historic radio address from his London exile—"*Whatever happens, the flame of French resistance must not and shall not die*"—inspiring, indeed *ordering* France to refuse the German barbarism, Jean Moulin never heard the voice of his future boss. He lay bleeding to death, by his own hand, in a Chartres prison cell.

*   *   *

Born in 1899, he'd loved drawing and painting since childhood, exhibiting his work, winning awards, considering art as a career but choosing instead the civil service. Over the years he collected work by Dufy, Rouault, Matisse, Marie Laurencin, de Chirico. It made sense he'd choose an apartment in *Montparnasse,* the *quartier* of painters and poets since the nineteenth century, known as "the cradle of modern art" into the twentieth. The cafés were crowded with Picasso and friends; refugees from Montmartre; the many refugee Russian artists; the writers Joyce, Pound, Beckett, and Apollinaire; the painter and poet Max Jacob who had first befriended Moulin when he was a prefect in Brittany; the sculptor Alberto Giacometti, who lived a few blocks west of Moulin on *rue Hippolyte-Maindron* (see p. 153).

For the Traveler

26, rue des Plantes, a modern building in the fourteenth *arrondissement* of *Montparnasse* was "full of painters" when Moulin moved in in 1934.

> DIRECTIONS: Exit the Mouton-Duvernet métro and walk
>   west, past the pretty *mairie* of the fourteenth, then
>   cross *avenue du Maine* and turn left.

He rented a top-floor studio, looking out over the roofs of southern Paris. Today a screen of good-sized healthy trees borders the front of the building. A plaque is affixed near the entrance, identifying Jean Moulin as the *First President of the National Council of the Resistance* (CNR), who, along with another resident, *Died As Heroes for the Salvation of France.* The place looks appropriately blank, its inexpressive architecture suited to the clandestine work and character of its most famous occupant. From the time he was a young student in Montpelier, an antiauthoritarian rebel, Moulin had kept his privacy intact. A second entrance to his building, made for quick getaways, is around the corner on *rue Bénard,* which ends two blocks west at the pretty *Place Flora Tristan.*

It would not have crossed Moulin's mind in 1934 that someday a plaque honoring his patriotism would appear on his building; or that a major road to the south would be renamed *avenue Jean Moulin*; or that a fifteen-minute walk north would lead to the rooftop garden of *Gare Montparnasse: Jardin Atlantique,* in the fifteenth *arrondissement*, where the *Musée Jean Moulin* (open daily, 10–6, except Mondays; www .museesleclercmoulin.paris.fr.) exhibits exhaustive documentary evidence, in print, films, and slides, of Moulin's political genius and courage. As De Gaulle's secret agent in France— Moulin's code name was "Max" or "Rex"—he worked with the many competitive networks of Resistance, military, Communist, Catholic, Socialist, labor unions, political parties right-wing, center-left, in the North and South, reconciling the conflicts among them, and finally—miraculously, some believed—uniting them into one French Resistance in May 1943: CNR—the National Council of the Resistance.

Moulin liked the plebian cast of his *quartier,* the legendary turf of *la vie bohème*. (Debris from nearby quarries formed a grass-covered mound where students came to read their poetry to one another, naming the place *Mount Parnassus* after the sacred mountain where Apollo communed with his Muses.) At the time Moulin moved in, he was temporarily out of a government job. He spent his free time going to art schools, painting, visiting the Pigalle brothels. With his artist friends he spent time in the cafés and brasseries on *boulevard du Montparnasse* (now serving as many tourists as locals): The art deco *La Coupole* at no. 102, with its original panels contributed by thirty artists, now part of a chain of eateries but still popular and fun at night, along with *La Rotonde* at no. 105, and *Le Dome* at no. 108, the café of the Bulgarian painter Pascin: art curators saw a resemblance between the drawings of Pascin and Toulouse-Lautrec and Jean Moulin's caricatures of fatuous politicians, smug bourgeoisie, and reclining prostitutes. Exhibited in Paris, Moulin's irreverent sketches were reviewed and praised by the renowned art critic (and poet), André Salmon.

There is a significant connection between Moulin's love of art and his brilliance as the leader of the Resistance. Apollinaire's description of *Montparnasse* as "so full of imagination" fits the profile of Moulin's personality and strategies. Only a man easy with multiple points of view, with the complexity and contradictions of things—a man with the soul of an artist—could have become a genius juggler of the multiple identities and aliases and code names of his Resistance soldiers, patiently, flexibly, calming their conflicting political passions that often threatened to destroy the Resistance, and all along, simultaneously, holding in his mind the times and places of the arms drops from London, the money drops, the soldiers of the night who would pick them up, the safe houses where they hid, the schedule of sabotages: of electricity stations, of trains carrying French captives to German camps and German soldiers into France, of transmitters blocking the BBC broadcasts from London. Although the fate of the Jews was not a top priority for the Resistance, among its most honorable acts was safeguarding the shelter extended to Jews by thousands of resisting anonymous

French citizens.* Moulin's orchestration of all of this was a kind of terrifying art.

Moulin, a government minister well-practiced in doubleness, would have appreciated the easy-going nighttime pleasures of his *quartier,* the bohemian subculture that lay along the transgressive streets a few minutes to the northeast of his apartment, off the long monotonous *avenue du Maine: rue de la Gaîté,* which got its name in 1830 for its culture of pleasure, the abundance of theaters, dance halls, *guinguettes,* of free-spirited locals. Still in business are Théâtre Montparnasse (no. 31), Théâtre de la Gaîté-Montparnasse (26), where Colette performed, the legendary Bobino music hall (no. 20) which often presented Édith Piaf (see p. 263) and the old Théâtre Rive Gauche (no. 6). At the end of *rue de la Gaîté,* you cross *Place Edgar Quinet,* bearing right into *rue Delambre,* with its artist studios, *crêperies,* cafés, and the Hôtel Delambre where Paul Gauguin and André Breton once lived.

Across *boulevard du Montparnasse,* is the *Carrefour Vavin,* the crossroads of boulevards *Raspail* and *Montparnasse,* where Rodin's statue of Balzac has stood on a small tree-shaded triangle since 1939, the year Jean Moulin was appointed prefect of Chartres.

That appointment pleased him. From Chartres, Gare Montparnasse and Paris nightlife were only an hour's train ride away.

> DIRECTIONS: These days, trains leave Gare
> Montparnasse for Chartres every hour on weekdays;
> there are fewer trains on weekends. The Chartres
> station is a short walk from the tourist office on *rue
> Jean Moulin,* just next to the cathedral.

* Julian Jackson, *France: The Dark Years, 1940–1944.*

Visitors to Chartres can join a walking tour at the
tourist office which tells the stories of the great figures
of the town of Chartres (www.chartres-tourisme.com
/fr/chemin-de-memoire). At the edge of the old town,
on the **boulevard de la Résistance,** you will see the
Memorial to Jean Moulin: a giant brown granite fist
holding a broken sword. Not every tour guide tells the
full story of why Moulin's memory is so revered in
Chartres or why his life in Chartres is configured in
the shape of a fist.

Shortly after the Nazis occupied Chartres in 1940, their
bombs having already torn the town apart, they demanded
that the prefect sign a document attesting that colonial French
troops—black soldiers from Senegal—were responsible for
the mutilated corpses of French civilians found at the bomb
sites. Moulin refused to sign. He knew the dead were victims
of German bombs. For his refusal, he was beaten and tortured. Left alone in a cell and realizing he was at the end of his
tolerance for continued torture—that he would eventually
sign—he cut his throat with a piece of broken glass rather
than dishonor the North African French troops with his signature. But he knew to cut it near the vein and the jawbone—
so that he bled profusely—but did not cut into the vein. He
was lying in a pool of blood by the time a Nazi patrol noticed
him and brought him to hospital. He was treated and nursed
back to health by nuns who, like their prefect, had refused to
flee before the Nazi invasion, staying to take care of the sick
and the old who, their homes in ruins, had taken shelter in
the crypt of the cathedral. (As part of the historical tour, the
crypt, one of the longest in Europe, is open to the public.)
Moulin, the lifelong anticlerical republican, wrote a beautiful

tribute to the nuns—"the merciful angels of our misery"—in *Premier Combat,* his account of what had happened in the town of Chartres in 1940.

A few months later, fired by the collaborationist French government at Vichy for refusing to cooperate with the Nazis, Moulin spent the next months collecting information about anti-German activities in Occupied and Unoccupied France. On the run for the remaining three years of his life— he never slept in his own bed again—flying to London to meet de Gaulle and deliver his information, always carrying fake identity cards, meeting with the various chiefs of Resistance networks, encouraging them to work together.

On May 27, 1943, at *48, rue du Four* in Paris (marked with a plaque) in a first-floor flat on the Left Bank just west of *rue de Rennes,* his brainchild, the CNR—the National Council of the Resistance—met for the first time and agreed to work as one unified Resistance. It adopted unanimously Moulin's resolution for the structure of France's post-Liberation government: its leader would be de Gaulle, "the soul of the Resistance in its darkest days." That the communists signed on was just more evidence of Moulin's brilliance as a leader and strategist. In 2013, a man who lived in *rue du Four* pointed me in the direction of the founding site of the CNR with visible pride and reverence. For the people of Paris, Jean Moulin remains the hero of the French Resistance.

Less than a month after Moulin's victory on *rue du Four,* he lay, once again, dying in a Nazi jail. Betrayed by someone who was never identified, he ended up under the fists of chief Gestapo agent, Klaus Barbie, former altar boy, son of a devout Catholic mother and an alcoholic father whose vicious beatings helped turn his son into a monster. Some say Barbie tortured his prize captive for two weeks, but "Max" was never broken. In the end, his handsome face—"those sparkling eyes," his grace and charm, "simply to be in his presence was a delight"*—had been gouged and smashed to bloody pulp. Barbie brought him from Lyons to Gestapo headquarters in Paris, at *84, avenue Foch* in Passy (see p. 219) where Moulin was unrecognizable. He died, according to the German death certificate, on a train bound for Germany. "He who knew everything, said nothing," in the words of his sister Laure. His silence saved his fellow *Résistants* from arrest, torture, death, or deportation.

The Resistance carried on.

On August 25, 1944, the German commander signed the surrender at (the old) *Gare Montparnasse,*† where Moulin, artist, prefect, playboy, de Gaulle's man on the ground, had so often departed and arrived from his day job in Chartres, walking about fifteen minutes to his apartment on *rue des Plantes* or to meet his artist friends in the cafés on *boulevard du Montparnasse.*

After D-Day, General Dwight D. Eisenhower, the Supreme Allied Commander, said that the Resistance had been "worth fifteen divisions": Without its secret war against the occupying Germans before the invasion and its open war against the retreating Germans afterward, the war would have lasted longer and cost many more lives. De Gaulle and the surviving leaders of the Resistance gave Moulin and his visionary policies the credit for preventing France from exploding into civil war after the Liberation. As head of the

---

*M. R. D. Foot, *Six Faces of Courage: True Stories of World War II Resistance Fighters.*

†In 1973, the old train station was replaced by the city's first skyscraper, the ugly Tour Montparnasse, adjacent to the new train station. An elevator goes to the "Panoramic" floor, worth the thirty-eight seconds it takes to ride to the top and see its great view of Paris.

Resistance, Moulin always had his eye on post-Liberation Paris, on how to prevent either a takeover of a communist dictatorship or an Allied occupation. His goal was to rebuild the Republic, with the support of the people.

André Malraux spoke on the cold day in 1964 when Moulin's ashes were placed in the Panthéon. Delivering one of the greatest speeches in French history, he called Jean Moulin "the face of France."

Nearby

LE SEVERO *8, rue des Plantes. Métro: Alésia or Mouton-Duvernet. A few blocks north of the corner of rue Benard and rue des Plantes. Open Mon–Fri for lunch and dinner. Tel: 01. 45.40.40.91. Reservations necessary. A renowned steak and frites restaurant.*

THE FOURTEENTH MAIRIE *On rue Mouton-Duvernet, near the métro of the same name, a three-minute walk (west across avenue du Maine) from Moulin's apartment. This Town Hall, where Giacometti and Annette Arm were married, is surrounded by a tidy green space with sculptures of mothers and children, and where Parisian students relax on the grass.*

CARTIER FOUNDATION FOR CONTEMPORARY ART *261, boulevard Raspail. Open Tues–Sun, 11–8. fondation.cartier.com. A wonderful exhibit space for contemporary visual art and all the performing arts, designed by Jean Nouvel. The unlandscaped garden behind the building is a bucolic hideaway.*

LE MONTPARNASSE 1900 *59, boulevard du Montparnasse. www.montparnasse-1900.com. A brasserie with pre–World War I art nouveau décor, serving traditional food. Open daily, 12–3 and 7–12.*

Alberto Giacometti: Rue des Thermopyles

ALBERTO GIACOMETTI:
WHAT YOU SEE IS WHAT THERE IS

LOCATION: *46, rue Hippolyte-Maindron,* Studio
MÉTRO: Pernety

As a schoolboy, Giacometti (1901–1966) was admired as a talented artist and brilliant student. He would become, in the words of art critic John Berger, "a most extreme art-ist," a contemplative sculptor and painter who believed that "no reality could ever be shared."

He grew up in a close family in a small village in the al-pine valley of Bregaglia in southeastern Switzerland, about twelve miles from the Italian border. From November until February the high mountain walls along the valley cut off all sunlight. Alberto, born in October as the sunless, austere sea-son got underway, had a profound connection with this place and his mother that lasted through both their lifetimes. As a child, his dearest friends were stones (more like boul-ders), a cave, and trees, the material of his future art. He loved to sit and read and illustrate his storybooks in his painter/father's studio; he loved the art of Dürer and Rembrandt. At fourteen, returning home from boarding school for vacation, he spent his train money on a book of Rodin reproductions, which meant he had to walk ten miles over the Alps carrying his precious book. At fourteen, he made his first sculpture, of his brother Diego's head.

Before he finally moved to Paris in 1922 just after his twen-tieth birthday, he had studied in Geneva, which he disliked,

Venice (*Women of Venice* would be one of his most renowned masterpieces), Florence, and Rome where he fell in love and began to visit brothels. He also developed some themes of his lifework: the universe now became alien, beyond his own self, altogether incomprehensible. Reality is unknowable. His later friend and walking companion, Samuel Beckett, agreed. Some artists, according to Giacometti, achieve a partial view; most stay blind. He was no Cartesian. *Seeing* is being. "The act of looking was like a form of prayer for him . . . a way of approaching but never being able to grasp an absolute."*

On his father's suggestion that he go to Paris to study with Antoine Bourdelle (Rodin's former assistant) at the Académie de la Grande-Chaumière, he worked for five years in Bourdelle's studio though teacher and student were never simpatico. The evidence of their radically different vision and gifts is on exhibit in Bourdelle's hard-to-find studio/museum north of the *Gare Montparnasse* (*16, rue Antoine-Bourdelle, www.bourdelle.paris.fr*) and in the many museums showing the sculpture and paintings of Giacometti (the Beaubourg, Musée d'Orsay, the Louvre, the Musée d'Art Moderne de la Ville de Paris, and others in New York, Chicago, Washington, D.C., London, Zürich, Rome, Turin, Venice, Vienna, etc.) Take a tour at www.fondationgiacometti.fr/en/16 discover -the-artwork/. Or google "Images from museums in Paris showing Alberto Giacometti's sculpture and painting."

Paris in the era when Giacometti arrived, just after World War I, had become the countercultural center of artistic life in Europe. Dada was the first of the movements formed to overturn traditional canons in visual and literary art, soon replaced by André Breton's Surrealist movement, which

* John Berger, "Alberto Giacometti" in *Portraits: John Berger on Artists*.

Giacometti joined in 1929 though he would eventually distance himself from Breton.

As his work became recognized in the international art world (France never held a Giacometti exhibition in his lifetime), he insisted, in writing, on what his sculpture did not signify. His essays and articles in the various cultural reviews of Paris, like his letters, are models of clear prose, exceptional intelligence, and powerful persuasion. Though friends with Beckett and Sartre, he argued against the critics' interpretation of his skeletal figures of men and women as the embodiment of Sartrean existential alienation or Beckettian solitude.

> *While working I have never thought of the theme of solitude. I have absolutely no intention of being an artist of solitude. Moreover, I must add that as a citizen and a thinking being I believe that all life is the opposite of solitude, for life consists of a fabric of relations with others. . . .* *

He thought the melancholy fixation on existential anguish in the cafés of **Saint-Germain** (see p. 134), was nothing new. Read the Greek and Latin writers, he said. Since childhood he had been a voracious reader.

Giacometti broke his friendship with Sartre after the revered philosopher lied about a detail of Giacometti's life in his autobiographical *Les Mots*, claiming the detail, which was important to Giacometti, was so trivial it did not matter whether it was told truthfully or not.

Truth, more than art, was what Giacometti cared most deeply about: to connect with it he unceasingly revised his

---

*James Lord, *Giacometti: A Biography*, the beautifully written source of most details of the artist's life cited in this book.

paintings and sculpture. In a late interview, quoted by James Lord, he voiced an artistic credo that never changed:

> *For me, reality remains exactly as virginal and un-explored as the first time anyone tried to represent it. That is, all representations of it made until now have been only partial. . . .*
>
> *Art interests me very much, but truth interests me infinitely more. The more I work, the more I see things differently, that is, everything gains in grandeur every day, becomes more and more unknown, more and more beautiful. The closer I come, the grander it is, the more remote it is. . . .*

For the Traveler

The métro leaves you at **rue Raymond Losserand** in the tucked-away *quartier* of Pernety. As you start your search for Giacometti's studio in the fourteenth *arrondissement*, everything depends on slowing down, taking it easy, opening yourself to the modesty of this old rural *quartier* once alive with goats and mules and horses. (Their stables were converted to the artists' *ateliers* you see throughout Montparnasse.)

This neighborhood appears so ordinary; many travel guides ignore it. But to borrow the insight of twentieth-century Montparnassiens James Joyce and Samuel Beckett, it's "the extraordinariness of the ordinary" you need to look for, wherever you are. In the backstreets of the fourteenth, the slower you go the more moments of surprise and pleasure you'll have. A friend who grew up in Paris and now lives in Queens, New York, told me his favorite street in his hometown is the one you are about to discover on your way to the Montparnasse of Giacometti.

Start at the corner of *rue Pernety* and *rue Raymond Losserand*. A block south of this corner, you'll find *rue des Thermopyles,* which runs east. It's scenic and charming like a movie set of a secret Paris though it feels—it *is*—lived in. (Supposedly the street takes its name from the narrow coastal pass where in the fifth-century BC, 300 Spartans of Greece, led by Leonidas, tried to hold back the Persian army of 150,000. They failed, the army of Sparta was wiped out. The name of the place of battle stands for great patriotic courage against overwhelming odds.) The narrow cobblestone passage is lined with flowering plants; overhead bright-colored posters hang, noting upcoming exhibits and concerts. The passage winds right at the end, passing on the left a sort of artists' commune, a cluster of low-slung houses, gardens, and *ateliers*. They face a long rectangle of green across the way.

This is the *Square Alberto Giacometti,* on the corner of *Thermopyles* and *rue Didot*. The plaque at the entrance says that Giacometti's studio is nearby. Inside the square, through the arbor, the grass is partly covered with people stretched out under a bright sun, reading, sleeping, toddlers playing on blankets and in the flower beds. The plaque gives a few details of Giacometti's years of living and working in the fourteenth, unsuccessful and, except for the money his mother sent him, almost destitute years, eventually to be followed by an explosion of recognition and praise. (Big money came his way but he gave it away, to friends and family in need, to the prostitutes he loved). The plaque mentions one of his masterpieces, the six-foot-tall bronze man— *L'Homme Qui Marche* (*The Walking Man*)—an image of a man at once humble and expressive of the essence and the glory of the human figure. Auctioned in 1961, it won the highest price ever paid for an artwork: $103 million.

One more block to the east, along *rue Olivier Noyer,* you come to *rue Hippolyte-Maindron* (named for a nineteenth-century French sculptor) where you turn right (south) for another block to arrive at no. 46 on the southwest corner: the double black doors framing another sign, will admit the public to Giacometti's studio and living quarters when its restoration is complete in late 2017. Since his death, it has, according to *The New York Times,* been tied up in the financial and real-estate feuds of the Giacometti family and Foundation.

The low walls surrounding the 15 × 16-foot space of hidden workshops and apartment border a deep garden, like a small forest, dense with tall trees, orange trees, a frantic rush of singing birds overhead. In Giacometti's time this plain street across from the beginning of *rue du Moulin Vert,* was lined with shabby small shops, cafés, houses, scraps of garden and farms; the artist and his brother Diego, moved in in 1927 to what Alberto called "just a hole. I planned on moving as soon as I could." It had neither electricity, heat, or running water. He and Diego stayed for thirty-eight years.

Montparnasse, the area surrounding the intersection of *boulevard du Montparnasse* and *boulevard Raspail,* was the hub of that world of experimental artists from many continents and countries who crowded into the *quartier* and its cafés until the sun came up. In his early years in Paris, before *rue Hippolyte-Maindron,* Giacometti occupied a series of cheap hotel rooms including a studio on *rue Froidevaux* (running along the south side of the Montparnasse cemetery), which he preferred as a workplace to master Bourdelle's studio. In the streets south, east, and west of *boulevard du Montparnasse,* you can still see tall-windowed artists' studios in apartment buildings, one of them the residence of Jean Moulin (see p. 143), another a setting in Patrick Modiano's novella "Afterimage" in *Suspended Sentences*.

Giacometti knew that the important place for him was the city of Paris. Paris was "the indispensable idea," the goal in the pursuit of achievement, "the place where the enactment of his destiny could attain the status of a creation in its own right" in the words of James Lord. When, during the German Occupation, he was trapped in Geneva without the necessary visa to return to Paris, he was miserable, longing to return to the place whose energy and tolerance were essential to his nontraditional art and nonconformist soul.

As a Parisian, he had from the beginning put on the mantle of modernism, embracing ambiguity, turning away from academic definitions and representation. Through the decades he lived there, his style changed and changed again, showing the influences of African, Asian, and Middle Eastern art; for ten years he meditated on the aesthetics of failure and experimented with tiny figures of human beings, always obsessed with the image of the human head and its gaze.

He also made many friends in the course of all-night conversations in **La Coupole, Le Select,** and **Le Dôme** as well as the cafés of **rue Didot** and **rue d'Alésia,** walking until dawn or taxiing through Paris, dressed like a hobo, chain-smoking, eating little, drinking heavily, visiting prostitutes in Le Sphinx, the best-loved brothel in Montparnasse. (His marriage to Annette Arm—Alberto, who had ambivalent feelings toward women, nicknamed her "Sound and Fury"—did not change his nocturnal habits.)

For the second production of *Waiting for Godot*, his night-owl friend Samuel Beckett asked Giacometti to create a new tree for the set (the tree of the original production had disappointed him). The middle-of-the-night itinerary of the two men whom Paris by that time considered two of its greatest geniuses took them all over Montparnasse (Beckett lived to the west on *rue des Favorites*). *Allée Samuel Beckett* is in the southern section in the middle of the sycamore-lined *avenue René Coty,* a short walk from *boulevard Saint-Jacques* where Beckett would later have another apartment (no. 38) and his favorite cafés.

The two artists were soul mates to the end. Both cared most deeply about truth, seeing it, shaping it, whether with language, bronze, or paint.

Nearby

RUE PERNETY   *Walk east toward* **Place Flora Tristan,** *detouring left into the* **Jardin de la ZAC Didot,** *a communal preservation with lovely sections of gardens, housing, playground, beds of grass, a school, basketball court, all leading through and around many hidden paths to Place Marcel Paul. This UDE complex—Urbanism and Democracy—has become a local symbol of resistance to demolition and new luxury housing.*

PLACE FLORA TRISTAN   *A small pretty outdoor terrace-café, filled with locals on weekends, chain-smoking through the afternoons of long shadows from the surrounding trees and high wall of the "Boulangerie." As told by James Lord in* A Giacometti Portrait *(about his weeks of sitting for Giacometti who painted his portrait) Giacometti had his lunch in the neighborhood cafés (on rue d'Alésia and rue Didot) most of them now gone. This café, off the beaten track, is a few blocks north of his studio.*

RUE DU MOULIN-VERT   *It starts across from Giacometti's studio on* **Hippolyte-Maindron.** *Follow this narrow old street* *east, passing the pretty Hôtel de la Louvre. At the end is Auberge du Moulin Vert, surrounding an old mill and covered in greenery. Open evenings. Bear left and explore the quiet empty streets and gardens behind* **rue des Plantes: rue Léonidas,** *named after the leader of the Spartans at the Battle of Thermopyles and* **rue Olivier Noyer.**

WESTERN PARIS

Francis Poulenc: Place des États-Unis

FRANCIS POULENC'S
SOUL MUSIC

LOCATION: *11, Place des États-Unis, Musée Baccarat*
HOURS: 10–6:30; closed Tues, Sun, and public holidays
    www.baccarat.fr.
MÉTRO: Boissière

"What Poulenc did, he did perfectly," wrote the great music critic Harold Schonberg. Since his death in 1963, Poulenc's music has enjoyed worldwide popularity. His *Gloria* is the second most-performed piece of French music in the world. For his friends, his art was an expression of his own irresistible personality. He was a man of lovely tenderness, intimate with grief, a natural in the registers of sheer fun. He played practical jokes on his friends, and even when it was dangerous, on the occupying Germans. He adored his native Paris though not the snobby eighth *arrondissement* on the Right Bank where he was born in 1899.

He was orphaned as a teenager, losing his parents within two years of each other. His mother had been musical and encouraged her son's talent in opposition to his father, a wealthy businessman who wanted a like-minded heir: He would have no part of *le conservatoire* for Francis. An uncle took him to Stravinsky's *The Rite of Spring* at the Casino of Paris, an ecstasy for the music-loving teenager but a scandal to conventional Parisian audiences.

Starting out, thanks to Papa, Poulenc received no formal

musical training: "*Mon canon, c'est l'instinct.*" ("My model is my instinct.")

It was probably just as well. *Le conservatoire* dismissed student Erik Satie (the Surrealist composer renowned for his humor) as "untalented," "worthless," the "laziest" student in the history of the school. In 1917, when Poulenc presented to the *conservatoire* his manuscript of *Rapsodie Nègre,* his ensemble for piano, voice, strings, and winds, dedicated to Satie, the professor, as Poulenc told it, "stood up and screamed at me: *Your work stinks, it's inept, infamous balls . . . I see you're a follower of the Stravinsky and Satie gang. Well, goodbye!*" Satie had accepted the dedication and praised the work and by then was a mentor to not only Poulenc but many French musicians of the early twentieth century, the high season of the avant-garde in all the arts.

In the twenties Poulenc met the members of his new adopted family: Darius Milhaud, Arthur Honegger, Georges Auric, Louis Durey, Germaine Tailleferre, Jean Cocteau, to name a few. At the age of twenty-three, he wrote the acclaimed ballet *Les Biches* for Sergei Diaghilev. A few years later, he began a serious study of the music of Bach. He and his friends Milhaud, Auric, Honegger, Durey, and Taillefierre were called *Les Six* after the Russian group known as "The Five" in the nineteenth century. Their collaborations, though few, created spectacular music such as *Monuments du Coeur* (1949) a suite of songs in memory of Poulenc's beloved Chopin on the centenary of his death (1849).

His best friend since childhood, Raymonde Lossier, also an artist, took him to Adrienne Monnier's salon-bookshop *La Maison des Amis des Livres* on **rue de l'Odéon** (across from her lover's Sylvia Beach's Shakespeare and Company where she and Joyce were publishing *Ulysses*). There he met the poets Louis Aragon, Paul Éluard, and Guillaume Apollonaire each of whom became a friend and a strong influence on his aesthetics. He set many of their poems to music during and after World War II. These pieces remain among the favorites of French music lovers.

Poulenc knew he was gay; he also dearly loved his friend Raymonde, the only woman he would consider marrying if only for companionship and appearances. But then Raymonde died unexpectedly in 1930. After that, he practiced his homosexuality openly, an acceptable lifestyle in the Paris of the twenties and thirties but dangerous when the Germans took over in 1940.

Poulenc, in 1936, had gone on pilgrimage in the French southwest. A baptized but nonpracticing Catholic, he found at the shrine of the Black Madonna in Rocamadour the tranquility of another world utterly remote from the high-society Paris *salons* on **avenue Foch** where Hitler, the Duke of Windsor, and Picasso were much admired. In the sanctuary, "a place of extraordinary peace," in his words, where he saw the statue of the Virgin carved out of black wood by Saint Rocamadour, Poulenc, who had become obsessed with death since his loss of Raymonde Lossier and other friends, felt a deliverance from a fatalistic despair to a calm and simple religious faith. (Benjamin Ivry's biography, preferring the stories of Poulenc's homosexual love affairs, questions the authenticity of this conversion that brought Poulenc's music to a larger and more original plane of artistic expression.) He began work on his *Litanies à la Vierge Noire* that same day at the shrine which subsequently he visited often. Later he would write to a woman friend, "*you know that I am as sincere in my faith, without any messianic screamings, as I am in my Parisian* *sexuality.*"* From 1936 on, he composed some of the most beautiful sacred music of the European canon. His *Stabat Mater*, *Sept Répons des Ténèbres*, and the *Gloria* as well as his opera, *Dialogues des Carmélites* (see p. 259), began at Rocamadour.

"I have the faith of a country priest," he told a friend. On one of his pilgrimages he thanked the Virgin Mary for the gifts of his opera *Dialogues des Carmélites* and his latest lover. "*She understands everything,*" he wrote.

For the Traveler

Decades before Paris fell in 1940, Poulenc became well-known as a prolific original composer, his music performed then—as it is now—in many Paris concert halls including the Paris Opera; the less lavish and smaller *Opéra Comique*; the *Salle Gaveau* at **45, rue La Boétie** (*www.sallegaveau.com*) and the newly restored **Salle Pleyel** at **252, rue du Faubourg Saint-Honoré** (*www.sallepleyel.fr*) named after music publisher and maker of pianos Ignaz Pleyel. Chopin would perform only on a Pleyel. It's pure delight to hear music performed in any of these venues though the acoustics of **Salle Pleyel** makes it a personal favorite.

Charming, insouciant, and full of an infectious good humor, Poulenc was invited to high-society parties in the *hôtels particuliers* of the Faubourg Saint-Germain and the luxurious summer residences in the south of France. One aristocratic hostess who welcomed him was Marie-Laure de Noailles, born to the fortunes of a German-Jewish banker father named Maurice Bischoffsheim and a Christian mother

* Hélène de Wendel, ed., *Poulenc: Correspondence 1915–1963.*

thought to be descended from the Marquis de Sade. Their daughter Marie-Laure married into the family and money of the Vicomte Charles de Noailles. Her palatial birthplace became the couple's home in Paris.

It still stands (and is open to the public) in all its magnificence at *11, Place des États-Unis* in well-heeled Passy, on the right-hand side as you walk into the spacious *Place* from the direction of *avenue Kléber* (which leads into *Place de l'Étoile* and the *Arc de Triomphe*). Today, in this square honoring Franco-American friendship, Bartholdi's statues of George Washington and Marquis de Lafayette still stand (just above the small square of Jefferson), but *no. 11* has, since 2003, become the Musée Baccarat, exhibiting the most spectacular collection of crystal in France. The art that Marie-Laure grew up with, the Goyas, Klees, Delacroixs, Watteaus, Rubens, and Rembrandts have been removed. Replacing them on the walls along the grand staircases and in the grand ballroom on the second story are frescoes of lute-playing women draped in cherubs, doves, lambs, and flowers. Such confection would never have suited Marie-Laure, an unconventional connoisseur with exquisite visual taste.

But the mansion's many floors of rooms looking out over the chestnut trees bordering the *Place* are the rooms Poulenc knew. The ballroom, lavish in gilt mirrors, the ceiling painted by Francesco Solimena, a student of Tiepolo, provided a wildly rococo performance space on the occasions he performed at the piano and from the conductor's podium before the assembled avant-garde, which the vicomte and vicomtesse funded and entertained: Cocteau, Dali, Luis Buñuel, Auric, Picasso, to name a few. "This was the heyday of Surrealism, make-believe anarchy and fun-house revolution," in the words of James Lord, Giacometti's biographer.

Marie-Laure and Charles, proud patrons of the bold new artists, bought their paintings, paid for the productions of Poulenc's *Aubade*—which he wrote in this house—and Buñuel and Dali's scandalous film *L'Age d'Or*. And throughout the thirties, indifferent to the ominous prewar politics of Europe, Marie-Laure and Charles kept their respective lovers in limousines, chauffeurs, travel, nights at Maxim's, naked parties, sex, and champagne.

Visiting the mansion/museum these days—climbing the grand staircases, walking the long marble corridors and sparkling galleries, stopping into the gold-trimmed restrooms—the concrete details of this twenties' and thirties' opulence add perspective to the story of the ruling classes' obliviousness between the wars.

During the Occupation, Poulenc's practical jokes showed a nervy courage. But Goebbels, Goering, Otto Abetz, and the rest of the (German) classical music-loving audiences, not known for their sense of humor (or their tolerance of homosexuality) were tone deaf to what biographer Ivry has called Poulenc's "Resistance" music: It expressed his rage against the pitiless Germans.

As they took over Paris, Poulenc stayed put. His close friend, Darius Milhaud, who was Jewish, was forced to emigrate (to Mills College in Oakland, California, where one of his students was jazz musician Dave Brubeck). Most Jews lost their jobs in Parisian orchestras, at least fifteen Jewish composers were deported and died in Auschwitz. Honegger, in various ways, was considered a collaborator, fairly or unfairly. French musicians formed a Resistance group called the *Comité de Front National de la Musique*; the members, including Poulenc, Auric, Durey, Henri Dutilleux, Claude Delvincourt (director of the Conservatoire de Paris), and

Charles Munch, all of whom supported their newsletter *Musiciens d'Aujourd'hui*, pledged and worked to keep alive banned French music, especially Milhaud's. Poulenc's letters to Milhaud during the Occupation tell his friend what was going on in the concert halls of Paris. As he said and wrote many times, Poulenc believed that music itself—and the making of music—was the strongest resistance to evil.

He inserted anti-Nazi twists in his music, risking exposure and deportation. In his ballet *Les Animaux Modèles*, presented at the Paris Opera, its seats usually filled with Germans, he wrote some lines from an anti-German patriotic French song: "*Non, non, vous n'aurez pas notre Alsace-Lorraine*" ("No, no, you will not have our Alsace-Lorraine"), a reminder of the loathing felt by the French toward the German takeover of the region of Alsace-Lorraine after the Franco-Prussian War from 1871 to 1918 and again in 1940.

Before another German audience, his song, "*Le Mendiant*," inspired by a song by Modest Mussorgsky, cried out for compassion in opposition to "*the damned race that feels no pity.*" The music threatens that "*the worm will turn.*" Again, his lyric sabotage fell on deaf ears.

The poets Louis Aragon and Paul Éluard were heroic Resistance fighters as well as writers who used poetry to express their contempt for the Occupation and their determination to overcome. Throughout the war they were hunted by the Gestapo. Friends since the twenties at *La Maison des Amis des Livres*, Poulenc put many of their poems to music, performing them in the concert halls popular with the German military, their antifascist invocations of freedom heard but not grasped by the Nazis. Paul Éluard's poem *Liberté*, which the French knew by heart having heard it read over BBC radio from London and having read it themselves in Resistance newspapers, formed the main cantata of Poulenc's *Figure Humaine*.*

Liberté is a homage to the love of freedom: "*I was born to know you / To name you—Freedom.*" Its twenty-one four-line stanzas were printed in London on sheets of white paper which were then dropped over France by the RAF. Éluard's subversive tribute to the soul of France made him and his poem into the public enemy most wanted by the Gestapo.

Poulenc used *La Salle de Bal* in the home of his old friend and patron Marie-Laure de Noailles for the *Figure Humaine*'s first performance in 1944. Whether or not he knew that Marie-Laure had taken a German lover, he could not have missed the sight of the German uniforms in the room he knew so well. The show went on, a tribute in music and lyrics to the spiritual tradition of France: the resistance of tyrants.

Another tribute to the soul of France was Poulenc's musical version of Éluard's poem "*Un Soir de Neige*" in honor of the *Résistant* and poet Max Jacob, friend of Jean Moulin (see p. 143), who died in Drancy on the way to Auschwitz.

Whether or not the serenity of the *Place des États-Unis* or Marie-Laure's *La Salle de Bal* was violated during that performance by the sounds of torture—throughout the Occupation, captured *Résistants* were jailed and interrogated in a mansion at 3 *bis* on the *Place*—is not known.

The German authorities who controlled the culture of music during the Occupation, respecting only German music, refusing to program many of the renowned French

---

* Alan Riding, *And the Show Went On: Cultural Life in Nazi-Occupied Paris.*

composers, disgusted the French musical world for obvious reasons. Yet it was the occupiers' disregard for the beauty of the city that rankled in memory: on the gorgeous marble Grand Staircase and along the marble corridors of the Paris Opera (or the *Palars Garnier,* named for its architect Charles Garnier), the German soldiers scuffed and clicked the heels of their army boots, damaging it badly in the course of four years of strutting military swagger.

One of the most beautiful buildings in the city, the Paris Opera, at the head of the *avenue de l'Opéra* facing the Louvre at the far end, has long been restored to its original splendor. The Grand Staircase alone, with its balustrades and chandeliers, is still a breathtaking sight as you ascend to the entrance to the interior stalls. Chagall gave the dome over the auditorium, with its five tiers of boxes, a new ceiling in 1964. *(Tours in English and tickets online at www.operadeparis .fr or at the box office.)*

Poulenc's Paris ends in the Latin Quarter. His apartment at *5, rue de Médicis,* bordering the east side of the Luxembourg Gardens, had a lovely view (there are now large photographs covering the tall black fence of the Luxembourg); there is a plaque noting his years of residence until his death in 1963. From here he walked everywhere, a *flâneur* of great bonhomie who savored the beauty of his city. *"I'm a visual person,"* he said, *"the opposite of abstraction. . . . I detest philosophy. I've never read a dozen lines of Sartre. The three things I like best are music, painting, and poetry."*

His funeral was held in the nearby church of Saint-Sulpice, to the organ music of Bach—"Bach was how I learned to write for voices." *Square Francis-Poulenc,* closer to home, on the corner of *rue de Tournon* opposite *le petit senat* on *rue de*

Vaugirard remains the *quartier*'s tribute to one of the most beloved of Paris musicians.*

Nearby

MUSEUM OF MODERN ART OF THE CITY OF PARIS (MAM)   *Poulenc, a pioneer in the composition of an interdisciplinary music, invoking painters and writers in his songs, said his music was most like the painting of Raoul Dufy. In this museum overlooking the Seine on **11, avenue du Président Wilson**—a fifteen-minute walk from **Place des États-Unis**—Dufy's superb* La Fée Électricité (The Good Fairy Electricity), *the largest painting in the world, brings to mind Poulenc's imagination, perhaps his music for wind instruments as well as his* Histoire de Babar *narrated by Peter Ustinov.*

PLACE DU TROCADÉRO   *Ten minutes south of MAM, on **avenue du Président Wilson,** you come to Trocadéro, and what many consider the city's best view of the Seine and the Eiffel Tower. There are so many treasures here: the Trocadéro gardens, the new Musée de l'Homme, the lovely Passy cemetery where Édouard Manet and Berthe Morisot are buried. It's across from (and behind) Trocadéro, up the hill of **rue du Schoesing.***

LE COPERNIC   *54, avenue Kléber, at the corner of **rue Copernic** and **avenue Kléber,** on the left as you walk northeast toward l'Etoile. A modest café/restaurant, nice at lunchtime, with friendly service and good food. The tables up the stairs, in the rear, are best.*

---

* An introduction to his music is on YouTube, Poulenc playing his *Les Animaux Modèles* inspired by La Fontaine's *Fables*, and his *Aubade*, a choreographic poem for piano and eighteen instruments. His masterpieces are available on Deutsche Grammophone.

POLIDOR   *Near his home street, off the Luxembourg,* **41, rue Monsieur-le-Prince**. *www.polidor.com. Tel: 01.43.26.95.34. Open since 1842. 12–2:30; 7–12. Diners have included Arthur Rimbaud, Victor Hugo, James Joyce, Ernest Hemingway, and fans of Woody Allen's* Midnight in Paris.

RARE BOOKSTORES—LIBRAIRIES ANCIENNES   *There are a number of wonderful rare bookstores on Poulenc's* **rue de Médicis,** *as you walk south.*

THE RIGHT BANK

Colette: Jardin du Palais Royal

COLETTE: HER GARDEN
OF LOVE

LOCATION: *9, rue de Beaujolais, Palais Royal*
HOURS: Daily, 7:30–8:30
MÉTRO: Palais Royal; Louvre

Though a prose writer (of over fifty novels and a journalist and memoirist of forty books of nonfiction), Colette (1873–1954) lives on in literary history as the poet of the flesh—male, female, androgynous, young, aging, old, animal, vegetable. Proust, who praised her "voluptuous and bitter" soul, wept over some of her pages, André Gide "devoured [her] at a gulp."

A country girl from Burgundy, she moved to Paris at twenty as a new bride. Her new husband made her laugh, taught her the city, the cafés, theaters, streets, the *quartiers* north and south of the Seine. Twelve years older than his blue-eyed girl with the five-foot-long, ash-blonde plait, he ("Willy") ran around town reviewing music and cheating on the naïve wife he left alone in a small apartment on the *rue Jacob* (no. 28)—marked with a plaque—between *rue Bonaparte* and *rue de Seine* to sit at a desk obeying her husband: writing stories about Claudine, the fictional/autobiographical naughty schoolgirl from a provincial village. Willy appropriated each volume (*Claudine à l'École*; *Claudine à Paris*; *Claudine en Ménage*; *Claudine s'en Va*), selling them, adapting them to the stage, to good profits. His name, not the author's, appeared on the book covers and the contracts.

After thirteen years of trying to ignore Willy's infidelities, the swindled wife dumped the Paris playboy. He got the copyrights, she got nothing.

The women friends she'd made in *fin de siècle* Paris were actresses, dancers, mimes, *salonnières*—straight, lesbian, single, married. She joined them on the stages of music halls, all still open for business: the Olympia on *boulevard des Capucines*; the Marigny at *Carré Marigny and Champs-Élysées*; the Mathurins on *rue de la Gaité in Montparnasse*; the Bataclan on *boulevard Voltaire* in the eleventh open again after being closed for repairs following the terrorist massacre of Nov. 13, 2015). She played *la chatte amoureuse* in *Ça Grise*. The part suited her: Colette's face had a feline look, her body a supple, sensuous fluidity. At the Moulin Rouge in Montmartre (now a touristy nightspot at *82, boulevard de Clichy*) she kissed her lesbian co-star passionately; she was playing the part of a mummy in *Rêve d'Égypte*. When the mummy stripped, unwinding the gauze that covered her flesh, her reputation was shredded. Colette never recovered from the publicity headlined by outraged male critics. "Missy," her costar, loved her but couldn't keep her.

Her music hall years made her self-supporting. As did the books she began to publish under her own name, to enthusiastic reviews and the censorship of booksellers and parents: Her books were locked away, forbidden to young girls. She was not afraid to write sex scenes or descriptions of her characters' bodies, their erotic pleasures and disappointments. She moved house many times, wrote more novels, became a popular and respected journalist.

She married again, another cheat, with whom she had a daughter. Her music hall reputation distressed his *faux* aristocratic family; after the Great War the couple divorced. In 1920 she published *Chéri*, considered her finest novel, a story of a love affair between a middle-aged woman, Léa, and a very young man, *Chéri*, who was thought to be based on her seventeen-year-old stepson. Bourgeois Paris erupted in fury, as much over Colette's outing of the demimonde of Parisian courtesans (all those churchgoing "respectable" customers, right out of Émile Zola's *Nana*) as for her portrait of Léa's boy lover.

Turning a dry eye on the furies, Colette spent more energy walking the green spaces of Paris to keep her country-girl loves close: the flowers and trees, the wildflowers in Montmartre cemetery, remembering her mother—Sido and her garden in Saint-Sauveur-en-Puisaye. With her friends, she rode a bicycle through the Bois de Boulogne (as "Gigi," the character of her novel *Gigi* would later). Moralistic disapproval, she well knew, ran in the veins of many Parisians; married women who had never had to support or think for themselves snubbed her at the formal dinner parties she loathed. The Church weighed in, as it added to the Vatican's Index of Forbidden Books yet another Colette title. As you read Colette, Voltaire's voice comes to mind as you feel the elation of her irreverent sense of humor, of her lacerations of hypocrisy, her intolerance of fixed ideas. As a schoolgirl, she had read Voltaire (and Balzac, and Shakespeare) outside of class; she read Zola in secret.

Her wisdom, like her mother's, was earthy, pagan, pantheistic. The many cats, dogs, and other animals she kept irritated her second husband. As Geneviève Dormann puts it in *Colette: A Passion for Life*, she was in love with everything delicious, good to look at, and pleasing to the senses: the bodies of men and women, the sea and the colors of the sea, flowers, fruit, fine wines, truffles, oysters, music, the soft fur of animals, the touch of human skin, the scents of the earth.

She loathed ideology, sadness, tears: *"Tears are as grievous to me as vomiting."*

For the Traveler

After more than forty years of writing, she moved into the **Palais Royal.** Here, in this "village" in the center of Paris, the myth of Colette still has life. In the flowering gardens, among the Parisians—silent, chatting, reading on benches—there is here, inside the fountains' mist, an echo of a turbulent history. There is, too, an awareness of her *joie de vivre*. In her words, *"When my body thinks . . . all my flesh has a soul."*

The **Palais Royal,** her last residence in Paris, was just across from the Tuileries and the Louvre. This gracious, fragrant place felt as if it had been made especially for her. Even today this jewel of the city center reflects a quiet beauty despite the clusters of tourists arriving through the south entrance on **Place Colette.** Often the visitors do not move beyond the *Cour d'Honneur* fronting the original seventeenth-century palace built by Cardinal Richelieu and now occupied by the Ministry of Culture and other government offices. The *Cour d'Honneur* presents 280 black and white striped columns (1986) and, recently, displays of glass balloons; along the arcades visitors wander in and out of small shops offering designer everything.

Walking on, inside the rows of clipped lime trees and surrounded by sixty arcaded buildings, you'll come into the rectangular heart of the **Palais Royal** where Colette felt blissfully at home. By the time she moved into her large, sunny second-floor apartment in 1937, overlooking the far end of the garden, she had become a famous wealthy writer; she was married again, to the Jewish Maurice Goudeket whom she called her "best friend."

In the flower gardens—yellow and white tulips in season, with pink cherry blossoms bordering the fountains—you can imagine her in the early morning hours leaning out her window to feed the pigeons, observing her neighbors on the benches around the fountains, later visiting with them under a wide sky of changing colors, morning and night the view a feast of light and dark. She loved the sociability of the place, knew her neighbors' names, and those of the hard-working janitors and gardeners, the chefs at *Le Grand Vé-four*, the elegant restaurant she liked in the northwest corner. (The menu names her, honoring her gourmet tastes.)

After World War II she published *Paris de Ma Fenêtre* (*Paris from My Window*), a collection of superb and moving pieces about living in Paris and the **Palais Royal** during the war. The first entry is dated June 1940, when the German army occupied Paris. What the entries make so clear is how completely the setting of her life—this beautiful garden—inspired and sustained her throughout the four-year nightmare of fear, humiliation, sickness, no heating oil, no coal through the winters of the early forties which were some of the coldest on record. ("Stay in bed," Colette advised in the columns she wrote for various newspapers.) Her biographer Judith Thurman says that she "worked more prodigiously during the Occupation than at any other period of her life," producing eight books. (At midnight she would cross town to the secret radio station on **rue de Grenelle** to broadcast upbeat talks about France to American audiences. Riding home, she cherished the view of the night sky over the Seine.)

She was pretty much confined to her apartment and the gardens as a result of severely arthritic hips; she could no longer cycle in the Bois de Boulogne or shop along nearby *rue Saint-Honoré* and *rue de Rivoli*. She could still attend the Théâtre-Français in the southwest corner of *Place Colette*.

She also agonized over the safety of her husband as the roundups of Jews increased. Trying not to call attention to herself as a writer who was boycotting the Vichy and Nazi-controlled press, she instead continued to publish in the censored journals. She hoped to distract or mellow the authorities into leaving Maurice alone. In 1941 he had once been arrested and deported to a concentration camp, then released, thanks to one of Colette's connections; then he escaped to the free zone, then he returned to the *Palais Royal* to take care of his "best friend." He hid through the nights in the secret closets and rooms of neighbors in the *Palais Royal*. (The gardens of the *Palais Royal* under the Occupation were called "A Coalition of Friends.") Colette kept writing through the insomniac hours. She and her neighbors dreaded the loud middle-of-the-night arrivals of the Gestapo trucks, the click of their Nazi heels on the stone pavement as they hurried along the arcades into the stairwells leading to the apartments.

Optimism, she believed, was the best resistance. Inspired by the beauty of the world, the "enchantment" of *Palais Royal* as a kind of emblem of the miracle, she turned it into the witness of her daily journals, records of what she saw from her front and rear windows (at *9, rue de Beaujolais,* marked with a plaque) as well as on her neighborhood outings along *rue de Beaujolais* and *rue des Petits-Pères* to such nearby destinations as the *Place des Victoires*. She said the most crowded road out of the *Palais Royal* led to *Église Notre-Dame des*

Victoires (1642) at *Place des Petits-Pères. (Métro: Bourse.)* She compared the church to the village fountain where all the thirsty come to drink. In the large side chapel filled with votive candles Colette lit candles for friends, soldiers, and the *Résistants*, who included her daughter. A baptized Catholic, Colette called herself an agnostic, seldom talking about religion except to say that hers was an earthly paradise.

If you leave the *Palais Royal* through the north end, you can explore her neighborhood, starting across *rue de Beaujolais* where you'll find the charming old covered passage of *Galerie Vivienne* on *rue Vivienne* and inside the excellent antiquarian bookstore *Librairie Jousseaume.*

Colette had lived in and traveled to many great cities, coasts, countries, and villages; brought many to vivid life in her book *Places*. But when the war and her pain imposed a fixed address in the *Palais Royal,* she stayed calm and measured:

> *If nothing was able to make me leave this place, . . . it is because my sufferings and felicities were better borne here than in any other place in the world. . . . To wait in Paris meant to drink from the spring itself, however bitter. Perhaps a woman who was born in the provinces draws a particular kind of faith from Paris . . . to admire the children, to admire the men and women of Paris. . . . their defiant bravery kept these incorruptible city dwellers on their feet.*

Some postwar critics insist she was too passive during the war, perhaps her spirit so weakened by her two ruthless husbands that she didn't have the power to rebel. Others believe she stayed on good terms with the German-controlled journals and newspapers to make money. Colette didn't explain. (Throughout the war she gave food, wine, clothing, and ration coupons to many of the residents in the *Palais Royal*. Her friend and neighbor Jean Cocteau talked about her anonymous generosity but not to her face; how she kept so many, including himself, in a state of hope.)

After the war, she refused to join the *épuration*, the punishment and execution of collaborators. For one thing, she knew the history of the place where she lived. Not only was it the hotbed of the French Revolution, chaotic with argument, drunkenness, radical politics, but since its seventeenth-century beginnings it had been known throughout Europe as the home of French hedonism. "Ladies of pleasure" looked out from the windows of the brothels, viewing the human traffic in and out of the gambling dens, the taverns, coffeehouses, and their own houses of "ill repute." (In one of them the young Napoleon lost his virginity.) Colette enjoyed a communion with the ghosts of these "ladies of pleasure," imagining their view of the night sky after business hours or their fears that that night they would again be arrested by the French police. She knew what it meant to be on her own, a self-supporting working girl without protection.

As ever, and especially after the war, Colette would not judge. (Though in a few memoirs she did seek revenge against those treacherous husbands.) Ordinary people earning their bread, for themselves and their children, the weak and criminal and compromised, what they did to survive during the war was their own business. Maybe, like her friend the novelist François Mauriac, a *Résistant* and Catholic (who tried to persuade her back to her Catholic roots) she believed in forgiveness.

But the Church was not forgiving. Remembering her mummy act, her young-woman flesh bared on a public stage, it denied her a funeral Mass. (The three marriages and sexy novels weren't the problem.) The French State held its own, giving her the first state funeral ever given a woman. Thousands of Parisians filed past her bier in the *Cour d'Honneur*, leaving behind bunches of the wildflowers she loved.

She was laid to rest among the twelve thousand trees in *Père Lachaise*, beneath a living green canopy of sycamores, cypresses, chestnuts. (From the entrance at **rue de la Roquette** walk straight ahead, then left.)

"What a wonderful life I've had," she wrote toward the end. "I only wish I'd realized it sooner."

Nearby

LE NEMOURS   *To the right on **Place Colette** as you approach the entrance to the **Palais Royal**. A convivial café, serving a tartine citron beyond description. François Truffaut in his youth used to sit here all night talking with friends about films.*

LIBRAIRIE DELAMAIN   *155, **rue Saint-Honoré**, across the street from Place Colette and around the corner from the Hôtel du Louvre. A fine (and the oldest) bookstore, stocking many foreign writers.*

LE GRAND COLBERT   *2–4, **rue Vivienne**, beyond the rear entrance to **Palais Royal**. www.legrandcolbert.fr. Once a workers' café, now a glittering brasserie.*

LE GRAND VÉFOUR   *17, **rue de Beaujolais**, inside the northwest arcades of the **Palais Royal**. Closed Fri night, Sat, Sun and* *holidays. www.grand-vefour.com. The oldest restaurant in the city (originally Café de Chartres in the eighteenth century), it presents a beautiful ambience, superb food, and a hefty addition.*

BIBLIOTHÈQUE NATIONALE RICHELIEU   *58, rue de Richelieu. visites@bnf.fr. Colette did research in the archives. The Reading Room shows the ironwork of architect/engineer Henri Labrouste. A long restoration will end in 2019.*

Frédéric Chopin: Square d'Orléans

FRÉDÉRIC CHOPIN'S
FALLEN ANGEL

LOCATIONS: *16, rue **Chaptal**, Musée de la Vie Romantique; 80, rue **Taitbout**, Square d'Orléans*
HOURS: 10–6, except Mon
MÉTRO: Saint-Georges

The early death of the great nineteenth-century composer and pianist Frédéric Chopin (1810–1849) at the age of thirty-nine can be read as a kind of romantic agony though the composer himself was as much classicist as romantic. (Mozart, Haydn, and Bach were his inspirations.) When his end finally came, it struck not with a furious crash but as a prolonged measure in a sorrowful minor key following his breakup with his lover, the novelist George Sand (1804–1876). His friends said this cross-dressing vampire woman had killed him; hers said it was her care and devotion through the eight years they were together that had kept him alive. A few years after Sand abandoned him, his friends moved him out of the home they'd shared in the artsy ninth *arrondissement* to the *Place Vendôme*. His deathbed faced the wide square with Napoleon's column; it was filled with light. Sand seemed to have vanished from Paris, but as Chopin lay dying she was once spotted walking alone, along the quays. For those who had known the couple in the time of their rapture, her absence from his funeral at the Church of the Madeleine on October 30, 1849, felt more like a haunting presence.

For the Traveler

The prosaic street address of their idyllic hideaway at *16, rue Chaptal* in the ninth *arrondissement* (it runs between *rue Blanche* and *rue Pigalle*) hardly prepares you for what you find when you climb the path leading to its entrance: the *Musée de la Vie Romantique,* a sanctuary in shades of green, set into a garden of flowering bushes under the shade of tall old chestnut trees that seem to reach the sky. Sometimes there is the sound of quiet talk from the small tables in the outdoor garden café. Always you hear the singing of birds nesting in the chestnuts. You're free to sit here, relishing the peace and beauty, for as long as you like. (There is an excellent card and bookshop at the entrance.)

The city feels far away on this hill leading up from Lower Montmartre to *La Butte Montmartre.* The garden and house belong to the story of the love affair between Chopin and George Sand when their love was new. They were frequent visitors here starting in 1838 when they became a couple. The painter Eugène Delacroix often joined his friends in the garden, the three of them guests of the painter Ary Scheffer who owned the house and worked in the upstairs studio. (Inside there's a small museum, with locks of George Sand's hair, her letters, jewelry, and a cast of Chopin's hand.)

From the outside, the love affair appeared as charmed as this setting. The serene beauty of the place was a perfect backdrop for the story of two passionate lovers: one a bold and prolific novelist—George Sand, the pen name of Aurore Dupin Dudevant—who wrote about the sexual desires and pleasures of women and denounced marriage as "one of the most barbaric institutions society has engendered"; the other Europe's genius musician, a "divine" composer and pianist who had come to France from Poland in 1831, at the age of twenty-one. Sand called Chopin her "angel." The music he composed and performed in the salons and Pleyel concert rooms of Paris brought his lover to ecstasy. Chopin called her *Aurora*, his "Dawn."

The lovers sound transported to a world of joy and delight in their early letters to friends. *"My God, if you knew him as I do now, you would love him even more,"* Sand wrote. She praised her angel for his "kindness, tenderness, and patience. . . . *I imagine that his sensibility is too finely wrought, too exquisite, too perfect to survive for long in this rough life."* She worshipped his innocence, the purity of soul that she said had transformed her own. *"If God sent death for me one hour from now,"* she declared, *"I would not complain at all since these three months have been pure intoxication."*

To his best friend, a Polish exile like himself, Chopin wrote, *"You know, you would love her still more if you knew her as well as I do at this moment."*

"For you, Aurora," he wrote in his diary, *"I would lie on the ground. Nothing would be too much for me, I shall give you all! . . . I do not want to live except for you."* He expressed his most profound love in the music he wrote after they became lovers: the mazurkas, ballades, scherzos, preludes, études that thrilled the audiences at his public concerts. Friends heard his music as an *homage* to George.

Yet the French, who value appearances, also realize their deceptiveness. How they lie. *La vie romantique* is not immune from reality, no matter how pretty its setting. A seductive reaction against the order and conventions of the Age of Reason, the Romantic movement glorified extravagant emotions and unconventional life choices. But the real world of the lovers' histories, the losses and grief—inevitably their buried sorrows—poisoned the garden of love, their metaphoric life in the *Musée de la Vie Romantique*. And from the beginning, Chopin's music had expressed as much sadness as joy. As if he *knew,* intuitively, that their dreamworld would not last.

At first they lived nearby to Ary Scheffer in Pigalle. Summer and fall, they traveled south to Sand's ancestral home in Nohant, in the Berry region, usually accompanied by Sand's two young children, Maurice and Solange. Chopin's frail health went along too, a kind of fellow traveler with an ominous hacking cough. Always he felt stalked by death, which had already claimed a number of his consumptive Polish friends in their thirties. But no matter where they lived or traveled, in the early days of their romance, Sand was for Chopin his lover, muse, friend, mother, manager, nurse.

Some summers they stayed in Paris because Sand could not afford to open the house in Nohant. Their social life, a nightly round of theater, concerts, parties, dances, dinners, cost a fortune. Overnight they'd find themselves in debt up to their necks. Gallivanting around "the capital of the world" from November to April required a horse, two carriages, a full-time coachman. Chopin's fussy tastes for handmade shirts and leather gloves, to be purchased only in the pricey arcade shops of the *Palais Royal* (see p. 179) matched Sand's preference for the finest cigars, cigarettes, and the fabrics used to decorate herself and the salons of the house. Chopin's income rose or fell depending on the number of concert bookings and the demand for his private piano lessons; Sand's money came from the novels she wrote as fluently as their stream of houseguests talked through the night in Polish and French and smoked like chimneys despite Chopin's chronic cough, how hard he had to fight to breathe.

After four years in Pigalle, the couple moved. A short

walk downhill (south) from Ary Scheffer's pastoral retreat, you come to *rue Saint-Lazare,* running east/west. Turn left (east), then left again into *rue Taitbout* which in a short distance brings you to the entrance of *Square d'Orléans.* You are free to enter this private enclave where Chopin and Sand lived, worked, entertained, and, in time, found no escape from the real world of their troubled emotions.

This expensive district in post-Napoleonic Paris was called *La Nouvelle Athènes* (the New Athens), in recognition of the many painters, writers, singers, actresses, and poets who lived in the surrounding streets—*rue de la Tour-des-Dames, rue de La Rochefoucauld, rue d'Aumale.* The Square has not changed much since Sand and Chopin fell in love with it in 1842 and signed two leases, one on the ground-floor no. 9 apartment for Chopin, and the larger no. 5 near the cobblestone carriage entrance, for Sand and her children. (There are plaques on both buildings.) As artists, who both worked at home, each needed their own space; Chopin cared about the propriety of appearances. All the apartments today face a central fountain (a new addition) and a lovely courtyard planted with magnolia trees where discreet visitors are free to wander.

It was in their common life here that the seeds of the conflicts they'd buried for years began to grow. Despite their extravagant testimonials in diaries and letters, their lives in *Square d'Orléans* were increasingly strained.

There were the debts, the pressure to earn more money. The children were difficult. Maurice disliked Chopin and his mother's relationship with him. The mother adored her son and disliked, in fact hated, her daughter Solange, who liked Chopin. Chopin felt sorry for the little girl, gave her piano lessons, played checkers with her. Health crises, which included Sand's migraines and Chopin's depression, mood swings, and worsening consumption wore them out. Always, Chopin was homesick for Poland, for the sound of the Polish language, for his family. There was sexual tension. Did Chopin enjoy sex? Did he detest sex? Did he and Sand have sex? Biographers make conflicting claims: no, he didn't; yes, he did; *she* certainly did: enjoy, desire, and deny. George Sand of the multiple lovers, usually younger unhealthy men who needed her mothering, at some point insisted on abstinence. She worried about Chopin's diseased lungs, his lack of stamina.

But there is no consensus about any of it, including the claim that Chopin was asexual. The lovers' letters offer no conclusive evidence, Chopin's because he was too private to ever write about his sex life and Sand's because what she wrote or told to friends cannot be trusted. She changed her tune about almost everything in the course of their years together. She, who in the beginning had called him "the love of her life," later claimed to have lived like "a nun," "a virgin," for nine years; she'd turned herself into an old hag for his sake. In time, their conflicts sprouted into full-grown monsters. Sand's childhood traumas had wounded her deeply. Unacknowledged, unhealed, the wounds became the nasty running sores of her jealousy of her daughter.

Sand had been neglected and abandoned by her mother; exiled to the Nohant home of her judgmental repressive grandmother; sent off to a convent school—the nuns turned out to be her least cruel caretakers; at eighteen she was given in marriage to a man nine years older, dull, adulterous Casimir, passionate about hunting. After nine years of depression and disgust, she took off for Paris alone. Eventually the children and a series of lovers joined her.

Researches upon her family tree turned up her mother's years of prostitution as well as her lies about who her unloved daughter's father actually was. Throughout Sand's childhood, she had longed for her absent mother, and thought herself worthless. When she grew up, she came to believe—long before Freud—that a person's relationship with their mother created the template for all later adult relationships. For her, who had desperately wanted her mother but was rejected, no matter how many lovers she would have as an adult, there was, for her, no one there. Lovers, and the love they professed, were absences, like her mother, Sophie, far away in Paris, always absent, as if her daughter Aurore did not exist. That Sand saw soon enough—or thought she saw—that the woman Chopin loved most in the world was *his* mother didn't help to change her belief that trusting other people was absolute delusion.

Such was the unraveling that began in the idyllic setting of the *Square d'Orléans*. As the increasingly disenchanted lovers hurried back and forth between Chopin's rooms in no. 9 and Sand's in no. 5, welcoming their many artist friends, admitting Chopin's piano students, avoiding journalists, cooking their dinners, attending to finances, supervising the children who were growing up, such real-life responsibilities became overwhelming. The courtyard's lovely sheltering magnolias made little difference.

With her daughter Solange, Sand repeated her mother's pattern. Though Sand advertised herself as the most generous loving mother on earth (or certainly in Paris), she sent her daughter off to a boarding school the girl hated, rarely allowing home visits, never visiting herself. Chopin visited. Solange's mother kept a cold unloving distance. Chopin disapproved.

Sand's venomous relationship with Solange caused the final break between the lovers. When Chopin took the newly married and pregnant Solange's part in a dispute with Sand over money, Sand accused him all over Paris of being secretly in love with Solange. The renowned painter, Eugène Delacroix, a neighbor and regular visitor to the evenings of music and conversation at *Square d'Orléans,* was horrified; he wrote in his Journal of the "cruelty of [her] passions, the impatience so long repressed."

The final rupture came in July 1847. Chopin lived on, alone and sick, in his rooms at *Square d'Orléans* until, toward the end, he was moved to the *Place Vendôme*. Sand exchanged him for the radical politics of the 1848 revolution and a new lover. (The conservative Chopin had called her beloved proletariat—her "proles"—fools.)

A few biographers claim that Chopin died alone. Like many romantic glosses, this one is wrong, betrayed by the evidence cited by Benita Eisler's wonderful biography, *Chopin's Funeral*. Chopin's favorite sister, to whom he had written long letters ever since he first came to Paris, traveled from Poland to be with her brother at the end. Solange was there. Also attending were several close friends, including a Polish priest from whom Chopin was said to accept the last rites of the Church. Although he had long kept his distance from institutional religion, according to friends and his diaries, he was a believer. The friends at the deathbed also said later that Chopin died in the arms of the despised daughter Solange as she offered him water. "I finished growing up under Chopin's piano," Solange told a friend, "and the magic of his divine music remains in my soul among the fond memories of my childhood, which are few and far between."

Except for a plaque at no. 12, there's not a trace of Chopin in the *Place Vendôme* today, now home to luxury shops and government ministries.

Three thousand people attended his funeral Mass at the Madeleine. Afterward some mourners, mostly women, walked the three miles to *Père Lachaise* behind the hearse that carried his coffin.

It is possible their route to the northeast followed a portion of the ancient *boulevard Poissonnière* where Chopin had rented his first apartment in Paris at no. 27 in November 1831. He'd loved this wide tree-lined street and his room "beautifully furnished in mahogany on the fifth-floor . . . with a balcony over the boulevards, from where I can see from Montmartre to the Panthéon and the whole lovely world along with it."

Today the old building is gone and *Poissonnière* is all stores and traffic, but above the new building, an old stone pediment inscribed in gold letters bears witness to the site's most famous resident: *Frédéric Chopin Habita Cette Maison 1831–1832.*

Nearby

PLACE SAINT-GEORGES   *Leaving the métro, you see in the center of Square Alex-Biscarre a fountain with a statue of Paul Gavarni, famous cartoonist of the nineteenth century and colleague of **Honoré Daumier**. Two elegant mansions at 26 and 28 frame the square. At 26, the former residence of Adolphe Thiers, there is a "secret garden" of the Fondation, Dosne-Thiers, a pretty sunny space where neighborhood children have a good time. The popular café facing the fountain serves a good "Salade Saint-Georges."*

PLACE GUSTAVE-TOUDOUZE   *Named for a writer/journalist (1847–1904) who was born in the year Chopin and Sand parted so bitterly. Tall trees shade the wide terrace and the "No Stress Café" and other cafés. The mood is calm but alive, the news kiosk excellent. It's just north of* **Place Saint-Georges,** *on* **rue Notre-Dame-de-Lorette** *and* **rue Henri Monnier** *(Truffaut country—see p. 203).*

François Truffaut: Cité Charles-Godon, near rue Milton

RAISING HELL IN PIGALLE: FRANÇOIS
TRUFFAUT'S *THE 400 BLOWS*

LOCATIONS: *33, rue de Navarin; rue des Martyrs; rue Milton; Place Pigalle,* Streets of the Ninth Arrondissement
MÉTRO: Notre-Dame-de-Lorette

F̄ar more than any natural mother or father, the streets of Paris, especially those of the ninth *arrondissement,* nourished the identity of one of France's favorite filmmakers, François Truffaut (1932–1984): They created the imagination of the artist he would become. Their rambunctious energy kept alive in the unwanted child the curiosity and desire that his nasty childhood somehow didn't destroy.

Born to a single mother, who lived at *21, rue Henri-Monnier* with her Catholic family, François was handed over at birth to the care of a wet nurse. Almost three years later, his grandmother, Geneviève de Monferrand, rescued him for the second time (three years earlier she had talked her eighteen-year-old daughter out of aborting him); when she discovered the baby sickly and half-starving, she brought him home to live with her and her family. A woman who loved music and literature—she wrote a novel, was a passionate reader who read to little François every day, and walked him to bookstores and the local public library—she protected him from his mother/her eldest daughter when she came (rarely) to visit and criticize François.

Truffaut's grandmother died when he was eight. His

stepfather, Roland Truffaut, insisted—against Truffaut's mother's wishes—that the boy move in with him and his unloving mother. This change of address, with its loss of affection and new portions of adult heartlessness, marked Truffaut's memory forever.

For the Traveler

The best introduction to the Paris of Truffaut's art is his five-film saga about troubled youth: *The 400 Blows, Antoine and Colette, Stolen Kisses, Bed and Board, Love on the Run,* all available on DVD as "The Adventures of Antoine Doinel." His street world is the setting of many of these films but especially the first one, the autobiographical *The 400 Blows* (*Les Quatre Cent Coups*), for which he won the Best Director award at Cannes in 1959 at the age of twenty-seven.

This film, like Truffaut's young life, unfolds along the streets of lower Montmartre between *rue Blanche* and *rue des Martyrs,* a web spreading east and west of the main north/south streets that lead uphill to Pigalle and the *butte* (hill) of Montmartre: *rue Notre-Dame-de-Lorette; rue des Martyrs; rue Saint-Georges, rue Henri-Monnier.* Climb them, zigzagging east, west, right, and left, as you walk the home ground of one of the great directors in French film history.* His neighborhood's vitality, seediness, and local color make a perfect backdrop for the film's emotional texture, the patches of cruelty, a child's misery, the adolescent's joy of escape.

There are moments when the streets of the ninth seem to be the movie's main character, or better, Truffaut's muse. They are made of moving light, people, concrete. More than

---

* The Ninth is a maze. Bring along the folding pocket-sized (3 ½ × 8 inches) *Streetwise Paris* or the 4 × 6-inch *Paris par Arrondissements.*

anything, Truffaut loves the open everyday world as opposed to the impersonal abstraction of intellectual analysis. As his mentor and friend, the film director Jean Renoir (son of the painter, Auguste Renoir, who also lived in the ninth), taught him, "Reality is always magic."

Start at the bottom of the hill of *rue Notre-Dame-de-Lorette* at the rear of the church of the same name (where *rue Saint-Lazare* ends); follow it uphill (north) as it forks left, across *Place Saint-Georges,* bearing right—or really straight uphill, into *rue Henri-Monnier.*

The busy sex trade along these streets took off in the nineteenth century, observing a definite hierarchy: the *lorettes,* named after the church, were middle-ground female prostitutes, serving the area's dense theater trade; lower than the grand-dame courtesan-mistresses installed in the new *hôtels particuliers* (on and off nearby *rue de La Rochefoucauld* in the area called *Nouvelle Athènes* where Chopin and Georges Sand lived in *Square d'Orléans* (see p. 195); and higher than the plain freelance streetwalkers of the *Quartier de Breda.* The *lorettes'* trade overlapped with the *Quartier de Breda,* where impoverished street prostitutes walked the *rue de Breda,* renamed *rue Henri-Monnier* in 1905. *Place Pigalle,* a few blocks to the north, parallel to *boulevard de Clichy,* was the largest meeting ground of prostitutes in the ninth. It was understood that they lived outside conventional Parisian society, engaged in an illicit profession.*

For Truffaut, who crossed the *Place* often, the sex trade simply came with the territory. (He set the scene of his mother's marital infidelity in *The 400 Blows* on *Place de Clichy.*) He would grow up to visit prostitutes in their Pigalle

*Luc Sante, *The Other Paris.*

and Montmartre brothels on a regular basis, his "relationships with women . . . in tune with the frenzied life he lead"—his liaisons matching his insatiable appetite for films, as his biographers put it.*

When François was ten, he moved into *33, rue de Navarin* (right, off *rue Henri-Monnier,* now marked with a plaque). The street matches the bleakness of the five years François (called "Antoine Doinel" in *The 400 Blows*) lived there with his parents, a time of heartbreaking neglect only relieved by his days at school where he made a few good friends and had fun running the streets on the days they played hooky: *rue Milton* (east off *rue des Martyrs*) and at the bottom of a long winding hill where his school was located and is still in operation; *rue de Douai* (southwest from Place Pigalle) where his friend Robert lived; the shops along hilly *rue des Martyrs* where the truants turned into petty thieves. The movie theaters on *Place Pigalle* and *boulevard de Clichy* (the dividing line between the ninth and the Montmartre *butte* were their favorite escapes. Back then, during the Nazi Occupation—though Truffaut's movie is set in the fifties— there were twenty movie "palaces" between *Place de Clichy* and *rue de La Rochechouart*. (In postwar Paris there were four hundred movie theaters, half of them near the Truffaut apartment.) Weekends (and three Christmases in a row) François/Antoine was left alone by his parents who liked mountain climbing; they ridiculed the boy's preference for roaming the *lorettes* to climbing the hills of Fontaine-bleau. On his own he saw some movies as many as twelve times; he and his friends wrote a film newsletter which they

---

*Antoine de Baecque and Serge Toubiana, *Truffaut: A Biography*. A comprehensive biography, the source of my information about Truffaut's life.

peddled along *rue des Martyrs,* Truffaut's debut as a film critic.*

By the time he was twelve he was reading three books a week (mostly Balzac and Dickens, as a truant holed up in his friend's apartment on *rue de Douai*) and, also as a truant, sneaking into three films a day. "Life was the screen," he said later.

The little outlaw was punished severely at school and home. Some nights he slept in alleys rather than face the severe consequences of his truancy and cover-up lies. In the film we see Antoine/François running in the pale light of dawn to wash his face in the icy water of the pool in front of the **church of** *Sainte-Trinité,* on the east side of *la Place d'Estienne d'Orves* and *rue Saint-Lazare.* We also see him running along the bridge of *rue Caulaincourt* above the Montmartre cemetery, carrying the typewriter he'd stolen. Despite the trouble he winds up in, we can feel his elation not so much over what he thinks he's getting away with as his sense of the wind at his back, the freedom of the open street. He knows the ninth like a conductor knows his orchestra or a different child might know his home.

The career of the street urchin/movie journalist ended when he was thrown out of school and home and locked up in a juvenile detention center. But the boy genius of fast escapes and street smarts broke free to run north, pursued by the forces of law and order he would always despise, ending up on the Normandy coast facing the undefined freedom of the vast open sea.

The 400 Blows' win at Cannes brought invasion of his

---

*François Truffaut, *The Films in My Life*. He saw four thousand films between 1940 and 1955, was regarded by other critics as a "living *cinémathèque*." He praised many American films, and all the work of Alfred Hitchcock.

privacy; but with his new wealth he made loans to friends and family, helped them pay off debts and back taxes; his celebrity enabled him to keep on working, continuously, producing a steady often prize-winning run of popular films. (*Small Change, Jules and Jim, Mississippi Mermaid, The Wild Child, Fahrenheit 451, Two English Girls, The Story of Adele H., Day for Night*, and his last and biggest box office success, *The Last Métro*, some of which was shot in *Le Théâtre Saint-Georges*, on the left as you ascend ***rue Saint-Georges*** and enter the *Place Saint-Georges. You may visit the lobby but not the actual theater.*) Travelers who have the time to wander along the streets of lower and upper Montmartre, will enjoy being able to recognize many Truffaut settings in the five-film saga featuring Antoine Doinel.

Truffaut, in the fifties, became the founder of the New Wave (*Nouvelle Vague*) movement that began to change the look of French movies. With his friends and fellow directors Claude Chabrol, Jacques Rivette, Éric Rohmer, and Jean-Luc Godard, he adopted techniques that corresponded to the way he had seen the world—in particular the streets—since he was a child: their quick, spontaneous rhythms, informal and vaudevillian characters, the simplicity of the outdoor settings. As a New Wave director he used rapid filming, young actors, natural lighting rather than interior studio sets. At the same time he turned away from the "psychological realism" of past French movies, the directors' so-called true-to-life characters, always base, infamous, vile, spineless, for whom the directors and screenwriters have contempt. Instead, wrote Truffaut in the prestigious *Cahiers du Cinéma*, "the director should have the same humility toward his characters that St. Francis of Assisi had toward God."

Above all, he wrote, movies should have a pulse—like his

rue des Martyrs in early morning when the street markets open and local shoppers and vendors greet one another by name. (Elaine Sciolino's *The Only Street in Paris: Life on the Rue des Martyrs* guides us along this old multiculti street of unpretentious Parisians, making a delightful companion on our exploration of Truffaut's world.)

Truffaut died of a brain tumor in 1984 at the age of fifty-two. If he'd lived a long life, he would still recognize the streets of his youth. There is gentrification in this part of the ninth but it has not destroyed its original heart and soul.

Some changes would no doubt please Truffaut. Across *Square Berlioz* at the end of *rue de Douai* (where the ninth gives way to the eighth), as you follow *rue de Bruxelles* downhill, you pass on the left the house—*21 bis, rue de Bruxelles*—where Émile Zola died in his bed of asphyxiation, a revenge killing, it is thought, for his attack on the army and support for the convicted—but innocent—Jewish soldier Alfred Dreyfus in his article *"J'Accuse!"*—the chimney flue was found stuffed. There is now a plaque on the building's exterior and quotes from his article on the walls of its inside lobby, all of it a validation of Zola's courage. Truffaut, as a director, a film critic, and a human being always identified with the underdog. Street prostitutes, working men down on their luck, lonely children—in Truffaut's movies, we feel only his sympathy and respect.

Returning to—and crossing *Square Berlioz* again—turn left into *rue Blanche,* a street Truffaut knew well: It leads up the hill to the movie theaters of Clichy. As you climb the hill of *rue Blanche,* you'll be approaching the Moulin Rouge, once a windmill, now a touristy cabaret in the eighteenth *arrondissement*, the *quartier* of *Clichy*. The multiplex on *Place de Clichy* is crowded day and night; Parisians love the cinema, and they still turn out for a Truffaut retrospective (as cinèphiles do for Truffaut festivals at New York City's Film Forum).

One block west along ***boulevard de Clichy*** and off to the right is ***avenue Rachel,*** the only entrance to the cemetery of Montmartre, which lies beneath the ***rue Caulaincourt*** bridge. Truffaut is buried here in Division 1, under a simple black onyx stone in the company of artists. Berlioz, La Goulue, Degas, Rodin, Heine, Zola (before his remains were moved to the Panthéon), Stendhal, Nijinsky. In his movie *Love on the Run*, Truffaut buries his/Antoine Doinel's mother here. The cemetery, originally a gypsum quarry, is quiet, shadowed with tall trees and a groundcover of the wildflowers Colette used to come here to pick. Visitors leave single red roses on Truffaut's grave.

Standing here in the first light of morning, I like to remember words he said to an interviewer:

> *I see life as very hard. I believe one should have a very simple, very crude and very strong moral system. One should say "yes; yes," and do exactly as one pleases.*

This is quintessential Truffaut, to the end the canny little rebel of his native streets, the lifeline of his hardscrabble world in northern Paris.

Nearby

LE BON GEORGES   *45, rue Saint-Georges on the corner. Tel: 01.48.78.40.30. www.LeBonGeorges.com. A lively good bistro, crowded at lunchtime.*

PÈRE TANGUY *14, rue Clauzel, right off rue Henri-Monnier at Place Gustave Toudouze. The art shop of Père Tanguy, where Cézanne, Gauguin, Renoir, Toulouse-Lautrec, and Vincent van Gogh met, bought oil paints, displayed their work, and van Gogh saw Japanese prints brought from Japan by Père Tanguy. Van Gogh painted his portrait (now in the Rodin Museum). Père Tanguy was the only person from the Paris art world to attend van Gogh's funeral. Many prints are on sale. Across the street, on the south corner of rues Clauzel and Henri-Monnier is a Japanese restaurant, Yumiko.*

*Three-year-old François Truffaut attended his first school, a nursery, on **rue Clauzel** where today a public school (you hear the voices of teachers and students through the open windows) is a few doors down (east) of the art shop.*

LA PRAIRIE *Boulangerie at **50 bis, rue de Douai** as you face **Square Berlioz**. (Métro: Blanche; Place de Clichy.) The proprietor serves excellent pastry and clear directions to Zola's last home in Paris.*

SACD, SOCIETY OF AUTHORS AND DRAMATIC COMPOSERS *www.sacd.fr. **11, rue Ballu**, a beautiful streetscape with stunning architecture. Turn left into **rue de Clichy** from Zola's **rue de Bruxelles**, then left again and straight ahead into **rue Ballu**. Truffaut, who was active in defending his industry from censorship, unfair contracts, and government meddling, supported the SACD, founded in 1777 by the comic dramatist Beaumarchais (*The Marriage of Figaro*) to defend the legal rights of writers, dramatists, and in our time, filmmakers and other artists. You may enter this gracious building—and its annex just down the street—where the members of SACD meet in a lovely salon facing a garden in which a bust of Rabelais has pride of place.*

LE DIT VIN   *No. 68 on the corner of **rue Blanche**. The owner of this charming little wine bar is an engaging storyteller who shares stories of the ninth's past as a playground for wealthy tycoons, actresses, opera singers—the originals of Zola's characters.*

Patrick Modiano: Place Émile-Goudeau, La Butte Montmartre

PATRICK MODIANO'S
MISSING PERSONS

LOCATION: **Rue Berthe** and **Place Émile-Goudeau,**
La Butte Montmartre
MÉTRO: Lamarck-Caulaincourt

The name Patrick Modiano drew a blank in the States when he was awarded the Nobel Prize for Literature in 2014. But in Paris, his home city, his many novels (more than thirty) are read, the screenplay he wrote for Louis Malle's masterpiece *Lacombe, Lucien* remains a favorite, and the songs he wrote for Françoise Hardy you hear in cafés and on the radio. Still, Modiano, as man and artist, remains a mystery man. The search for phantoms of history is his basic plotline, the searches as well as the enigmatic love stories, all of which take place along the streets of Paris.

In the face of mystery, however, Modiano has one clear focus. In his early novels, he is obsessed with the crimes committed by Nazis and their French collaborators during the Occupation of Paris in the Second World War. He was one of the first writers to address the question of French collaboration. (Perhaps this is why some Parisians do not like Modiano's writing.) Born in 1945, he thinks of himself as a child of the Occupation nightmare. He wants to find out what happened in the years just before he was born and just after, uncover the secret stories of the victims, the criminals, the disappeared.

Modiano is the narrator of his searches. The one phenomenon he knows with certainty as he walks and walks is the map of Paris. To follow him along the streets, through all the neighborhoods included in the contents of this book, is to feel both the urgency and the sadness of his pursuits. His theme is said to be memory, its many faces, the loss of it, how over time it changes and lies. The streets do not lie. Their names are specific; they lead him to specific destinations. Most of the destinations tell only partial stories. Some tell nothing. There is one dead end after another.

The grimness of the history he is investigating distracts him in many places. But in the end it is physical place that offers some connection, even moments of happiness. On the *butte* of Montmartre, he feels "the joy of the hill," in the words of Eric Hazan. Maybe the word "joy" is a little much for the antiromantic Modiano. But from one angle, Montmartre, in the here and now, does deliver him from the tomb of the past.

To begin at the beginning, Modiano grew up as the elder son of a father of Italian-Jewish origins who kept his distance from his children, leaving them with crooks, gangsters, fellow black marketeers, actors, eccentrics, with whom he did his shady business deals; the mother was a failed Belgian actress who had no interest in her children, showing nothing but "insensitivity and heartlessness." Patrick's younger brother Rudy died of leukemia when he was ten and Patrick was twelve. He never got over the loss, and has dedicated seven of his books to the memory of the younger brother he loved so much. Both his mother and father were always broke or absent. Destitute himself much of the time, Patrick wandered the streets and quays alone, was often sent away to boarding schools which he hated. He ran away regularly, read without ceasing, and like many truants (Truffaut comes to mind—see p. 207), he hung out in bookstores and movie theaters. He won literary prizes in the schools he didn't run away from.

Trying to figure out how his Jewish father, who rarely talked to him, survived during the German Occupation during World War II, he picked up a few details: his father refused to wear the yellow star, carried no identity papers if he even possessed them, escaped from the French Gestapo more than once, avoiding deportation to a concentration camp. But for the most part he remains in the dark about his father's history and, therefore, his own identity.

For the Traveler

His first novel *La Place de l'Étoile* (*The Place of the Star*, 1968), published when he was just twenty-two, reinvents his father as a Jewish Nazi sympathizer and collaborator called Raphael Schlemilovitch. It's a shock novel, ugly with anti-Semitism, the Gestapo, Auschwitz, betrayal, torture (waterboarding, in particular), Modiano's anger. It's the first story in the series of three novels the publishers titled *The Occupation Trilogy*.

The settings of the trilogy mark the exact locations where the crimes of the Occupation and the collaborators occurred. The novel's title—the *Étoile*, with its iconic Arc de Triomphe rising from its center as well as its significance as the symbol the Nazis forced the Jews to wear on their clothing—mocks this site of French military glory. The *Étoile* during the Occupation is an image of the utter defeat of the French military and the French soul, the pictures of Hitler's army marching under the Arc de Triomphe on June 14, 1940, combined with the pictures of Jews wearing the yellow star on their clothing are forever inscribed in the city's collective memory of shame. The **Place de l'Étoile** (now called

Place Charles-de-Gaulle) has twelve avenues radiating in a star shape from the Place, around which traffic flows. At the top of the *Arc de Triomphe* is an observation platform with a view down the *Champs-Élysées,* "the major axis of Paris collaboration"* and of all the other streets.

> MÉTRO 1 TO L'ÉTOILE. Open April–Sept, 10–11; Oct–
> Mar, 10–10:30. Walk through a tunnel from the métro
> exit to get to the booth for tickets to the top of the Arc.
> There is also an elevator. The eternal flame of the
> Unknown Soldier is midway up, on the same level as the
> ticket booth. The view from the top, at night, is superb.

Modiano shows us this long street as the center of the war's black market, the *quartier* where gangsters ran their dirty illegal business. He underscores the moral filth of the racketeers who got rich while most of Paris went hungry. Some also belonged to the French Gestapo whose headquarters were nearby.

The words *"Avenue Kléber,"* one of the twelve streets ending at the Étoile, named after one of Napoleon's generals, is invoked in the novel as a refrain signaling the omnipresence of the victorious Nazis; it leads in the other direction to the Boissière *quartier* and *93, rue Lauriston,* another site of Occupation criminality, where the black market gangsters did double duty as members of the French Gestapo. Walk southwest along the *avenue Kléber* of hotels and offices to *rue Boissière*—or take the Kléber métro to the Boissière métro—then turn right and walk one block up the hill of *rue Boissière* to *rue Lauriston*. (You're walking in the direction of Place Victor-Hugo.)

* Eric Hazan, *The Invention of Paris: A History in Footsteps.*

Turn left, walk about half a block on the south side to no. 93. In the cellars of this building, now painted a creamy beige, the French Gestapo—as the plaque on the building recounts—interrogated, tortured, and murdered members of the Resistance. The place was notorious during and after the war. Several of Modiano's scenes in the second novel of the trilogy, *The Night Watch*, are based on historical records: His main character works for the Resistance and the Gestapo, informing on both to each one, the actual record of Jo Attia.* The whole operation was under the control of the brutal Bonny-Lafont gang.† "For some people," writes Eric Hazan, "the very words *rue Lauriston* still raise a shudder."

Ten minutes away on foot (or take the métro to Porte Dauphine), at *84, avenue Foch,* the widest avenue in Paris, you will see on the northwest side, the six-story mansion which during the Occupation was the headquarters of the German Gestapo. (The sixteenth *arrondissement* and Passy, so quiet and orderly, was the favorite neighborhood of the German high command.) There's a sign on the grass across from the stately mansion: *Pelouse Pierre Brossolette*. A leader and hero of the Resistance, arrested and tortured here in 1944 (almost a year after Jean Moulin's mutilated body was brought here from Lyons—see p. 143), Brossolette, afraid that he would finally break and talk, jumped to his death from an open window on the fifth floor to avoid further torture. His remains were transferred to the Panthéon in May 2015.

The crimes of wartime and postwar Paris become Modiano's story of origin: in other books, too, he describes the dark aftermath of the Occupation, his personal experience of

*Luc Sante, *The Other Paris*.
† Murielle Neveux, *Paris Criminel*.

the years of *épuration*, a kind of civil war in which scores were settled ruthlessly. What he suffered was the betrayal of the "first relationship" as psychology calls it: *"my mother . . . I seldom saw her. I can't recall a single act of genuine warmth or protectiveness from her."*

The menace of the Occupation recedes in the later books, in which Modiano's fixation shifts to the processes of memory and his need to find missing persons, who are usually women. He roams the city, his plain sentences an incantatory naming of places: the Pont des Art, Pont Neuf, Vert-Galant, the Louvre, the quays (Conti, Orfèvres, Tournelles, Orsay, Célestins), Pigalle, Clichy, Saint-Germain, Parc Monceau, Pont de l'Alma, the Bois de Boulogne, Hôtel de Ville. *"I was happy when I walked the streets of Paris by myself."** The names of places come across as fixed points—the only fixed points—familiar, reliable presences. Paris as mother surrogate. But they almost never help him solve the mystery.

In *Paris Nocturne*, Modiano takes us to the lovely Trocadéro gardens, south of avenue Foch. (*Métro: Trocadéro.*) Other searches take place along **rue de Grenelle;** the streets of the Latin Quarter, now lost, as he says, to boutiques and leather shops (*In the Café of Lost Youth*); of Montparnasse (*Suspended Sentences*); along the quays (*After the Circus*); over the Seine bridges. The steep narrow streets of Montmartre (*In the Café of Lost Youth*) where he imagines the loss of one of his most moving characters, the child-woman, Louki. His love for her is genuine; but she is unknowable, like Paris, her history a secret.

Perhaps his most compelling book, *Pedigree* (2005), is almost an *homage* to the saving streets of Montmartre. A

* Patrick Modiano, *Pedigree*.

memoir of his first twenty-one years, many of its incidents, characters, places will be familiar to readers of his novels. But what comes across toward the end of the book is the narrator's sudden lightness of being, moments of feeling more insistent than memories of cruel history. He forgives his mother. Despite the horrors, which include his parents' cold indifference and his city's wartime past, Modiano now sees the beauty of the world. The vision changes him. The particulars move him.

> *I spent my days in Montmartre . . . I felt better there than anywhere else. The metro stop Lamarck-Caulaincourt, with its rising elevator. . . . For brief moments, I was happy. . . . The icy handrail on Rue Berthe . . .*

If you climb the steps from the Lamarck-Caulaincourt métro exit up to *rue Caulaincourt,* as you walk straight ahead and then up the steps into *Place Dalida,* you can follow Modiano's wanderings in several directions through the old streets of Montmartre (where the social misfits Vincent van Gogh and Erik Satie lived, painting and composing respectively, both lonely and ridiculed). Despite gentrification and the tourist buses around Sacré-Coeur, it is possible to walk in peace on the *butte.* Many places recall Montmartre's layered past: The *Allée des Brouillards* ("Fog Alley") to your right, and next to it *Square Suzanne-Buisson, Résistante,* with the statue of Saint-Denis holding his severed head, his legend the origin of the word "Montmartre": *Mons Martyrum,* the mountain of execution. Both Buisson and Saint-Denis were victims of totalitarianism. In the other direction, follow the pretty, slightly uphill *rue de l'Abreuvoir,* crossing *rue des Saules* into *rue Cortot.*

From van Gogh's *rue Lepic* (he lived at no. 54, with his

brother, Theo, 1886–1888), you wind uphill past Le Moulin de la Galette (now a tourist restaurant, on your left as you climb this old quarry road); van Gogh painted it—there were more than twenty-five windmills in his time; he, too, walked the streets of Paris, painted *en plein air,* and sent postcards to friends. *"Paris is Paris . . . the French air clears up the brain and does one good—a world of good."* Just past the windmill, turn right at the corner into the steep downhill *rue de la Miré* which ends in *rue d'Orchampt.* Turn left, walking straight ahead. *Rue Ravignan* winds left, uphill, forking into several streets.

Here at this small picturesque crossroads, you also find the end of Modiano's uphill *rue Berthe* with its handrail still in place, in front of the pharmacy (where Giacometti had his prescriptions filled). Turning to face south (*rue Berthe* is on your left) you see a welcoming square, with a Wallace fountain in the center, a few benches, and shaded by chestnut trees, *Place Émile-Goudeau* (formerly called Place Ravignan). Under the breeze of the hilltop you can sit to overlook the steep streets below and in the distance the expanse of the city. *Rue Lauriston* has its place in that distance—Modiano never denies the dark side—but from up here, his view of Paris has a wider more forgiving focus.

(On the west side of the Place is the restored *Bâteau-Lavoir* where Picasso and many other artists lived in the early twentieth century, working in penury—no water, no heat, no food. Camus lived up here, on *rue Ravignan,* when he first came to Paris and lived like a hermit, finishing his novel *The Stranger*—see p. 130.)

On weekdays, Place Émile-Goudeau offers an unusual haven of solitude in the old village of Montmartre where the ethos of Modriano's novels feels true: *"I was really myself only when I could be alone in the streets."*

Following in Modiano's footsteps, from Place Émile-Goudeau, climb up to *rue Lepic* and explore the nearby *avenue Junot, rue Norvins, rue Saint-Vincent, and rue du Mont-Cenis* where Berlioz lived when he wrote *Symphony Fantastique*. Or, returning to Place Émile-Goudeau, descend the steep *rue Berthe,* bearing right into *rue des Trois-Frères* and then *rue Yvonne-le-Tac* into *Place des Abbesses* ... You don't need a map up here. Just keep walking, up and down the narrow cobblestone streets and the long flights of steps, in whatever direction you choose, meandering, forgetting, returning, like the movements of memory itself.

Avoid the *butte* on weekends, if you can. On weekdays, off-season, there is solitude and a haunting silence and bracing fresh air.

The multiple personalities of the streets of Paris—dead ends, zero zones, sites of beauty and of memory—have been Modiano's lifetime companions; the web of streets has shaped his multi-angled consciousness. Sometimes they provide clues about the past. To keep track of them, he lists addresses and phone numbers along with the names of the missing. Not as often as he includes this data but often enough he uses the word "kindness," for him an important clue in the face of the unknowability of every human being. It was a friend of his mother's, a kind man, who helped the abandoned teenager move forward, into his future as a writer. Raymond Queneau, the French writer (*Zazie in the Métro*), read Modiano's first attempts at a novel; he encouraged him to keep writing and talked about him to his publisher—who would become Modiano's—Gaston Gallimard. Queneau understood Modiano, saying that he himself was happiest the afternoons he wandered alone on the out-of-the-way streets of his city.

In 2015 Paris recognized Modiano's historical contribution to the excavation of its hidden shameful memories—and the identification of the thousands of missing persons from the war years—when it named a promenade in the eighteenth *arrondissement* (Clignancourt) after Dora Bruder, the name of a fifteen-year-old girl who went missing from that neighborhood in 1941. She became the subject of Modiano's search for her and the focus of his sorrowful meditation on loss, told in the novel *Dora Bruder* (1997), *The Search Warrant* in English. He finally tracked her down: her name appeared on the lists of deportees to Auschwitz.

Another young Parisian Jewish woman, Hélène Berr, was found long after she had been deported to Auschwitz in 1944 and then marched to Bergen-Belsen where she was murdered in 1945. Hélène Berr had left behind her voice in her *Journal*: we meet her during the Occupation when she was a student at the Sorbonne and a volunteer in the underground networks that rescued and smuggled Jewish children out of Paris. Her journal was found after the war and published in 2008.

Patrick Modiano wrote the introduction:

> *It is necessary to listen to the voice of Hélène and walk by her side. Hers is a voice and a presence that will stay with us for our whole life.*

Berr's philosophical intensity reminds him of Simone Weil (see p. 91), but her desire for happiness as she walks around Paris is different from the ascetic Weil. A best seller in France—24,000 copies sold in two days—Hélène Berr's *Journal* is, according to Modiano and many reviewers, "a truly great book." Her final words in it are from Shake-speare's *Macbeth*: *"Horror! Horror! Horror!"* The victims of the horror, their loss and namelessness, drive most of Modiano's searches and meditations. He finds out nothing about Dora Bruder. But Hélène Berr assumes identity in the pages of her memoir, a similar revelation to Modiano's *Pedigree*.

She grew up about half an hour away from *la butte Montmartre* (by métro), just beneath the Eiffel Tower at no. 5 *avenue Elisée Reclus,* one block south of *avenue de la Bour-donnais.* The manuscript of Hélène Berr's *Journal* is in the archives of the Shoah Memorial, www.memorialdelashoah .org. (In the *Marais* section of this book—see p. 239.)

Nearby

Roaming around Montmartre as a truant teenager, Modiano spent a lot of time in bookstores.

LIBRAIRIE VENDREDI   *67, rue des Martyrs, on the left as you climb north. librairievendredi@wanadoo.fr. A good selection of Modiano's novels in stock.*

LIBRAIRIE DES ABBESSES   *30, rue Yvonne-le-Tac, on the right, near the corner, as you head into Place des Abbesses. Excellent, with many Modiano titles in stock and a children's section.*

ANIMA   *Small, on the left as you climb toward Place Émile-Goudeau on rue des Abbesses.*

L'ATTRAPE-COEURS   *On the left side—4, Place Constantin-Pecqueur—as you approach the stairway up to Place Dalida from Rue Caulincourt. An excellent selection of French titles and some contemporary American writers, with a large children's section in the back.*

LE RELAIS DE LA BUTTE   *Directly below **Place Émile-Goudeau**, at the head of a very steep street, a bistro with a large outdoor terrace overlooking the city. Good service, good food, a friendly place to relax under a wide sky.*

Reine Margot: Hôtel de Sens, rue du Figuier

The Marais

REINE MARGOT:
LEGENDS AND LIES

LOCATION: *1, rue du Figuier, Bibliothèque Forney,*
  Hôtel de Sens
HOURS: Tues, Fri, Sat 1–7:30; Weds, Thurs 10–7:30
MÉTRO: Pont Marie; Sully-Morland

Centuries of chroniclers bearing grudges have left us an ugly portrait of Marguerite de Valois—*La Belle Reine Margot*—youngest sister of the four Valois sons of Catherine de Medici and at eighteen the first wife of *Henri IV* (see p. 37). According to the mythmakers, Marguerite as girl and woman amounted to little more than a lying whore, fat, nymphomaniacal, homicidal (like her mother). She deserved every humiliation her families dealt her, the Catholics of the House of Valois and the Protestant House of Bourbon which she entered by marriage. The "Margot" of these so-called historians is made in the image of her treacherous, malevolent mother, gifted in the "arts" of poisoning.

These days, however, historians examining new and old evidence are proving conclusively that Marguerite de Valois—*Reine Margot*—and Catherine de Medici were not a case of like mother like daughter.* They depict a far more complex and sympathetic princess than the depraved gargoyle of earlier storytellers.

The cruelty inflicted on Margot (1553–1615) began in the

---

* Nancy Goldstone, *The Rival Queens: Catherine de Medici, Her Daughter Marguerite de Valois, and the Betrayal That Ignited a Kingdom.*

nursery of the Louvre palace where her own mother and brothers colluded on how they could best use her to eliminate their enemies and strengthen their own power.

Black-haired, dark-eyed Marguerite had been the favorite of her father, Henri II. Extremely pretty and bright, she was ignored or controlled by her ruthless mother, whose heart belonged to her son Henri. Catherine's maternal agenda was to groom her three daughters for power marriages with other royal European thrones. As a teenager Marguerite was severely beaten by her brother King Charles IX and Queen Catherine for flirting with the Duke of Guise and maybe ruining her chances to snare a richer and more prestigious husband than the duke.

The princess's refuge was books. She read in the sanctuary of her grandfather King François I's royal library, becoming fluent in Italian, Spanish, and the only member of the royal family who could read, write, and converse in Latin. She was also admired as a graceful dancer, gifted lutenist, and poet. She studied history, art, philosophy, and Catholic theology though pious Catholic hatred ran in her Medici mother's milk.

At court, her interests aroused suspicion. Defenseless, she became the sacrificial victim of her mother and brothers' marriage politics. They arranged to marry the "belle of the Valois court" to Henri, the Bourbon son of the Protestant kingdom of Navarre in France's southwest. This union, they thought, would reconcile the two opposing religious tribes fighting the civil Wars of Religion: by 1572, the year of the marriage, papist Catholics and heretic Protestants had soaked France in the blood of innocents and bankrupted the State. Neither religion would submit to making peace. The marriage, according to Catherine and her sons, would force a peace. Margot, their pawn, wept, begging to be spared a life sentence of a loveless marriage. Witnesses of the wedding, held in front of, not inside the Cathedral of Notre-Dame (Protestant Henri was not fit to enter this heart of Catholic France), noticed the misery of the bride's expression.

There was dutiful sex but no chemistry between Henri of Navarre and Marguerite de Valois. From the start, the two teenagers mostly maintained an emotional distance, preferring the company of their lovers. The accomplished, cultured Marguerite was said to intimidate the crude garlicky military man of the south. Neither one would consider converting to the faith of the other though Henri IV eventually became adroit at converting from Protestant to Catholic to Protestant to Catholic.

Five days after the grim wedding and the attendant nights of dancing and partying, fireworks accompanying the lovemaking and drunkenness throughout the Louvre and its courtyards, the Catholic Catherine and her fanatical advisers and sons orchestrated the slaughter of those same guests and their co-religionists—the loathsome heretics spawned by Martin Luther. That orgy of murder became known as the Saint Bartholomew's Day Massacre of an estimated five thousand to fifteen thousand Protestants. For more than a century this episode of royal butchery lost France the respect of governments in England, Spain, the Netherlands, and Germany.

Throughout those days and nights of late August 1572, the Protestant bridegroom's life was in danger. A prize target of the crusading Catholics, with the Catholic Margot's help, he hid all over the Louvre, under his bed, in the corridors and closets of the bedchambers of both his mistress and his Paris bride, the new Queen of Navarre. Protestant Henri and his Catholic wife realized how close to death the bridegroom— and perhaps his new wife—might be; he in turn wondered if she had betrayed him, if she would lead the ax-wielding soldiers to her bedchamber. She knew that had she chosen to betray him, to lead the Catholic courtiers to the closet where she'd hidden him, she could have escaped the hated marriage into which she had been sold.

Instead Margot saved Henri's life. She also saved the lives of a number of his Huguenot friends. During the next four years when her husband was held a virtual prisoner in the Louvre, she saved him again despite the humiliation of watching Henri's nightly visitations to his mistresses and hearing the gossip that entertained the court.

Finally, when he escaped the Louvre, pretending to be off to the hunt, Margot covered for him. Loyalty to her husband and to their marriage vows mattered to her. The disappointing sexual relationship they did not have was far less important than the integrity of her soul. (And she knew the consolations of her lover.) Perhaps her steadfast loyalty evolved in reaction to her mother and brothers' history of treachery, their betrayals of one another and of their friends. The corrupt Valois brothers and their mother changed sides as fast and as strategically as they changed horses and dogs during the royal hunts at Fontainebleau, Boulogne, and Vincennes. Betrayal was the twisted heart of Valois politics, spying and lying its daily liturgy. Refusing their politics, Marguerite acted as the rebel Queen of Navarre, standing by her man, risking her life.

After Henri got away, Marguerite remained confined to

the Louvre. Her brothers and mother had always suspected she had a soul of her own. All those books! The salon discussions, the poets she preferred to all-night dancing (though she loved to dance). She was closely watched, her every attempt to organize a getaway and head south to Navarre foiled.

Six years after her wedding, she was permitted to travel south and reunite with her husband. Henri wanted an heir, she wanted her freedom; possibly she also hoped to find a loving, grateful husband in Gascony. At Nerac they set up their ecumenical court, with Protestants and Catholics getting on together. (Both king and queen liked to party.) Scholars and poets visited the festive court of Navarre, including Montaigne who in his youth as a courtier in the Louvre (see p. 63) had known Margot. He dedicated the first edition of his *Essays* to her, describing her as resembling *"one of those divine, supernatural and extraordinary beauties that one sometimes sees shining like stars through the veils of an earthly body."* Shakespeare heard about the spirited court of Navarre, which inspired his first play *Love's Labour Lost*, set in the "kingdom of Navarre."

At times Henri and Margot got along like old friends. But the massacre on the night of their marriage had damaged Henri's trust in his Valois bride for life. She had saved his life; but ever since 1572, her brothers had strategized how to eliminate him. The wedding night murders, more than his dalliances (or halitosis) are said now to have ruined their chances of a happy marriage from day (night) one.

Like her husband, she was happiest when she was in love. She'd had and continued to have several passionate affairs; her courtier lovers usually died or were killed in the name of religion. She was "a pioneer of that sex equality," to quote

Charlotte Haldane, that women in her day would not dare to claim publicly.

Her brothers in Paris condemned her disgraceful sensuality. Long before gender studies and the dogmatism of evolutionary psychology, men of power enjoyed their infidelities and promiscuous lives without censure. Then, as now, the "evo-psycho set"—the phrase is Natalie Angier's— believed, on the basis of a few self-serving surveys, that men are innately more sexual than women, can't help acting on their desires. Women, on the other hand, want (or should want) a provider, children, monogamy. The discrepancy in male-female sexuality, according to the evolutionary psychologists, is as certain as the difference in male-female anatomy. By their standards, Margot was a common whore. Her whoring brother King Henri III called her out publicly in court during one of her return visits to Paris and eventually exiled her to a remote mountainside château, Usson, for eighteen years.

Instead of going mad, she created a library and salon for intellectuals, philosophers, writers, and poets. Her library held titles by Dante, Petrarch, Boccaccio, Ronsard, du Bellay. Montaigne's niece was her librarian. She began to write her memoirs, which she called "history." The Académie Française would pronounce them "one of the masterpieces of French literature."

Husband Henri did not rescue her from Usson. He was occupied fighting more religious wars, outwitting Marguerite's brother Henri III, and, after Henri III was assassinated (on the toilet), fighting to win the crown he had inherited, besieging Paris, converting, once again, to Catholicism, then drafting divorce papers: Henri knew he needed an heir if his throne was to be safe. Margot had never conceived, perhaps, according to one modern biographer, because she suffered from hypothyroidism, which would also explain her weight gain as she aged. Though what did not suffer was her very active sex life: She took many lovers in "old age"—her forties and fifties—giving her puritan critics ammunition and evidence of how "unnatural" she was.

For the Traveler

The *Hôtel de Sens* in the *Southern Marais* figures as the setting of one of the mythical Margot's most vindictive mad scenes. It is repeated in old biographies and even now, rehashed in popular guidebooks.

> Walk west from the Sully-Morland métro, along Quai des Célestins, with its lovely views across the Seine of Quai d'Anjou on Île Saint-Louis; bear right at the pretty Square Marie-Trintignant, stopping at the angle where rue du Figuier and rue du Fauconnier meet. Cross rue du Figuier to the front entrance of the Hôtel de Sens. Or you can approach from the Pont Marie métro, walking east along the Seine and bearing left into rue des Nonnains d'Hyères, cutting through the sunken garden in the back of the Hôtel.

The fifteenth-century residence (1475–1519) of the Archbishops of Sens, older than the Hôtel de Cluny (the only other important example of fifteenth-century domestic architecture in Paris), the building was eventually rented out by the archbishops after they relocated from Paris to Sens.

In 1605, Margot, freed from exile, and divorced—amicably—from Henri IV, became Sens' most famous resident. Just as Henri had never been without a mistress throughout their twenty-seven-year marriage so the passionate Margot had enjoyed the pleasures of a string of lovers. In the courtyard of the *Hôtel de Sens,* or so the story goes, she showed one of them the depths of her rage after he had murdered one of her favorites.

The sunken garden behind the castle—*walk away from the front entrance (and the Seine) and bear left through the gate on rue du Figuier.* Here is a quiet haven, an off-the-beaten-track landscaped garden in which to sit and consider the legendary story of *La Reine Margot,* which culminates in the front courtyard of this medieval residence. The popular myth has it that this was the site of an atrocity that was used for centuries to defame a female royal, a woman who in fact had refused victimhood, making herself into a respected and courageous advocate for peace despite the murderous enmities between the two barbaric Christian sects of sixteenth-century France, both of which would like to have seen her dead.

With Henri of Navarre finally on the throne and living in the Louvre, Margot was free to return to Paris. She had always loved the capital, its gaiety a life force, long denied her in the Huguenot towns. After she'd agreed to a divorce, it had taken at least five years before the pope had given up his signature. Once legally free, Henri imported a new wife, the wealthy Italian Marie de Medici who had plenty of money to pay France's war debts as well as the hormonal balance to produce an heir. The future Louis XIII was born, Marguerite arrived, and "so began the most peaceful and congenial years of Marguerite's life," in the words of biographer Nancy Goldstone.

She became a close friend of Marie, of baby Louis. At long

last she and Henri "got on." There was warmth and respect between them. In 1605 he installed her in the magnificent Hôtel de Sens, only half a mile from the Louvre. *(To reach her childhood home, walk west along the quays—Célestins, L'Hôtel-de-Ville, Gesvres, Mégisserie, and right into rue de l'Amiral-de-Coligny. Cross to enter the Cour Carrée.)*

But less than a year in residence at Hôtel de Sens, she had to move again. According to the slanderous chroniclers, one of her ex-lovers had been murdered in the courtyard by her present lover as Marguerite stepped down from her carriage.

In fact, the victim, Saint-Julien, had been her protégé— no evidence exists that they'd been lovers—and the murderer had played a part in a conspiracy against Henri's throne: He believed the victim had passed along information about the conspiracy to the Crown. The murder was a crime of political revenge having nothing to do with Marguerite's erotic whims. She complained at once to Henri about the political assassination that had bloodied her courtyard.

King Henri captured the murderer and had him hanged the next day in the same courtyard so that his ex-wife could observe the rite of royal justice from her high window in the Hôtel de Sens. Many fictitious details color the event: that Margot screamed and yelled with glee as the murderer was beheaded and the courtyard ran with his blood (just as her brother had screamed in approval the night of the Saint Bartholomew's Day Massacre). Like brother like sister. Not.

In disgust, she left the Hôtel de Sens six months later to build a splendid château on the Left Bank, across from the Louvre, behind the Quai Malaquais, where the École des Beaux-Arts is now located.

Like Queen Margot herself, her salon became popular for its exuberance and intellectual heft. Paris loved having her in residence again, her taste in fashion and the decorative arts, in poetry and music, creating a sparkling presence in the capital once more. Helpmate to Henri (she spied for him), godmother to his second child, friendly with Marie de Medici, a generous benefactor to the poor, especially the poor Irish refugees fleeing the murderous Tudors, she became a beloved elder royal. Paris was glad to be rid of her mother when she died; it mourned openly when Marguerite died, crowds of Parisians queuing to view her body and pay their respects.

Still. Until recently she was remembered almost exclusively for her sensuality which overshadowed every other aspect of her life. That the sexual behavior of her brothers and husband dwarfed her own did not matter. That most of her love affairs were passionate rather than opportunistic affairs of state has hardly mattered. That Margot was a modern woman centuries ahead of her time, centuries before the feminist movement confronted the hypocrisy and double standards of masculinist sexual mores, has only recently been acknowledged: "The queen of Navarre was so much more than the sum of her affairs," to quote Nancy Goldstone. And in saving Henri of Navarre's life on their wedding night, it is no exaggeration to say that La Reine Margot saved France.

Looking south toward the Seine from *rue Charlemagne* in the *Southern Marais,* you see the length of the very pretty *rue du Figuier* (Fig Street), dating from the thirteenth century. Walking, you pass on the left the Square Roger-Priou-Valjean (named after a *Résistant,* the founder of Libération-Nord).

Legend has it that fig trees were cut down to widen this street for Margot's carriage. Like the garden of the *Hôtel de Sens,* the Square, dense with lilac bushes in spring, is a fine place to look across at the turrets of the Hôtel and take aim at the reigning theories surrounding Marguerite de Valois. Like many defiant, sensual, and intellectual women in history, Margot's life was refigured as a gothic fairy tale by men who for centuries condemned women who do not conform to man-made moral codes. (Ninon de l'Enclos of the *Northern Marais* seemed to welcome the risks of ignoring these codes—see p. 243.) Today the Hôtel de Sens houses the *Bibliothèque Forney,* a library of art and architecture. Queen Margot, who loved books and beauty and the arts of interior decoration, would like that. When the sun is shining, the courtyard is a hushed and pleasant place, bibliophiles crossing it to return and withdraw books, stopping to greet friends, maybe unaware of the modern historians who have liberated this ancient place and its notorious royal from the bloody legend that has long disfigured her.

Nearby

THE SHOAH MEMORIAL   *A few minutes west of Hôtel de Sens, along **rue de L'Hôtel-de-Ville**, turn right into **rue Geoffroy-l'Asnier**, no. 17. Open Sun–Fri, 10–6; Thur 10–10; closed Sat. www.memorialdelashoah.org. A moving exhibition of photos, archives, chronologies, with a good library/bookstore at the entrance. The names of 76,000 Jews deported from France—with photos—are engraved on the Wall of Names in the forecourt. The Wall of the Righteous bears the names of those who helped Jews find safety.*

CAFÉ LOUIS PHILIPPE   *Continuing west from Hôtel de Sens on rue de L'Hôtel-de-Ville. At **66, Quai de L'Hôtel-de-Ville.** Tel: 01.42.72.29.42. A friendly restaurant, serving hearty French food, with a beautiful view of the Seine and Île Saint-Louis. In the other direction, you face the lovely **rue des Barres,** behind Église Saint-Gervais and the elegant restaurant Chez Julien.*

Ninon de l'Enclos: Arcades in Place des Vosges

NINON DE L'ENCLOS:
VOLTAIRE'S FIRST COURTESAN

LOCATION: *34, rue des Tournelles, Hôtel de Sagonne*
MÉTRO: Chemin Vert; Saint-Paul

Born in Paris in 1620, a child of a religious skeptic father and a devoutly Catholic mother—and, as an accomplished lutenist and linguist, a prodigy like Voltaire—by the time she was a teenager she'd become a much desired courtesan and *salonnière* in the Marais. The very beautiful Ninon received her guests and lovers (she called them *Les Oiseaux des Tournelles*) at her *hôtel* and later the *Hôtel de Sagonne,* just off the northeast corner of Place Royale (Place des Vosges) on *rue des Tournelles.* She was nicknamed Notre-Dame des Amours (Our Lady of Love).

During the reign of Louis XIV (1661–1715), her salon attracted the *crème* of Paris, powerful statesmen (including Madame de Sévigné's husband and son); clergy, including Voltaire's godfather, Abbé de Chateauneuf, and Cardinal Richelieu whose erotic interest she did not return; and artists Lully, Racine, La Fontaine, La Rochefoucauld, Boileau, and Molière. Ninon and Molière were especially close friends. Although he mocks the silly conversation of the salons and their *salonnards* (sycophants) in his play *Les Précieuses Ridicules* (*The Pretentious Young Ladies*) he had a warm regard for the mistress of the salon on *rue des Tournelles.* "Ninon has the keenest sense of the absurd of anyone I know," he wrote. *Tartuffe*, his anticlerical play about hypocrites, received its first reading in her salon. Outranking her sister *salonnières* (Mesdames de Sablé, de Rambouillet, and de Scudéry to name a few), the brilliant and nonconformist Ninon (a story goes that refusing to get married, she withdrew to a convent as a teenager) was reputed to host the most prestigious literary salon of her era. She required originality from her guests, barred the door against pedants.

Most salons were presided over by women. As Stacy Schiff puts it, "the women of France . . . kept the salon, which was the equivalent of running the newspapers." The sharing of gossip about who was doing what with whom around town, in and out of bed, was one of the salons' most delicious party games. Political debates and new philosophical speculations added to the effervescence of the talk that sparkled until the sun came up over the rosy-colored stone and mansart roofs of the new Place Royale.

Ninon de l'Enclos was not a *salonnière* whose primary role was to flatter male wits or keep the hors d'oeuvres moving. Among cultural historians there is now a controversy about whether women actually contributed anything substantive to the conversation or whether they performed merely as pretty *objets* offering every variety of hospitality. But no one disputes that Ninon had her own ideas: "*Feminine virtue*," she insisted, "*is nothing but a convenient masculine invention.*" She scorned organized religion, especially monastic and ascetic Christianity and the priests and bishops who denounced her amoral salon from the Sunday pulpit after enjoying themselves there on Saturday night. Her credo affirmed the primacy of pleasure and the duty to avoid pain.

All that I can say in favor of love is that it gives us a greater pleasure than any of the other comforts of life. It pulls us out of our routines and stirs us up.

Her ethical horizons focused on the renewed Epicureanism that had inflected the French Renaissance. Her disdain for Plato's spiritual universe was matched by her enthusiasm for the earthbound essays of Montaigne.

More than for the licentiousness of her gatherings or the gossip about her serial lovers, it was for the philosophical transgressions voiced inside her salon and reported in the streets of the *Marais* that moved the pious Queen Anne of Austria, mother of the Sun King (Louis XIV), to send Ninon to jail for a few months. (In fact, the jail was a convent.) Mademoiselle de l'Enclos was simply too unorthodox and permissive to avoid the silencing and condemnation of the censors in royal Catholic Paris. But the memoirist Saint-Simon took notes, Ninon herself wrote letters, and over the next three centuries her reading audience was charmed.

For the Traveler

There is a white plaque on the black façade of *34, rue des Tournelles,* identifying Ninon as the *hôtel*'s renowned philosophe and courtesan.

> *NINON de L'ENCLOS (1620–1705) Femme de lettres, Femme de pouvoir.*
> *In the Hôtel de Sagonne lived one of the most powerful women of her time. Ninon de L'enclos was a philosophe and*

courtesan of the 17th century. In her salon she received
Lully, Moliere, Racine and la Fontaine.

Location was on her side. ***Rue des Tournelles,*** opened in
1400, extending from the ancient Roman road ***rue Saint-
Antoine*** on the southern end to ***boulevard Beaumarchais***
on the north, was on the site of the original royal lands of
the Château des Tournelles, the royal residence where
Henri II died after a jousting tournament. After his death,
Henri's queen, Catherine de Medici (choreographer of the
Saint Bartholomew's Day Massacre), had the château razed.
The Tournelles district turned into a sort of dump and
horse market until Henri IV, the ultimate *galant* urbanist
(see p. 45) orchestrated the building of the glorious ***Place
Royale*** (Place des Vosges). In the *hôtels* of the Place and its
surrounding streets—***rue des Tournelles*** parallels the east
side of the Place, ***rue de Turenne*** the west, and ***rue de Béarn*** leads north of the Queen's Pavillion out of Place des
Vosges—the city's wealthiest and most fun-loving aristocrats settled in.

Even though Henri IV didn't survive to enjoy the beauty
or the nightlife of what Joan DeJean calls the "fun part of
town," from the outset this elegant enclave observed rituals
of pleasure that would have suited Henri's taste for good
times and beautiful women: tournaments, balls, fairs, fireworks, weddings, duels, and the specialty of *le grand siècle*,
the salon.

Perhaps Ninon got some of her nerve from the currents
of change moving Paris into the "modern" world, not just
inside the ***Marais*** salons but in public, under the influence of
the mover-and-shaker King Louis XIV. Absolutist in the
practice of statecraft, when it came to the reputation of his

city, he was determined to compete with the the rival cities of Europe. Throughout his long reign, in addition to waging hugely expensive wars and persecuting Protestants, he transformed Paris into a place of public pleasures and leisure. He broadened many streets, creating the first boulevards and getting rid of the garbage that had always been thrown in the gutters; he made carriage traffic practical, added street lanterns, and, thanks to the genius of his landscape artist André Le Nôtre who turned the *Tuileries* into a public park and promenade, he opened this former royal preserve to the working class who lived beyond the city center. Walking became the favorite Parisian leisure activity in Ninon's day, enabling women to show off new dresses, and both sexes to flirt.

Ninon's Paris now became the must-see city in Europe. The *Tuileries,* as the "first truly public Parisian garden," became the "prototype for public gardens" all over Europe. A twenty-minute walk to the east of it, the *Place Royale* was described as "the most beautiful spot, not only in Paris, but in any city in the world."* And women, long cloistered like nuns and drones inside what Ninon saw as their domestic marital prisons, were allowed this beauty. A friend of the prolific letter-writer Madame de Sévigné (after she forgave Ninon for sleeping with her husband and son), Ninon, no doubt, joined her on the paths through the *Tuileries* (and the Place) where men and women walked and drank and talked together. Madame de Sévigné described it all in her famous letters to her daughter.†

As the relaxed gender relations of the *Tournelles* salon

---

* Joan DeJean, *How Paris Became Paris: The Invention of the Modern City.*
† Madame de Sévigné, *Letters,* ed. Leonard Tancock.

moved outdoors, liberating the pleasures of the streets, parks, and the royal Places, many of the writers who lived in *rue des Tournelles, rue de Turenne,* and *rue de Béarn* and hated the idea of ever moving away wrote about the crucial role that "proximity to a beautiful spot," such as the *Place Royale,* played in their daily lives.*

Ever since the era of Ninon de l'Enclos, Paris writers have sung the joy of life in a place where the marriage of beauty, pleasure, and friendship feels like love.

A biographer of 1903 described the presiding *philosophe* and courtesan of *rue des Tournelles* as:

> *the most beautiful woman of the seventeenth century. For seventy years she held undisputed sway over the hearts of the distinguished men of France; queens, princes, noblemen, renowned warriors, statesmen, writers, and scientists bowing before her shrine and doing her homage. Even Louis XIV, when she was eighty-five years of age, declared that she was the marvel of his reign.†*

As a nine-year-old prodigy, Voltaire was taken to meet the aging Ninon who had heard about him from his godfather/her lover, the *Abbé Chateauneuf.* The boy recited from memory many verses of poetry. He was struck by her old wrinkled skin. Wrinkles, opined Ninon, are a sign of wisdom. She died soon after meeting Voltaire and rewriting her will to leave him a generous bequest for the purpose of buying books.

---

* Joan DeJean, *How Paris Became Paris: The Invention of the Modern City.*
† Robertson and Overton, *Life, Letters & Epicurean Philosophy of Ninon de l'Enclos: The Celebrated Beauty of the Seventeenth Century.*

Nearby

CHEZ JANOU   *2, rue Roger Verlomme and rue des Tournelles.*
*A friendly provençal bistro and restaurant open every day, midi
et soir. Tel: 01.42.72.28.41.*

LE PETIT ITALIEN   *Entrance at 5, rue Saint-Gilles but facing rue de Béarn (the street that leads north out of Place des
Vosges). Excellent food and service. A two-minute walk, through
an archway, from the lovely Jardin Saint-Gilles-Grand-Veneur
to the north, with stately seventeenth-century mansions. Tel:
01.42.71.05.80.*

LE PETIT MARCHÉ   *9, rue de Béarn. Tel: 01.42.72.06.67.
Very good food and ambience on the terrace in season, looking
down the street at the Queen's Pavillion on the north end of the
Place des Vosges.*

HÔTEL DE SULLY   *2, rue Saint-Antoine, the residence of the
Duke of Sully, Henri IV's able Calvinist finance minister. Walk
straight, into the pretty orangerie. The archway in the northeast
corner leads into the Place des Vosges. The excellent bookstore in
the southwest corner—**Librairie des Monuments Historiques**—
stocks books about Paris in every genre. Open Tues–Sun.*

PLACE DU MARCHÉ SAINTE-CATHERINE   *Turn right into
rue Caron as you walk west, along **rue Saint-Antoine**. The little
street leads straight into this small square facing **rue d'Ormesson**.
Benches and bistros under the trees. **Le Marché, 2, Place du
Marché Sainte-Catherine,** serves good simple food in a comfortable old dining room.*

MUSÉE CARNAVALET   *23, rue de Sévigné. Métro: Saint-Paul.
Hours: Tues–Sun, 10–5:30. Walk west from Place des Vosges*

across rue de Turenne, continue one block west along **rue des Francs-Bourgeois** *until* **rue de Sévigné.** *Turn right. The Renaissance mansion of Madame de Sévigné (1626–1696)—now the Museum of Paris—where she lived for the last twenty years of her life and wrote many of the thousands of letters she is remembered for has a sculptured garden and exhibits providing a rich introduction to the history of Paris starting with the Romans. But Madame du Sévigné's letters tell the story of life under Louis XIV like nothing else.*

RUE PAYENNE   *Walk another block west along rue des Francs-Bourgeois and turn right into* **rue Payenne,** *a street of treasures, especially* **Square Georges-Cain** *on the right. Farther west is the heart of Marais museum country: Musée Picasso, Musée d'Art et d'Histoire du Judaïsme, Archives Nationales de France, and the Musée de l'Histoire de France (with the only contemporary portrait of Joan of Arc and Marie Antoinette's last letter to Louis XVI).*

The Carmelites: Picpus Cemetery

Around Bastille and Northeastern Paris

"PERMISSION TO DIE, MOTHER?": SISTER CONSTANCE AND THE DIALOGUES OF THE CARMELITES

LOCATION: *Place de la Nation*
   35, rue de Picpus, Picpus Cemetery: *The Walled Garden of Memory*
HOURS: Weekdays, winter, 2–8; weekdays, summer, 2–4
MÉTRO: Nation

Eyewitnesses told afterward of the mob's counterrevolutionary tears, the cups of water offered to the nuns by the usually ferocious spectators. It seemed not to care about the women's guilt: expelled from their monastery on September 14, 1792, their convent dissolved, they'd refused to sign the new separatist oath of submission to the "the King, the Law, and the Nation." In secret, they had united in an "act of consecration" whereby the community vowed to offer itself to God as a sacrifice that "the ills afflicting the Church and the unhappy kingdom of France might cease." They were arrested on June 21, 1794, charged with counterterrorism and for assembling illegally in a small prison in Compiègne where they'd been confined by the men in charge. In a courtroom of the Palais de Justice, the Revolutionary Tribunal, finding the women guilty as "enemies of the Nation," had sentenced them to death by guillotine.

For the Traveler

Late in the afternoon of July 17, 1794, two wooden carts without springs set out over the cobblestones of the *Île de la Cité*. Their two-mile journey from the Conciergerie prison to the *Place du Trône-Renversé* (Place of the Toppled Throne) in eastern Paris, now the **Place de la Nation,** was joined by the usual jeering mob. The carts—*tumbrils*—carried many prisoners, including the sixteen nuns from the town of Compiègne, about fifty-two miles northeast of Paris.

At some point along **rue Saint-Antoine,** the main east/west artery of ancient Paris, the mob following that day's batch of condemned fell silent. What silenced them was the Carmelites themselves. Had they gone mad? The women were neither weeping or crying out or tearing at their white cloaks. As the carts clip-clopped over the cobblestones, headed toward a collective decapitation, the nuns had begun to sing.

First, the *Miserere*. Then the Divine Office that they chanted every day in their convent chapel at Compiègne. "*Have mercy upon me, O God, after thy great goodness . . . Create in me a clean heart, O God, and renew a right spirit within me. . . .*" So serene were their faces, it was as if they were back in Compiègne praying in their convent choir stalls, intoning and kneeling and bowing through Vespers and Compline, the canonical hours sung at the end of the day.

The eyewitness accounts, preserved in diaries and referenced in histories of the French Revolution, all tell the same story.

The journey to the scaffold along **rue Saint-Antoine** took about five hours. Today the walk takes about three: from the Conciergerie across the **Pont au Change,** passing the **Tour**

Saint-Jacques, then, farther along, past *Hôtel de Sully* and *Place des Vosges* into *Place de la Bastille.* Its prison had been destroyed by the mob on July 14, 1789, a guillotine set up in its place; now, five years into the Revolution, the housewives and mothers of the Bastille/Saint-Antoine district, sickened by the stench from the guillotine, had recently protested to have it relocated to *Place du Trône,* another mile to the east. The walk today, from Bastille, along the final stretch of *rue Saint-Antoine* is without charm.

Following the chanting of Vespers and Compline, the nuns, whose hair had already been cut short in preparation, sang the ancient *Salve Regina*, the hymn to the Virgin Mary. "*Mater misericordiae, vita, dulcedo et spes nostra salve . . . O clemens, O pia, O dulcis Virgo Maria.*"

In early evening, the tumbrils reached their destination. At the center of the large open space of *Place du Trône-Renversé,* framed by the tall Vincennes pillars (which still tower above *avenue du Trône*), the scaffold and guillotine were in place. Beneath the huge naked blade, the execution-er's blood-stiffened leather bag was open, ready to receive that day's severed heads. On sight of the blade, mounted on the high scaffold, the Mother Superior of the Carmelites, Mother Teresa of Saint Augustine, or Madame Lidoine in the world, sang forth the words of the *Te Deum*: "*It is Thee whom we praise, O God!*" The nuns answered: "*It is Thee whom we acknowledge to be the Lord!*" Hearing the Latin words, perhaps composed by Saint Ambrose as he baptized Saint Augus-tine, the mob that gathered every day to enjoy the specta-cle of executions, was again stunned to silence.

At the end of *Saint-Antoine,* at Place de la Nation (*Place du Trône*), you are facing the large circle that surrounds the monumental statuary in the center of the *Place*. From any angle you can stand here and imagine the scene of 223 years ago. Inside the circle, you feel an unmistakable bleakness.

In 1794 the air over the ***Place du Trône*** was thick with the stink of putrefying flesh and blood that evening. The Reign of Terror (1793–1794) in 421 days murdered 2,800 people by order of Robespierre. The corpses were dumped into open pits throughout the city and piled high in public squares.

The nuns continued singing. *"It is Thee, the Father everlasting, whom all the earth does worship. . . . It is in Thee, O Lord, that I have put my trust: O never let me be confounded!"* The tumbrils came closer to the platform; the singing became louder as they stopped at the scaffold. The condemned women seemed oblivious to the stench of the open pits as well as to the smell caught on the wind from the nearby Picpus Cemetery. In the last month, one thousand corpses and heads had been thrown into the pits at Picpus. (The Terror, according to Simon Schama, "was merely 1789 with a higher body count.") No amount of lime could cleanse the air blowing west from Picpus, a neighborhood where, before the Revolution, religious communities had built convents and the well-heeled their summer mansions to escape the heat of the inner city. (Ninon de l'Enclos had had her summer retreat here—see p. 243)

Standing at the foot of the scaffold, Mother Teresa intoned the *Veni Creator Spiritus* as each nun placed her hands between her own and renewed her vows of poverty, chastity, and obedience. Bystanders taking notes mentioned their "loud and intelligible voices," their faces *très calmes*.

Then Sister Constance, the youngest nun, knelt first before Mother Teresa, kissing the tiny clay image of the Virgin and Child she held in her hand. Her head bowed, she called out:

"Permission to die, Mother?"

"Go, my daughter."

Climbing the steps of the scaffold, Sister Constance called out for the last time: *"Laudate Dominum omnes gentes!"* It was the first line of the psalm sung by Saint Teresa of Avila at the founding of her Carmelite Order in Spain in the sixteenth century.

Waiting at the foot of the scaffold, Sister Constance's fifteen sisters took up the chant.

> *Praise the Lord, all ye nations!*
> *Praise Him all ye people!*
> *For His mercy is confirmed upon us,*
> *And the truth of the Lord endureth forever!*
> *Praise the Lord!*

They kept chanting as they heard the thud of each head as it fell and hit the chopping block of the scaffold. Mother Teresa/Madame Lidoine had been sentenced to be the last to die.

In silence the bodies and heads, thrown into carts painted red, were taken away in the direction of the cemetery.

Today, **Place de la Nation** is dominated by a huge triumphant statue of Marianne, symbol of the Revolution, encircled by fierce lions and, presumably, male and female revolutionaries bearing weapons and babies. If you start from where Marianne's left hand is pointing and leave the Place de la Nation following in that direction, you will find the shortest route to the cemetery: follow **rue Fabre-d'Églantine** (named for an aristocrat who was slaughtered just across the way in **Place du Trône**), a long block that bends left into **rue de Picpus.** The entrance to the grounds of the cemetery, less than a ten-minute walk from *Nation*, is on the left, at no. 35. Stop at the gatehouse inside the entrance for a sheet of information in English. *(Admission, 2 euros.)*

You will find the cemetery grounds through a blue gate to the left of the chapel. At the end of a long expanse of garden plots, deathly bare in February, bright green in spring, along the narrow paths lined with poplars, you will come to the cemetery entrance. On its far rear wall, you will find the memorial plaques to the Carmelites and other victims of the Terror—1,306 of them between June 14 and July 27, the date of Robespierre's execution and the end of the Terror. You are facing the gate at the entrance to the space where open pits or mass graves received the dead bodies and decapitated heads on the night of July 17, 1794. The names of the nuns are incised on the wall on either side of the entrance to the pits. Sister Constance, less than thirty years old, grew up in the *quartier* of Saint-Denis in Paris. Her worldly name was M. J. Meunier.

This is a place of silence and severe solemnity. I have never heard visitors speak as they look through the bars of the locked iron gate leading to the pits. There is more than death on the air at Picpus. The place seems to hold the memory of an unearthly courage and faith as if it is a living thing. In spring, the garden walls are covered with climbing roses; in winter the walls and garden plots are naked as corpses.

A look into the chapel that stands at the entrance of the Picpus Cemetery is a fitting end to your visit. Because there had been no religious ceremony at the time of the burial of the ***Place du Trône***'s 1,306 victims, their families built a chapel on the grounds of the cemetery and invited a religious order of nuns to offer perpetual prayer here, on their behalf. The order is still in residence. The Carmelites' names are incised on both left and right marble walls of the chapel's sanctuary.

Picpus has the atonal austerity of some of Francis Poulenc's choruses of women's voices confessing the starkness of belief in the face of death. It brings back the spell cast over the house of the Metropolitan Opera at the end of his opera, *Dialogues of the Carmelites* (1957). A strange hush. No one in the audience moved or made a sound. It took some time before the applause broke out.

Poulenc's sacred music expresses his own faith in the significance of the nuns' martyrdom. After a pilgrimage to Rocamadour in southwest France in 1935, he told of a mystical experience—in the church of Notre-Dame, he saw the Black Madonna carved by Saint Amadour—an event that inspired his return to Catholicism (see p. 165). Much of the sacred music he composed after 1936 had Marian themes: the *Litanies à la Vierge Noire*; the *Stabat Mater*. His *Gloria* carries the spirit of joy he found at the heart of Catholic mysticism.

The mass graves of Picpus, dug in gardens belonging to an order of Augustinian nuns and requisitioned by the Revolution, were closed and filled in in 1795; a few years later, they were bought by the families of the victims buried here. The tombstones record the presence of many aristocratic families prominent in French history, many of whom, as members of the Resistance, were deported and murdered by the Nazis. Lafayette is buried here because several women in his wife's family were guillotined during the Terror.

For a long time, the slaughtered Carmelites were forgotten. But as scholars continued to research the story into the twentieth century when the nuns were beatified (1906), a cult developed. Then, in the 1930s, reminded of the Terror by the rise of Hitler, a German writer, Gertrud von le Fort, wrote a novel about the event, *The Song of the Scaffold*. Georges Bernanos, the French Catholic novelist (*The Diary of a Country Priest*) wrote his *Dialogues of the Carmelites* as a screenplay in 1952, as he was dying.

Francis Poulenc was inspired to use Bernanos's text as the libretto for the opera he composed in 1953–1955 about the death of the Carmelites. All three writers fictionalized the story to include a main character, Blanche de la Force, who never existed. Sister Constance, however, the youngest nun, did exist. She was, in fact, the first to die.

Nearby

L'ÉGLANTINE   *21, rue Fabre d'Églantine. The terrace, full of local people, faces Place de la Nation where Fabre d'Églantine was executed. Friendly service. Peaceful in the late afternoon, with good desserts.*

LE BISTROT PAUL BERT   *18, **rue Paul Bert**. Tel: 01.43.72.24.01. Reservations suggested. Métro: Faidherbe-Chaligny. Open Tues–Thurs for lunch and dinner. Fri and Sat dinner only. A popular and lively bistro with excellent simple food.*

MEDIATHÈQUE HÉLÈNE BERR   *70, **rue de Picpus**, on the corner of rue de Picpus and **rue Santerre**. Named for the martyr and Résistante who left behind her* Journal *(see p. 224), the library is a quiet, well-lit space with a garden and a music room upstairs in memory of Berr's love of music. There is a photo of her on the left in the entrance lobby.*

FONDATION DE ROTHSCHILD   *76–80, **rue de Picpus** and **rue Lamblardie**, about a block southeast from Picpus Cemetery.*

Rothschild Orphanage, where Résistante Hélène Berr volunteered to help with the abandoned Jewish children during the Occupation, was on 19, rue Lamblardie. The plaque affixed to the building commemorates the members of the foundation's staff who saved the lives of many children and adults during the war and were themselves deported and murdered in the years 1941–1944.

Édith Piaf: Rue des Cascades

ÉDITH PIAF: THE LITTLE SPARROW

LOCATION: *72, rue de Belleville, The Hills of Belleville, Ménilmontant, and Rue Oberkampf*
MÉTRO: Belleville; Ménilmontant; Belgrand; Filles-du-Calvaire

Belleville gets a bad name from people who've never been there or who feel threatened by diversity. Immigrants and refugees from all over—Vietnam, Cambodia, Japan, Algeria, Morocco, Senegal, Ivory Coast, Pakistan, Greece, Armenia, Poland, Russia, Auvergne and many French provinces—have settled here and worked side by side throughout the last two centuries. And still they come. The cobblestone high streets are dense with vendors, children, neighborliness; headscarfed women, bearded Orthodox men, artists, squatters, students, teachers, vagrants—people stop in the street and markets to pass the time of day. Historian Richard Cobb has called immigrant Belleville/Ménilmontant (which includes the nineteenth and twentieth *arrondissements* as well as the tenth and eleventh, both down the hill)—*"the high citadel of l'esprit parisien."*

Édith Piaf (1915–1963), considered by many the greatest of the great French singers, began here. And forever, she said, *Belleville* was inside her.

From the beginning (December 1915, the second year of World War I), Édith Piaf's existence—her birth name was Édith Giovanna Gassion—was enough to make you weep. As a baby, a child, and an adolescent, she was a starveling.

She needed affection and food; she received almost nothing except neglect. As an adult, this utter deprivation left her yearning for love, always looking for human tenderness, no matter what kind of man was offering, and, after a while always needing comforting addictive substances. Her fans adored her because she sang from the heart about what every human being knows: pain, suffering, despair.

In 1915 her father was away in the war. Her mother was a penniless street singer who left the baby day and night either alone or with her mother; by the time Édith's father returned in 1918, the mother had abandoned the child. (Later it was said the mother left when Édith was two months old, an abandonment that haunted Édith Piaf for her entire life.) The father, finding the child malnourished and weak, moved her to his mother's house in Normandy. The house was a brothel. The grandmother showed her new charge no affection, the father returned to his itinerant life as an acrobat and circus man. Other children threw stones at Édith, this "child of the devil's house."*

At four, Édith was already singing in public, at night standing on tables in cafés with her grandparents. She also sang for the prostitutes she lived with and who were kind to her. They said she had a "magical" voice, that she could remember song lyrics as well as any grown-up.

Her housemates, *les filles perdues* (the lost girls), and her grandmother took her to Lisieux, the Carmelite shrine of Saint Thérèse of the Child Jesus, the "Little Flower," whom they implored to cure Édith of the acute keratitis (an inflammation of the cornea) that made her blind. After a number of unsuccessful pilgrimages, when she was about four or five

---

* Carolyn Burke, *No Regrets: The Life of Edith Piaf.*

years old, Édith's eyes opened at Lisieux: she could see. The lost girls and Édith believed the saint had performed a miracle for her. For the rest of her life she prayed to Saint Thérèse, wore her medal, and professed herself a person of faith though she didn't practice Catholicism. "My faith in something bigger, something stronger and more pure than what exists on this earth"—her faith in that "world beyond" she called immense according to her biographer. In times of crisis, she visited Paris churches to ask God for help. She claimed that "miracle" at Lisieux was her first and, for many years, her only happy memory.

When Édith's father, Louis Gassion, showed up in Normandy, he took his seven-year-old daughter on the road with him, as part of the Caroli Circus. Louis was an acrobat and contortionist with a short fuse; Édith kept house in their trailer, sang a few songs, passed the hat. When she made a mistake, he smacked her around. Then, in a temper, he quit the circus and he and Édith went on the road as a vagabond itinerant duo. He stood on his head; the little girl sang racy songs, *"La Marseillaise," "L'Internationale."* He picked up girlfriends, brought them along. In interviews and memoirs, Édith described those years on the road as an education: she learned "street smarts" and how to survive among many different kinds of people, mostly outcasts like her and her abusive father. Refusing to give in to adversity—to crumble—became a theme of her life as it was the ethos of the streets of Belleville/Ménilmontant.

They returned to Belleville—father, new girlfriend, daughter—when Édith was ten. She learned how to belt out the ballads called *chansons réalistes*—sad, sentimental songs about the hard lives of workers and their lovers. Édith was pretty much on her own, earning her way by singing in the cafés along the *boulevard de Belleville,* in the squares of Belleville and Ménilmontant, which adjoins Belleville from the east on the steep hill of *rue de Ménilmontant,* a continuation of *rue Oberkampf* in the eleventh.

Despite her skinny, small body—she never grew taller than four feet eight inches—Édith had a deep, strong voice—someone called it "assaultive," another a "velvety vibrato"; she had the defiant, saucy manners of the *Belleville* street. The locals in the cafés and music halls of her home territory cheered her on. But usually she was almost penniless. She got pregnant, married the father, took a room in Romainville, then later in the eleventh. They ate out of cans.

Word spread beyond Belleville about this birdlike singer with the haunting voice. "*That kid sings straight from the guts,*" Maurice Chevalier, who grew up in Ménilmontant, exclaimed the first time he heard her perform.

This was in 1935, two years after she'd moved out of Belleville. "*This stinking poorhouse*"—she wanted to get as far away from it as she could. And yet the compassion came through in her songs, her identification with the "underclass"—she may have moved but she never left her birthplace. When she moved to upper Montmartre and then Pigalle, a district of pimps and prostitutes and the mafia, she had her toddler daughter Cecelle with her. She nursed her, took her along as she traveled from gig to gig on the métro. Soon, the father of the child reclaimed her, bringing her back to Belleville where the baby died of meningitis, a paralyzing loss to her teenaged mother. There was no comfort (and almost no money) on the streets of Pigalle. She had the baby's coffin blessed in *Saint-Pierre-de-Montmartre,* a small ancient church tucked into the back of *Sacré-Coeur*; she buried Cecelle in a pauper's grave.

In the next few years, thanks to radio broadcasts and the records produced by Polydor, she was discovered, lionized, idealized, exploited. All along she would have many lovers, favoring men in uniforms, and three or more husbands. Her first manager, a fatherly gangster, gave her the name that he felt suited her: she was a true Paris sparrow, *un moineau*. He used the slang sparrow: *piaf*. "*La môme piaf*"—"The Little Sparrow" or "The Piaf Kid"—who made the sign of the cross before she entered the stage the night of her first real opening, in her ratty black skirt and hand-knitted sweater still missing a sleeve. Her first song was straight out of **Belleville**: "*Les Mômes de la Cloche.*"

> *We're the poor girls, the poor kids*
> *We roam around broke,*
> *We're the outcast girls*
> *We're loved for a night, it doesn't matter where.*

The "*bravas*" that cheered the song about her own life story roared through the cabaret. That was the night Maurice Chevalier first saw her perform.

She learned the art of singing, wrote some of her own songs, worked long hours with her composers and lyricists. But she never learned the conventions of the bourgeoisie. She was indifferent to saving any of the money she earned. She gave it away, to her father, her mother—a street singer who had become a drug addict and a hysterical stalker beneath Édith's windows—to friends, relatives, and hangers-on. Bums on the sidewalks of New York received nothing less than a twenty dollar bill the times she came to sing in Carnegie Hall.

During World War II, she supported and hid Jewish

friends. She traveled to Germany to entertain the troops, carrying with her phony identification cards, maps, and compasses given to her by the Resistance to hide on her person and give to imprisoned soldiers who were then able to escape. After the war, during the *épuration,* purge panels accused her of collaboration just for traveling to Germany. Proof from 118 prisoners of war who had escaped because of the material she carried to them and the cash she contributed saved her career. The penalty of proven collaboration would have been the removal of her songs from French radio forever and perhaps imprisonment.

For the Traveler

According to legend, she was born at *72, rue de Belleville* (there's a plaque), a short steep climb up from the main street, *boulevard de Belleville*. Bearing right into *rue Piat* (your back to the spot where Édith's mother supposedly went into labor), it's another easy hike up to the entrance of the lovely Parc de Belleville. It has a higher view over Paris than Montmartre.

But you'll find Édith Piaf's actual rather than legendary birthplace in a hospital another half-hour walk away into the southeast—you can descend through the park (in June, the roses are gorgeous, the many children so full of fun) to the exit into *rue des Couronnes*; then zigzagging north, then southeast through the old streets of Ménilmontant you'll come into *rue de la Chine* where Hôpital Tenon extends to *rue Belgrand*. The no-frills *Place Édith-Piaf* facing the trafficked *rue Belgrand* makes you wonder if Paris meant this square to celebrate or mourn the life of its most famous singer.

The down-and-out *Place Édith-Piaf,* however, is in many

ways appropriate as a nod to Belleville's most revered international celebrity. She did not abandon Belleville. She returned often to visit her father whom she said she never stopped loving.

Because the policies of Léon Blum's Popular Front government had brought reforms to the working classes in the thirties—higher wages, a shorter work week, health care, soup kitchens—Édith Piaf in later years did not see the same destitution on the streets of Belleville and Ménilmontant that she had grown up with. But these hills above Paris were still a world apart, still true to their history as the site of revolution and union protests. (Hitler had planned to bomb the northeast—it had no factories, was good for nothing but rebellion and Resistance; he hated the windmills of Pantin.)

Walking up these hills and zigzagging east and west, you can still feel yourself in an outsiders' *quartier*: in the almost rustic simplicity of the backstreets and their plain houses you're feeling the pulse of the working-poor world that shaped Édith Piaf. A route she would have known and serves as an enlightening example of both the charm and the dreariness of these outskirts begins about midway up *rue de Ménilmontant* off to the left behind the beautiful **church of Notre-Dame-de-la-Croix**. You are at the beginning of the *rue de la Mare,* an old riverbed that ran into a pool (*mare*) on the spot where the church now stands. The bookstore/gallery *"Le Monte-en-l'Air"* (with an outdoor terrace), at *2, rue de la Mare* sits in a curve of the street. The shop has a first-rate collection of French literature, especially poetry. As Piaf began to write her own lyrics and work on improving her French, she became an ardent reader of poetry, reciting Baudelaire with one of her best friends/lyricists; she loved Ronsard; her close friend Jean Cocteau (who made a movie for her), recited his poems to her; she in turn recited the classic French poems she had memorized.

Leaving the bookstore, wind right and along the *rue de la Mare*. A stairway crosses over the old railroad tracks—*l'enceinture*—behind the bookstore. *Rue de la Mare*'s uphill curves continue until you come to *Place Henri-Krasucki,* named for a Polish immigrant. Krasucki (1924–2003), a hero of the Resistance, was deported to Germany and tortured brutally in the presence of his mother. He escaped and returned to Belleville to become secretary of the Communist Party and a fierce supporter of workers' rights. The square was named for him in 2005, at the intersection of five streets: *rue Levert, rue de la Mare, rue des Envierges, rue des Couronnes,* and *rue des Cascades*. Local elders say that the square has not changed a lot (except for the cars) since the early twentieth century when Édith Piaf was young, singing and passing the hat in the squares of these hidden streets. Locals hang out in *Les Mésanges* at *82, rue de la Mare,* a low-key pleasant bistro, serving good food (*mesanges.krasu@free.fr*).

Bear right into *rue de Savies,* empty, quiet, and mysterious in the late afternoon. At the top of it is the *Regard Saint-Martin* (1722), a small stone building with a pointed roof. This was an inspection point at the place where springwater flowing down from the hills was collected and carried to Paris in an aqueduct built by monks. As you walk, you pass old stone walls covered with moss, patches of wild grasses, and deserted gardens. Bear right again into the charming *rue des Cascades,* with its many springs and a few more stone buildings that were part of Belleville's acqueduct in the time of Philippe Auguste (1180–1223). *Rue des Cascades* looks like a set for a film about Old Paris. (Jacques Becker had it in mind when making *Casque d'Or* [1952] with Simone Signoret.)

The street leads back into *rue de Ménilmontant* just above where this walk started. Descend toward *boulevard de Ménilmontant*—where, a block to your left is *rue des Panoy-aux,* another movie set of a street, beautiful in its simplicity. (At no. 15 you'll find *La Boulangerie*—www.laboulangerie .fr—a fine old restaurant, formerly a bakery, closed Mon, Sat lunch, and Sun.)

Jean Genet offers a poetic introduction to the walk out of Ménilmontant and up and down the hill of *rue Oberkampf* in the eleventh *arrondissement* where Édith Piaf once lived and sang when she was nobody.

> *Giacometti and I . . . know that there exists in Paris, where she has her dwelling, a person of great elegance, fine, haughty, vertical, singular and grey—a very tender grey—known as* **Rue Oberkampf,** *who cheekily changes her name and is called higher up* **Rue de Ménilmontant.** *Beautiful as a needle, she rises up to the sky. . . . she opens up as you climb, but in a singular manner: instead of re-treating, the houses converge . . . truly transfigured by the personality of this street, [they] take on the quality of a kind of goodness, familiar and distant.* *

To your left, as you head downhill (walking west) is *5–7 rue Crespin du Gast* and the off-the-beaten-track *Musée Édith Piaf* (closed June and Sept., open erratically, 1–6, Mon and Weds). The museum is filled with old photographs, clip-pings, mementos, one of Piaf's stuffed teddy bears, some little black dresses.

So many nearby streets in the eleventh—*rue Jean-Pierre*

* Jean Genet, *L'Atelier de Giacometti.*

Timbaud, in particular—have retained their personality against the onslaught of gentrification that endangers—and has destroyed—the soul of many old neighborhoods. Named for a steel workers' union leader and a *Résistant* who sang the "Marseillaise" as he faced the firing squad at Châteaubriant in 1941, his hill street is a dynamic ethnic mix, with a few good cafés. *Cannibale, no. 93,* has music at night and an interior full of light.

Near the corner of ***Oberkampf*** and *rue Saint-Maur* (named for the seventh-century *Abbaye de Saint-Maur* in the south-east of the eleventh), if you turn right, you can follow it north-west down to *l'Hôpital Saint-Louis,* founded and designed by Henri IV, its courtyard an exact copy of his Place des Vosges; leaving the hospital, you're a block away from the lovely Canal Saint-Martin in the tenth.

Returning to *rue Oberkampf,* you pass a few lively cafés near the corner of ***rue Saint-Maur, Chez Justine*** and ***Café Charbon,*** serving simple good food, their interiors and sur-rounding streets popular for their energetic night life. Across ***avenue de la République*** and ***avenue Parmentier, Oberkampf*** continues along its downhill slope, past small food shops, fruit markets, pâtisseries, florists, parents pushing strollers—some hurrying downhill, others uphill in the direction of Belleville. The motion of bodies flowing along these streets brings to mind the ballet called *La Voix* that was once planned as an homage to Piaf; it featured dances set to songs she would sing in celebration of the street life of Paris—the people, kiosks, métros, shops, the Parisians' habit of stroll-ing around—a kind of lighthearted sung dance. *La Voix,* never finished, was seen on French TV after her death.

Rue Amelot is off to your left a block before you reach the end of ***Oberkampf*** at ***boulevard des Filles-du-Calvaire.*** It is a narrow street of secret *passages, impasses,* and tragedy: walk down to *no. 36* (passing four separate stairways leading up to *boulevard Beaumarchais,* which must have served as escape routes) and read the plaque on the restored building. During the Occupation, a shelter for hunted Jewish mothers and children—*Le Comité Amelot*—operated here under the direction of David Rapoport from the Ukraine, who was arrested and deported in June 1943. The rest of the staff was also deported in the following months but not before they'd sent the children and their mothers to safe hiding places throughout France and Switzerland.

Returning to *rue Oberkampf,* passing the legendary bistro *Le Centenaire* on the corner, you turn to look up toward the top of the hill where you started out: Genet's words about *Oberkampf* ring true. *"Beautiful as a needle it rises up to the sky."* The view is especially moving at dusk, just before dark, and again the next day, as the sun rises to cover this cheeky person in brilliant morning light.

This is a *quartier* of workers, artists, shopkeepers, young freelancers, and families. *Rue Oberkampf* and its side streets are vital with diversity, an unaffected courtesy, and good humor. The luxury shops just a block away on *boulevard Beaumarchais* (the continuation of *boulevard des Filles-du-Calvaire*) threatens the eleventh's identity. Residents look on the expensive new eateries and clothing shops as a blight.

For now we're still on Édith Piaf's turf, remembering her music. In the spirit of the eleventh and Belleville/Ménilmontant, some of it celebrates the *je-m'en-foutisme* ("I don't give a damn") street culture of northeastern Paris. Many of her songs are "tough-minded," as Carolyn Burke puts it, born of these streets, "a refusal of sentimentality." The people of this *quartier* saw themselves in Piaf; in Charles Aznavour's words, they heard her "anarchic laughter." Duke Ellington and Louis Armstrong cherished her as a great musician, they flew from New York to Paris to catch her last triumphant shows at the Olympia.

When her hearse passed through these streets on the way to *Père Lachaise* in October 1963, forty thousand mourners followed it, closing the streets of Paris for the first time since the Liberation. Her coffin held her tiny body, her medal of Saint Thérèse of Lisieux, and her stuffed animals. The hearse did not stop at the Belleville church—Saint-Jean-Baptiste at the top of *rue de Belleville*—where she'd been baptized and her father's death had been blessed with the Mass of Christian burial. The Vatican refused the request for a funeral Mass for his daughter: She had lived in a state of sin, it said, and as an icon of false happiness. Besides herself, her grave in section 96 holds her father and her baby daughter.

Nearby

SQUARE DE LA ROQUETTE   *Five minutes away from the Roquette entrance to* **Père Lachaise** *along* **boulevard Ménilmontant.** *Piaf's people sit on the benches at the entrance on* **rue de la Roquette.** *The "History of Paris" plaque tells the story of the women's prison that once stood here, a facility for "incorrigible" girls, and later, during the Occupation, four thousand women of the Resistance. The guillotine across the street is now just a marker in the sidewalk. The flower gardens are lovely in season, the shouts and laughter of children in the playground a kind of music.*

LE LABO DE L'ABBÉ   *25–27,* **rue Oberkampf,** *on the left as you head up toward Belleville. An Emmaus House foundation, the work of Abbé Pierre on behalf of the Paris poor and homeless,* with many Paris and international outlets. The sale of the secondhand merchandise supports fair housing. Headquarters is in Romainville (where Édith Piaf lived with her baby).

HÔTEL BEAUMARCHAIS   *3, rue Oberkampf.* Tel: 01.53.36 .86.86. www.hotelbeaumarchais.com. *A friendly, modestly priced hotel, with an outdoor café. A minute from métro Filles-du-Calvaire and two minutes from the Marais. Within walking distance of Bastille in one direction and Place de la République in the other.*

CIRQUE D'HIVER *(Winter Circus)*   *110, rue Amelot.* *Exquisite architecture (built in 1852), unusual circus events, attended by Picasso, Toulouse-Lautrec, and swarms of families on public holidays.*

IMAGIGRAPHE   *84, rue Oberkampf.*   *Excellent Librairie & Contemporary Art Gallery.*

À LA BOULE MAGIQUE   *98, rue Oberkampf, 75011. An inviting, funky jewelry boutique. Christine is the helpful owner/proprietor.*

ACKNOWLEDGMENTS

AND THANKS TO

My husband, Tom, whose enthusiasm, humor, and original insights light the roads we travel in the good times of our lives.

St. Martin's Press: *The Streets of Paris* is made in memory of the late Matthew Shear (1955–2013), inspiring publisher and a man of unforgettable kindness and courage.

At St. Martin's, it has once again been my pleasure to work with my editor Charlie Spicer. His knowledge and love of Paris and publishing have sustained this project with a wise realism and a gracious and much appreciated courtesy.

His assistant April Osborne has given this book an unstinting and astute professionalism. Rob Grom, art director, has designed another beautiful cover and book, worthy of the City of Light. David Stanford Burr has also contributed to the clarity of the text.

My agent John Thornton has, as always, contributed his friendship and seasoned suggestions.

Friends in Paris and New York who have shared their memories of the City of Light as well as suggestions about not-to-be-missed treasures and off-the-beaten-track surprises:

Suzanne Ranoux, indefatigable walker, host, and insider guide to her favorite *quartiers*. The very gracious Pamela and Jim Morton, Catherine de Vinck, Elizabeth Cullinan, Shirley Abbott, Bill and Judith Moyers, Elaine Drootin, Jack Becker, Jo Lowrey of American University in Paris, Armand Jayet, Allon Schoener, Frances Hill and Leon

Arden, Renée Wiener, *Résistante* and *Commandeur de Légion d'Honneur*, Donald Spoto, Betsy Blachley and Henry Chapin, Nancy Lefenfeld, Anne Marlborough, Michelle Marlborough Lynch, John Laffan, Carolyn Waters of the New York Society Library, Maureen Waters and David Kleinbard, Linda Kunhardt, and the late Lois Wallace.

Nina Cahill, *Parisienne*, has been my muse for ten years.

The booksellers in Paris and the United States who have been faithful friends of all my travel books but especially my first book about Paris, *Hidden Gardens of Paris: A Guide to the Parks, Squares, & Woodlands of the City of Light*:

Louise H. Jones of Northshire Books in Manchester, Vermont; Elaine Petrocelli of Book Passage in California; Chris Doeblin of Book Culture in New York City; Nathalie Lacroix of the Albertine French bookstore in New York City; Linda and Olivia of Shakespeare & Co. in Paris; Anne of Galignani; Sylvia and the staff of W.H. Smith, and Odile Hellier of the legendary (and much missed) Anglo-American bookstore in *Rue Princesse*, who gave me the gift of the *Journal* of Hélène Berr.

SOURCES

The dates of publication refer to the year of the editions the author has read, consulted, or cited in the writing of this book.

Angiers, Natalie. *Woman: An Intimate Geography*, 2010.

Armingeat, Jacqueline. *Daumier: Lib Women*, trans. Howard Brabyn, 1974.

Atwood, William G. *The Parisian World of Frederic Chopin*, 1999.

Baecque, Antoine de and Serge Toubiana. *Truffaut: A Biography*, 2000.

Bakewell, Sarah. *How to Live or a Life of Montaigne*, 2010.

Baudelaire, Charles. *The Painter of Modern Life and Other Essays*, 1863.

Berger, John. *Portraits: John Berger on Artists*, ed. Tom Overton, 2015.

Berr, Hélène. *Journal*, 2007.

Brown, Frederick. *Zola: A Life*, 1995.

Burge, James. *Héloise and Abelard: A New Biography*, 2003.

Burke, Carolyn. *No Regrets: The Life of Édith Piaf*, 2011.

Bush, William. *To Quell the Terror: The True Story of the Carmelite Martyrs of Compiegne*, 1999.

Cahill, Susan. *Hidden Gardens of Paris: A Guide to the Parks, Squares and Woodlands of the City of Light*, 2012.

Camus, Albert. *Notebooks: 1935–1951*, trans. Philip Thody and Justin O'Brien, 1998.

———. *Notebooks: 1951–1959*, trans. Ryan Bloom, 2008.

Camus, Catherine, ed. *Albert Camus: Solitude & Solidarity*, 2013.

Char, René. *Furor and Mystery and Other Writings*, 2010.

Chazan, Robert. *The Trial of the Talmud: Paris, 1240*, 2012.

Child, Julia. *My Life in France*, 2007.

Chopin's Letters, ed. Ethel L. Voynich, 1931.

Cobb, Matthew. *The Resistance: The French Fight Against the Nazis*, 2009.

Cobb, Richard. *Paris and Elsewhere*, 2004.

Cole, Robert. *A Traveller's History of Paris*, 2008.

Colette. *Chéri*, 1920.

————. *Earthly Paradise: An Autobiography*, 1966.

————. *Places*, 1971.

Craven, Thomas. *The Story of Painting from Cave Pictures to Modern Art*, 1943.

Curie, Eve. *Madame Curie: A Biography*, 2001.

Curie, Marie. *Autobiographical Notes: The Story of My Life*, 1923.

Dallas, Greg. *Métro Stop Paris: An Underground History of the City of Light*, 2008.

Davidson, Ian. *Voltaire in Exile*, 2005.

DeJean, Joan. *How Paris Became Paris: The Invention of the Modern City*, 2014.

Desmard, Laurent. *Abbé Pierre: Images D'Une Vie*, 2006.

Desmons, Gilles. *Walking Paris*, 1999.

Donaldson-Evans, Lance. *One Hundred Great French Books*, 2010.

Dormann, Geneviève. *Colette: A Passion for Life*, trans. David Macey and Jane Breton, 1986.

Dronke, Peter. *Abelard and Héloise in Medieval Testimonies*, 1976.

Druon, Maurice. *The History of Paris from Caesar to Saint Louis*, 1966.

Dumas, Alexandre. *La Reine Margot*, 2008.

Eisler, Benita. *Chopin's Funeral*, 2003.

Foot, M. R. D. *Six Faces of Courage: True Stories of World War II Resistance Fighters*, 2000.

Frame, Donald M. *Montaigne: A Biography*, 1965.

Genet, Jean. *L'Atelier de Giacometti*, 1963.

Gildea, Robert. *France Since 1945*, 2002.

Goldsmith, Barbara. *Obsessive Genius: The Inner World of Marie Curie*, 2005.

Goldstone, Nancy. *The Rival Queens: Catherine de Medici, Her Daughter Marguerite de Valois, and the Betrayal That Ignited a Kingdom*, 2015.

Gray-Durant, Delia. *Blue Guide: Paris*, 2015.

Green, Julian. *Paris*, 2012.

Haldane, Charlotte. *Queen of Hearts: Marguerite of Valois ("La Reine Margot") 1553–1615*, 1968.

Harlan, Elizabeth. *George Sand*, 2004.

Hawes, Elizabeth. *Camus: A Romance*, 2009.

Hazan, Eric. *The Invention of Paris: A History in Footsteps*, 2010.

————. *A People's History of the French Revolution*, 2014.

Hazareesingh, Sudhir. *How The French Think: An Affectionate Portrait of an Intellectual People*, 2015.

Horne, Alistair. *Seven Ages of Paris,* 2002.

Ivry, Benjamin. *Poulenc,* 1996.

Jackson, Julian. *The Fall of France: The Nazi Invasion of 1940,* 2003.

———. *France: The Dark Years, 1940–1944,* 2000.

Jones, Colin. *Paris: The Biography of a City,* 2004.

Jones, David-Pryce. *Paris in the third Reich: A History of the German Occupation 1940–1944,* 1981.

Josephson, Hannah, and Malcolm Cowley, eds. *Aragon: Poet of the French Resistance,* 1945.

Kaplan, Alice. *The Collaborator,* 2000.

Lafayette, Madame de. *The Princesse de Clèves,* trans. Terence Cave, 1992.

Larkin, Oliver W. *Daumier: Man of His Time,* 1966.

Lipton, Eunice. *French Seduction,* 2007.

Liscio, Lorraine. *Paris and Her Remarkable Women: A Guide,* 2009.

Lobrano, Alexander. *Hungry for Paris: The Ultimate Guide to the City's 102 Best Restaurants,* 2008.

Lord, James. *A Giacometti Portrait,* 1965.

———. *Giacometti: A Biography,* 1985.

Malecot, Claude, and Caecilia Pieri. *Le Monde de Colette au Palais-Royal,* 2005.

Malcolm, Janet. *Two Lives. Gertrude and Alice,* 2007.

Marnham, Patrick. *Resistance and Betrayal. The Death and Life of the Greatest Hero of the French Resistance,* 2000.

Martines, Lauro. *Furies: War in Europe: 1450–1700,* 2013.

Maurois, André. *From Proust to Camus: Profiles of Modern French Writers,* 1966.

———. *A History of France,* 1956.

McCarthy, Patrick. *Camus,* 1982.

Mitford, Nancy. *Voltaire in Love,* 1957.

Modiano, Patrick. *The Occupation Trilogy,* 2015.

———. *Pedigree,* 2015.

———. *Dora Bruder 1997. (The Search Warrant),* 2000.

———. *Paris Nocturne,* 2015.

———. *After the Circus,* 2015.

Montaigne, Michel de, *The Complete Essays of Montaigne,* trans. Donald Frame, 1958.

———. *The Essays: A Selection.* trans. M. A. Screech, 1993.

Neveux, Murielle. *Paris Criminel,* 2013.

Packer, George. "The Other France," *New Yorker,* August 31, 2015.

Pearson, Roger. *Voltaire Almighty: A Life in Pursuit of Freedom*, 2006.

Pétrement, Simone. *Simone Weil: A Life*, 1976.

Poulenc, Francis. *Dialogues of the Carmelites*, 1956.

Radice, Betty, ed. and trans. *The Letters of Abelard and Héloise*, 1974.

Ranke-Heinemann, Uta. *Eunuchs for the Kingdom of Heaven: Women, Sexuality, and the Catholic Church*, 1990.

Riding, Alan. *And the Show Went On: Cultural Life in Nazi-Occupied Paris*, 2010.

Robespierre, Maximilien. *Virtue and Terror*, 2015.

Robertson and Overton. *Life, Letters & Epicurean Philosophy of Ninon de L'Enclos: The Celebrated Beauty of the Seventeenth Century*, 1905.

Rose, Jacqueline. *Women in Dark Times*, 2015.

Royal Academy of Arts. *Daumier, Visions of Paris*, 2014.

Ruelle, Karen Gray, and Deborah Durland DeSaix. *The Grand Mosque of Paris: A Story of How Muslims Rescued Jews During the Holocaust*, 2008.

Sante, Luc. *The Other Paris*, 2015.

Satloff, Robert. *Among the Righteous: Lost Stories of the Holocaust from Arab Lands*, 2006.

Schiff, Stacy. *The Great Improvisation: Franklin, France, and the Birth of America*, 2005.

Schoenbrun, David. *Soldiers of the Night: The Story of the French Resistance*, 1980.

Schurmann, Michael. *Paris Movie Walks*, 2009.

Sciolino, Elaine. *The Only Street in Paris: Life on the Rue des Martyrs*, 2015.

Sévigné, Madame de. *Letters*, ed. Leonard Tancock, 1982.

Seward, Desmond. *The First Bourbon: Henri IV of France and Navarre*, 1971.

Solnit, Rebecca. *Wanderlust. A History of Walking*, 2001.

Szulc, Tad. *Chopin in Paris*, 1998.

Thurman, Judith. *Secrets of the Flesh: A Life of Colette*, 1999.

Todd, Olivier. *Albert Camus: A Life*, 1997.

Truffaut, François. *The Films in My Life*, 1975.

Valensi-Levi Jacqueline, ed. *Camus at Combat*, 2006.

Valois, Queen Marguerite de. *The Entire Memoirs of Marguerite de Valois: Queen of Navarre*, 1813.

Von le Fort, Gertrud. *Song of the Scaffold*, 1931.

Weil, Simone. *Waiting for God*, 1951.

————. *War and The Iliad*, 2005.

Wendel, Hélène de, ed. *Poulenc: Correspondence, 1915–1963*. 1967.

Wills, Garry. "My Koran Problem," *New York Review of Books*, March 24, 2016.

Zaretsky, Robert. *A Life Worth Living: Albert Camus and the Quest for Meaning*, 2013.

Zerdoumi, Amir Jalal. "French Algerian or Algerian-French?," *New York Times*, August 16, 2015.

Zola, Émile, *The Quarry*, 1872.

Zweig, Stefan. *Montaigne*, 2015.

INDEX

ABOUT THE AUTHOR

Writer and editor, SUSAN CAHILL has published other travel books including the acclaimed *Hidden Gardens of Paris: A Guide to The Parks, Squares, and Woodlands of the City of Light* ("No matter how many times you have been to Paris," said one reviewer, "never go again without Susan Cahill"); *Desiring Italy: Women Writers Celebrate a Country & a Culture; The Smiles of Rome; For the Love of Ireland;* and, with her husband, Thomas Cahill, *A Literary Guide to Ireland*. She is the editor of the Women and Fiction series and author of the novel *Earth Angels*. She lives in New York City and spends a few months in Paris every year.

ABOUT THE PHOTOGRAPHER

MARION RANOUX is a freelance photographer and translator of Czech literature. A lifelong Parisian, she is currently doing graduate work in Visual Studies at the *École des Hautes Études en Sciences Sociales* (EHESS) with a focus on the power of the photograph and the creation of the historical record.